Great Restaurants of America

Antoine Gilly

1961

Great Restaura

By Ted Patrick

Drawings by

PHILADELPHIA & NEW YORK

nts of America

& Silas Spitzer

Ronald Searle

J. B. LIPPINCOTT COMPANY

PUBLISHER'S NOTE

Some sections of this book were written by Ted Patrick, others by Silas Spitzer. Some of the material was written jointly. The authors have preferred not to sign their contributions; hence the first-person singular pronoun, where used, refers interchangeably to either.

Printed in the United States of America

Library of Congress Catalog Number 60-14213

FIRST EDITION

Foreword

IT IS FITTING THAT WE TWO WRITE THIS book together, for we have traveled together along the richly scented road of fine food and fine wine. We came into the world not too many years apart, both endowed with inquisitive taste buds, lusty appetites and robust digestive apparatus. Both had parents who not only knew their way about a kitchen, but who believed in introducing their children to the wonders and delights of New York's better restaurants. And both had as a great and knowing friend, Douglas Hoxie Smith.

Doug Smith, artist and type-designer, wit and raconteur, musician and clubman, bachelor and man-about-town, was our first mentor in the niceties and enticements of the world of gourmandise. It was he who thought of and organized the Brillat-Savarin Club, and that started the whole thing.

The Twenties, the degrading days of Prohibition, were a black time for gracious living in the United States. The speakeasies were fun, and some of them served quite good food, but the liquor more often than not was atrocious, the wine was spurious, and the elegance which is a part of really fine dining was nonexistent. While Doug Smith spent a fair share of his life in these speakeasies, he missed more than most people the living of pre-Prohibition days. It was the longing for the restoration of this kind of living which gave birth in his ingenious mind to the idea of the Brillat-Savarin Club.

The Brillat-Savarin Club was a dining club of precisely six members, all male. It met approximately every six weeks in one of the fine restaurants of the metropolitan area, at a dinner planned well in advance, discussed thoroughly with the chef, and accompanied by classically proper wines.

Despite the presence and the aura of gangsters and thugs in the Prohibition era, there were many reputable and fervent practitioners of the culinary art. Mostly, they were in hotels, notably in the Hotel Ambassador in New York City. The chef there at the time was Sabatini, uncle of the then-famous novelist, Rafael Sabatini. Chef Sabatini was a huge man, six feet four in height, adorned with a terribly sincere red beard, a huge one, flowing down to the seventh rib.

The Brillat-Savarin Club called first upon M. Sabatini for its dinner. His six-feet-four rose to its full height; his red beard bristled, his culinary spirit glowed, and he produced one of the greatest dinners we have ever eaten. The wines? One of the six members of the Brillat-Savarin Club was Tubby Bell. Tubby was rich, a rather useful thing to be if you want also to be a gourmet. Because he was rich, and because he knew a great deal about wines (having traveled all over the wine countries of Europe with his father, who was an advanced wine-lover) we appointed him Sommelier of the Brillat-Savarin Club. This was not too tough a job. All he had to do was to drive up to Canada a reasonable number of days before the laid-on dinner, buy the wines which had been ordained in the solemn pre-dinner meetings, brazen them past the customs boys, and deliver them in time to be properly chilled and properly room-temperatured.

Brillat-Savarin dinners were held at the Colony, at the Ambassador, at Henri's in Lynbrook, at 21, at Zani's, at Papa Moneta's, at several other places.

[6]

All of these places spread themselves gloriously, as these were frustrating times for dedicated chefs and restaurateurs, who felt their art was unappreciated, and embraced almost touchingly the opportunity to be able to cook again in the great tradition. They longed to see their creations lingered over lovingly, to serve them with the proper wines and to behold them eaten with reverence.

The Brillat-Savarin died when Doug Smith died. It seemed almost sacrilege to meet under its silver plaque, which always hung on the wall behind the Brillat-Savarin table of the evening, without him. But it was the key which opened for us the door to the entire world of gastronomy. It influenced a study of food and wine, of cooking and eating, of restaurants and kitchens, which is still active and intense.

After a few years of holding Brillat-Savarin dinners in restaurants, it was decided to try our talents in our own kitchens and dining rooms. Each member had the obligation to devise a menu, shop for the dinner, and prepare it himself, from opening course to demitasse. At first, there was furious homework with the cookbook section of bookcases, solemn consultations with chefs we knew, explorations of the better markets and food shops. But under the inspiration of creating, and the solace of some surprisingly successful results, we went onward and upward with the art of cooking, until today a kitchen is a home, and an oven, a friend. Baptism in cookery started the acquisition of cookbooks, first as a crutch to our limping talents, then as what could be called, without too much pretentiousness, "a collection." They number several hundred volumes, in assorted sizes and languages, ranging in literary style from Fanny Farmer's "Add one level teaspoon of sugar," to William Hazlitt's

> Man has been distinguished from other animals in various ways; but perhaps there is no particular in which he exhibits so marked a difference from the rest of creation—not even in the prehensile faculty resident in his hand—as in the objection to raw food, meat and vegetables.

Much can be learned about food and wine from books, but as in all study, field trips also have a place, and give a firsthand knowledge not to be had even from the most ravenous reading. In 1932, we made the first of many trips to study wine and food, a trip from Paris to Nice, through the Burgundy country and the valley of the Rhone. We visited the famous vineyards, the respected *caves,* and the revered restaurants. It was on this trip that we discovered the Pyramide Restaurant in Vienne, and its then-youthful owner, Fernand Point, who was to become, indisputably, the greatest and best known chef in the world. Since that start in 1932, visits have been made to the vineyards of Bordeaux, the Rhine, the Moselle, Italy, Capri and Ischia, Spain, Portugal, Greece, and California. All of the best restaurants of the United States and Europe have been visited, the greatest of them many times. The food of other areas has been sampled in its native habitat, of Israel, of New Delhi and Calcutta, of Tokyo, of the Philippines and Hawaii. Good food and good wine were sought (and found) even deep in the bush of the Belgian Congo.

Our introduction to this most delicious of all worlds also led into other paths. In the 1930's, at the death of that miserable monster, Prohibition, we bought stock in the newly formed wine-importing firm of Bates & Schoonmaker, which was an invitation to a daily tasting and testing of the best wines then being brought into the United States, and exposure to the phenomenal knowledge of wines Frank Schoonmaker's extraordinary palate and mind had accumulated. The firm no longer exists, but the friendship and the access to Frank's knowledge endure, and are a cause for rejoicing.

In 1933, several of us, including Ludwig Bemelmans, whose idea and brainchild the project was, opened a restaurant in New York. It was the Hapsburg House at 333 East 55th Street. Bemelmans brought to the Hapsburg not only superb talents as an artist, but also a lifetime experience of the inn business gathered from his family's hotel in Bavaria and from the Ritz hotels in Paris and New York, in which his family were investors. He tramped the East Side streets of New York for a likely location, and found it in an old New Orleans style house on East 55th Street. It was charming, but as unlikely a spot for a restaurant as there could be. A lease was signed, however, and a chef hired; a doorman who looked exactly like Emperor Franz Joseph of Austria was extricated and extradited from Yorkville. When he wasn't hiring chefs and dishwashers and directing the layout of the kitchen, Bem was filling the walls of several dining rooms, all of which had been papered with drawing paper, with his inimitable and exquisite sketches. The rest of us bought the entire wine cellar which, while small, was, in the infant days of Repeal, probably the best in New York, and occupied ourselves with getting the place ready and seeing that the public knew about it. The Hapsburg bred many a headache, as any new business must, but in retrospect at least it was fun, instructing, and rewarding, and there were sighs of sadness mixed with the sighs of relief when it finally was sold. Today we still like to go into the kitchens and the wine cellars of restaurants, but as friends of the house, not as owners.

This way we keep in touch with the world of *haute cuisine,* this and through memberships in such organizations as the Confrérie des Chevaliers du Tastevin, the Vatel Club, La Société des Chefs de Cuisine, and others devoted to the philosophy, preparation, and consumption of food and wine. It's a fascinating subject, a fascinating world. And we hope this book might provide you with the key to it, as the Brillat-Savarin Club provided it to us.

When we undertook the task of writing this book, we knew that many restaurants worthy of inclusion would have to be left out. We could not possibly know all the good ones. It was only fair, we felt, to devote ourselves, one: to those we knew well personally, and, two: to those we knew both by reputation and by the candid reporting of knowledgeable friends who are qualified to pass judgment on restaurants.

We have made a careful selection across the country, and believe that the chosen ones are well worth your reading time and, whenever the occasion may arise, your actual patronage. As for the other fine restaurants which have been reluctantly bypassed, the fact that they were not included is in no way to be considered a reflection upon them, or a true measure of their quality. Many of them, we are quite certain, are as good as or better than some which we have given the full treatment.

Again we would like to emphasize that even though we get around a good deal, and are hungry three times a day, and are more than normally curious and exploratory about food, wines and people, no two human beings could ever hope to cover all the restaurants of the United States. This book, then, is in no sense intended to be a guide, except to the personal likes and dislikes of the authors. We can only hope that the reader shares our love of the endlessly varied pleasures and distractions of dining out, and that he ranks them as highly as we do among the privileges of being alive in a time of comparative civilization.

TED PATRICK
SILAS SPITZER

Contents

New York City

Baroque
Restaurant

14 EAST 53RD STREET

Owner: *Joseph Bugoni*
Maître d'Hôtel: *Paul Luchetti*
Chef: *Gaston Esnault*

I N WRITING A BOOK OF THIS KIND, YOU inevitably come to the need for a soul-searching decision; should a certain restaurant be included because it richly deserves to be or should it be excluded because you love it so much the way it is you don't want to attract new hordes to it.

Baroque posed precisely this problem. It's one of New York's best restaurants. It's one of the country's most elegant restaurants. It has a distinguished clientele of largely regular patrons, few strangers. It is always comfortably filled, but never crowded, so that the service and the atmosphere are always quiet, and collected, and unharassed. But it would be grossly unfair not to include it, so here it is.

The Baroque is a small restaurant, with a tiny bar on the right as you come in, a bar seating only ten people with surrounding tables seating perhaps ten or a dozen more. The dining room is beyond the bar, up a miniature stairway of five steps. The decorative scheme throughout is, appropriately, baroque, and a very pleasant setting for very pleasant dining.

The Baroque is soothingly quiet, a blessing rare in New York restaurants, and nicely, not stiffly, dignified. These qualities derive directly from the owner, soft-spoken, immensely dignified Joseph. Joseph is a consummate restaurateur, at home in the kitchen, in the wine cellar, and in the dining room. He is ably backed up by Maître d'Hôtel Paul and Headwaiter Giorgio, his brother.

The Baroque menu is classic and complete, but there is also a specialty served each day at dinner. My own favorites of these daily specials are *Le Suprême de Poularde Barcelonette,* served, at this writing, on Monday, and *Le Contre-Filet de Boeuf Armenonville,* served on Thursday.

When I go to Baroque, I rarely order from Joseph, but rather consult with him, discussing the food and the wine until both of us are content and happy with the prospect ahead. My most recent mutually arrived-at dinner started with Smoked Trout Chantilly, a delicately smoked fish, boned at the table, and served with a special creamed horse-radish sauce which had the titillating piquancy of fresh horse-radish, but not so much that it smothered the flavor of the trout. With this was a Danish aquavit, served in an ice-imbedded glass.

Following the trout was a cup of *Crème à l'Oseille,* with which Joseph insisted upon serving a small bottle of Puligny-Montrachet 1952. The entrée was *Carré d'Agneau Sardelaise,* one of the very best dishes on the Baroque menu, and especially irresistible when served with a bottle of Château Haut-Brion 1947, which accompanied it on this particular evening. With the lamb were feathery light, crisp *pommes soufflées* and *petits pois.* A soft, exquisitely ripe Brie did for dessert, and coffee, Armagnac, and a softly fresh Ramon Allones cigar did for me.

Baroque is not generally known to non-New Yorkers. Nearly everyone who comes is a friend of Joseph and his associates, and a very distinguished group it is. The upper echelons of Wall Street are usually represented along with editors, writers, literary agents, Shakespearian actors, oil and other tycoon types, moving picture producers, society (real, not café), and occasionally a Vice President (of the United States, not of an advertising agency).

Bo Bo's

20½ PELL STREET

Owners: *Unknown*

 SMALL CUBICLE MORE OR LESS HIDDEN IN the clutter and confusion of one of Chinatown's side streets, Bo Bo's (an oddly raffish name never clearly explained to the writer) is a place dear to the hearts and appetites of a comparatively few New Yorkers, who have sampled the food and grown fond of the help and the atmosphere. At this writing, it is not especially known to slumming uptowners and still retains its naïve charm to the cognoscenti.

The decor may be described in all honesty as Ugly Modern. All is strictly on the practical side. The street door opens narrowly on a quick-order lunch counter, equipped with stools, paper napkins and a Coca-Cola tank—enough to scare away the apprehensive at the very outset. The counter is patronized exclusively by Chinese patrons and an occasional truck driver or plain-clothesman. About a dozen chrome-and-plastic tables are jammed tightly into the remaining space. The kitchen, vaguely situated off the rear hallway and apparently not much larger than a phone booth, is yet mysteriously capable of producing an endless succession of luscious and intricately composed dishes, including one exotic and delicious soup known to old hands on Doyer Street as "Ten Things." The things are hard to count, being chopped small or ground fine, but their flavor is definitely connected with shellfish, chicken, duck, pork, and Bo Bo only knows how many vegetables.

Service is provided by two or three young and very attractive maidens, smartly dressed in tight-fitting sheaths, slit above the knee for maximum mobility. They wear a permanent smile and keep up a continual chatter in their native tongue. This lively approach is probably explained by the fact that in their spare time they are all actresses who used to play at the Chinese Theatre on the Bowery. Performances there followed no regular schedule, but when there was a play on, the chef at Bo Bo's vanished from the kitchen. At those times, he could be found in the orchestra, playing the drums.

There is no menu at Bo Bo's, apparently because the inspirations of the chef gifted with dual talents are difficult to translate. However, your wants will be well taken care of by a serene young woman who is most articulate in English and very helpful to dolts unfamiliar with the Cantonese dialect. At lunchtime, denizens of the quarter fill most of the tables, with a sprinkling of downtown office workers and even a few stray epicures from uptown. Luncheon consists of *Dem Sem,* which is, or are, a mixed covey of cooked pasties that come in various sizes and shapes and are filled with chicken, fish, lobster, duck, pork and vegetables, all finely minced and subtly seasoned. These pockets, envelopes and pillows of dough are somehow eaten with chopsticks by skillful guests, a trying stunt for knife-and-fork people, especially when they are confronted by the final goody of the meal, a dumpling about the size of a tennis ball.

At a recent dinner party for six, winter melon soup, which had been ordered a day ahead, was served as a first course. It consisted of a massive grayish-green melon of an unfamiliar variety, hollowed out and filled to the brim with what could well be the most wonderful soup ever invented. It tasted delicately of chicken, but there were many other flavors not easy to identify, and a cargo of precisely diced edibles that were crunchy, velvety or merely indescribable. This was followed by three separate courses of two or three dishes each, which were shared by all the guests. It was never clearly established what these items were called, but nobody minded. Bo Bo's is a place where names are not important. You are better off if you just accept what you are offered in a spirit of gratitude and without unnecessary palaver. Among the identifiable dishes were frog's legs in a mysterious sauce, dried abalone with pork and vegetables and black mushrooms under a filmy veil of white rice noodles, and a whole striped bass with elaborate garniture.

The restaurant is highly recommended, but only to those whose love of Chinese food amounts to a passion, and who are willing to take the long trip downtown and put up with rather cramped and drab surroundings in return for an unforgettable treat. No wines or spirits are available, but one can order bottled beer from an outside source. It arrives, icy cold and in a matter of minutes, cradled in the arms of a small Chinese boy.

The Brussels

115 EAST 54TH STREET

Proprietor: *Marguerite Pagani*
Maître d'Hôtel: *Leon Lievens*
Chef: *Pierre Rogalle*

MANY THOUGHTFUL GASTRONOMES BELIEVE that the artistry of the best Belgian chefs begins at a point where their French colleagues are content to rest on their laurels—or more properly, on their bay leaves. New York's only fine Belgian restaurant, the Brussels, is a good place to put that theory to the test.

Perhaps the most beautiful restaurant in New York, the Brussels occupies a white stone Renaissance mansion that was once the Frank Vanderlip town house. Handsome oil paintings abound; the carpeting is soft and lush underfoot and the magnificent wood-paneled and brocaded dining room is flooded with mellow golden radiance from clusters of chandeliers. Mrs. André Pagani, succeeding her late husband, carries on the tradition he began at the Belgian Pavilion of the New York World's Fair. She is nobly seconded by the manager and maître d'hôtel, Leon Lievens, and the head chef, Pierre Rogalle.

While the cooking is essentially French, the manner is Belgian, which means an abundance of cream, butter, wine and brandy in the sauces and an opulence of flavor in nearly every dish, in harmony with the amplitude of the menu and the sumptuousness of the setting. Besides the impressive main dining room, there are several private rooms upstairs, mostly decorated in the Florentine period. They are the scene of many splendid dinner parties of an intimate but lavish nature.

The Brussels dinner menu is almost baffling in its wealth of elaborate dishes. Even traveled and knowing guests of the fastidious kind will profit by consulting Leon when ordering a meal. Not only is it quite safe to leave the choice to him, but you will be sure to get things that are seasonally fresh and at their most desirable point of flavor. A few of the house specialties that I have tried and can recommend:

Sole d'Ostende sans Nom (apparently the anonymity is a chef's prank; the imported sole is also prepared in at least another ten different styles); *Homard aux Aromates* (not as good as plain broiled lobster in my opinion, but a nice change); Rack of Lamb *Brésilienne* with *Pommes Sardelaises* (exactly right for a dinner party of four or more, carved at your table with exquisite precision); *Suprême de Volaille Gismonda* (favored by blondes, who apparently instinctively prefer white breast of chicken in the most delicate of sauces); *Waterzooï de Volaille à la Gantoise* (the Flemish national dish which is really a double-rich chicken soup served with the boiled fowl and a side dish of boiled potatoes); *Crêpes Soufflées Sauce Sabayon* (the sort of dessert that causes necks to crane while it is being prepared at your table).

Victor Puppin, the sommelier, when questioned about the resources of his cellar, responded by lugging to my table six bottles which would be difficult to find anywhere outside of Paris or perhaps Brussels. They bore these impressive labels: Clos Vougeot 1915, Volnay Santenots 1919, Le Musigny 1929, Château Mouton-Rothschild 1934, Château Latour 1937, Château Lafite 1945. These, said Victor, merely nicked the surface. There were many other dust-covered bottles of the great vintage years, and he would vouch for the soundness of all of them. This is something I would not care to take for granted, and though I have great faith in Victor's probity I would like nothing better than the chance to sample every wine in turn, strictly in the name of scientific research.

Le Café Chambord

803 THIRD AVENUE

Maître d'Hôtel: *René Dufau*
Chef: *Fernand Desbans*

T HE CHEF DE CUISINE OF THE CHAMBORD once assured me, when I had complimented him on his artistry, that he did not find it difficult to prepare the classically great recipes of France for the patrons of that elegant rendezvous on Third Avenue.

"When you work for one of the most expensive restaurants in the world," he explained, "you have a great advantage. We pay the highest prices for beef, lamb, veal, poultry and game, all specially reserved for us. We have first pick of the finest fruits, vegetables and other materials, especially imported wines and spirits. How can I go wrong with such a head start?"

He might have added, if he had been less modest, that his skill and background were so well regarded by the owners that he was one of the highest paid chefs in his profession. Or that his kitchen assistants and the staff out front were rewarded on a similar scale of compensation. All this outlay, and other expenses of supply and maintenance, contribute to the high cost of dining at the Chambord. The average dinner check for two people, with apéritifs and wines, will run somewhere between forty to fifty dollars. This does not, as some may think, indicate that the restaurant makes a dizzy profit on its operation. On

[23]

the contrary, I was assured by the director that there are many large popular-priced New York restaurants where profits are proportionately much greater.

If you plan to dine at this quiet, conservative but sumptuous restaurant, be sure to reserve a table well ahead. You will be greeted by René, Paris or David, maîtres d'hôtel in that order of seniority. Unless you are opposed to advice, however expert, I would suggest that you permit one of these gentlemen to choose your meal, or at least guide you in building a well-balanced selection. With ordinary luck, it should be one of the memorable repasts of a lifetime.

Few restaurants, even the great ones of Paris, can improve on such Chambord masterpieces as: *Le Homard du Maine Flambé, Délice des Gourmets; Le Tendre Caneton à l'Orange et au Grand Marnier avec Pommes Soufflées; Le Roi Faisan à l'Estouffade Périgourdine; Le Carré d'Agneau aux Primeurs* or *La Grouse d'Ecosse, Flambée à l'Armagnac*. These are only a few meager quotes from one of the most lavish menus I have ever encountered. And if you happen to crave some dish you once enjoyed in France but which is not listed, the chef will usually make it for you without a quiver. It is no special bother, for everything is made to your order at the Chambord anyway, as in all great restaurants, except certain elaborate productions which require a little preliminary simmering before the final touch of the master.

Among the simple but highly significant symbols of the Chambord's excellence, a few are worth citing here. By far the best *pommes soufflées* I have eaten anywhere, each a delicate golden bubble, crisp and free from the slightest suggestion of grease. Butter of heavenly sweetness and creaminess. Bread that is almost like the good bread of a country bakery in France. One of the most beautiful broiled sirloin steaks that ever disturbed a hungry man's dreams, and plain broiled chops and spring chicken prepared with the same unvarying perfection. And, finally, coffee that could not be improved upon, roasted and ground freshly, I was told, from a specially prepared blend.

Having visited the cellar several times, with the sommelier as my guide, I can venture the statement that there may be larger collections, as for example the great cellars of the 21 Club, but none that is better balanced. If I was troubled by any doubts, they were prompted by the fantastic age of some of the specimens of which he was especially proud. There were first-growth Bordeaux of the years 1906, 1907, 1916, 1919, and 1921. I was shown a cobwebby, carefully cradled Côte Rôtie of 1895, a Château Latour of 1900 and a Château d'Yquem of the same year. These ancients were priced at $20 and upwards apiece. I wondered if, when opened and poured, they would live up to their romantic promise. The sommelier, however, assured me that all except a very few of his oldest bottles were sound and without a symptom of senility. But I remain skeptical. Wines of that great age, for the most part, are a gamble, as far as ordering goes. They are really showpieces, to be seen and fondled rather than to be drunk.

However, there are bin after bin of noble wines that can be ordered at the Chambord without the slightest apprehension. Among them I specially coveted a Richebourg 1915, a Montrachet 1945, a Romanée-St. Vivant 1937, a Château Haut-Brion of the fabulous vintage of 1929. These are wines that today are hard to find in European restaurants. It might be a good idea to sample one or two of them before they vanish utterly from the earth.

Café de France

T THIS LIVELY LITTLE SPOT WEST OF EIGHTH Avenue in the table d'hôte belt, the food is cooked as most French people like it—simply, unpretentiously and with all the savor and succulence inherent in provincial cuisine. Apparently there are plenty of New Yorkers who prefer their food in the same manner, for the tables are crowded to capacity, day and night. There are perhaps two or three restaurants of the kind in the city that do as good a job at such low cost, but this one offers the best fun.

Antoine Perrier, formerly co-owner of the Ambassador Inn of East Quogue, Long Island, works quietly and inconspicuously behind the bar, but supervises all details with a firm hand. And this, it should be noted, takes a bit of doing, for the tables are served by waitresses, all French, all pretty and vivacious in a style that suggests a party. The young ladies, unspoiled by the big city, are on excellent terms with their regular customers and often impulsively kiss the more attractive males on the cheek to show their good will.

At luncheon, the little room is filled with actors, clerical workers and journalists from the nearby offices of the *Times* and *Herald Tribune*. There is no menu or wine list, but the daily suggestions are chalked up on a wall slate. The place is not large enough to hold all the people who crowd it before theater-time. If you come early or late, however, you have a better chance to get a table.

Some of the chef's more notable achievements are: *Paté de Campagne, Escargots de Bourgogne, Filet Mignon en Croûte, Canard Rôti Sauce Bigarade, Soupe à l'Oignon, Coq au Vin* and an unctuously smooth *Mousse Chocolat* served in individual helpings. Most people drink wine by the glass, but if you want something better, you may choose from several sound French varieties, including white Puligny-Montrachet, red Beaujolais Brouilly and the pink Château de Selle. The room crackles with animated conversation, manners are informal, and if you are the sort of person who insists on decorum with your meals, you had better not go.

Café du Midi

311 WEST 48TH STREET

Proprietor and Maître d'Hôtel: *Jean Pujol*
Chef: *René Tariol*

THIS CROWDED LITTLE BISTRO IS TUCKED away in the never-never land west of Eighth Avenue, a section memorable for seedy lodging houses, steamy-windowed chili parlors and the fringe of furtive characters that haunt Madison Square Garden, many of them castaways of the rodeo, the circus or the fading world of the prize ring. Yet, in spite of its rather drab background, it overflows every evening with diners, many of them as knowing trenchermen as you will find anywhere. This is one of the favorite places of A. J. Liebling, the traveling journalist and articulate gastronome. Marlene Dietrich drops in to order the roast leg of lamb, cooked *à la française* with a juicy pink heart and a mound of green *flageolets*. Judge Medina is a regular customer. So is Nina Foch, the actress, and many others whose names are well known in the theater. The simple but delicious food and the friendly warmth of this little restaurant attract many who enjoy an occasional escape from the more luxurious establishments they patronize on the other side of Fifth Avenue.

The head man here is Jean Pujol, a large, beefy Frenchman who comes from the little southwest provincial town of Ercé, in the department of Ariège. He is one of that remarkable Pujol clan that has settled firmly in West 48th Street, to the marked benefit of dining standards in that scarred and battered neighborhood. The small restaurant called Pierre au Tunnel, across the street, is owned by his brother Pierre. Half a block farther east is the large and prosperous Les Pyrénées, operated by his wife, Odette, and his other brother, René. Odette Pujol, born and raised in Dijon, is related to the proprietors and directors of half a dozen other French restaurants in New York. Sitting with M. and Mme. Pujol over brandy in the late after-dinner hours always produces a stream of lively gossip about all the town's colorful restaurant people, from the great Henri Soulé (whose chef happens to be a cousin of Mme. Pujol) to Charlie, the owner-barman of the latest ten-table bistro on Ninth Avenue.

Jean has had a lively restaurant career since he started as an apprentice in Ercé, twenty-five years ago. He had a job at the Folies Bergère, an off-Broadway casino-type restaurant that flared briefly and expired without leaving a trace. He was *rôtisseur* in one of the kitchens of the Waldorf and cooked at the Biltmore, the sacrosanct Bankers Club and the Rainbow Room in Rockefeller Center.

"But we do not do the fancy cooking at Du Midi," he told me. "Here we make family style. My chef is young. He was born in my home town. He cooks like his mother taught him. He will make you a *gigot d'agneau Boulangère,* a calf's head *vinaigrette, raie au beurre noir* or onion soup, just as they were made in that part of France since the days when they plowed with a stick."

Among other modest triumphs of the shirt-sleeved chef is a lusty beef stew, laced with red wine, sprinkled with button mushrooms and small onions. There is an economical cut of steak that comes with crisp French-fried potatoes, and is served hot, juicy and full of flavor. Omelettes are excellent and so are the *escargots Bourguignonne.* The duck with black cherries and the roast filet of beef Bercy, are more festive dishes, and so is the whole roast squab chicken, with appropriate vegetables. Bread of a crisp and crackling freshness is almost as good here as it is in France. Beaujolais is the wine to drink with most red

[29]

meats, but there is also a good selection of popular favorites like Médoc, Châteauneuf-du-Pape, Pouilly-Fuissé, Neufchâtel and three well-chosen rosés—Anjou Perlé, Rosé de Provence and Tavel d'Or.

The Café du Midi is not far from the French Line pier, and there is always a clump of leathery-faced seamen in the little bar up front, which stays open until four in the morning. At most meals you will be almost sure to see a few dashing pilots from Air France and the air is usually full of animated French spoken by French-American members of the colony nearby, who know a bargain when they see it.

Chateaubriand

131 EAST 54TH STREET

Owners: *Alex Hounie and Roger Parizot* (Chef)

Maître d'Hôtel: *André*

N THE WANING DAYS OF 1933, WHICH WERE also the waning days of that most ignoble of Noble Experiments, new restaurants sprang up like mushrooms after a summer rain. One of these, still in its building stage, particularly caught my eye. It was on Third Avenue between 48th and 49th Streets, on one of the routes I took in walking home from the office at 40th Street and Madison Avenue to the apartment at 51st Street and the East River. Each evening I passed. I'd stop and look in to check the progress, the walls being painted, the small curved bar being set up and the leather-covered stools facing it, the carpet being laid, the kitchen taking shape behind the large plate-glass windows which were to permit the diners to watch the maestri in their acts of creation, the tables moving in, the chairs, and the final exciting preparation for the rising of the curtain. Everything about it, at least from Third Avenue peering in, had the look of an excellent restaurant, and my wife and I decided we most certainly would be amongst its customers on opening night. We were not amongst its customers; we *were* its customers. The only other people there were the owners and their relatives. The reason was simple; the wine and liquor license had not yet been granted, and the very attrac-

tive bar was non-operative, unpopulated in back, unpopulated in front. (In the first days of Repeal in New York, former speakeasies got their licenses immediately and without trouble, but new, legitimate restaurants had considerable trouble and, usually, in the end, expense quite a bit beyond the cost of the license itself.)

We were welcome to have dinner even though the whole place was *en famille,* but it was impossible for them to serve wine. The apartment was not too far away, so I volunteered to dash over and get some sherry as an apéritif, and some red wine to accompany the *coq Bourguignonne* we had ordered. These we shared, and the seeds of friendship were sown.

The restaurant was known then, and is known now, as the Chambord. But this essay is not at all about the Chambord, which is elsewhere in this book, but about the Chateaubriand.

There were four owners of the Chambord in its beginning. They were Alex Hounie, Roger Parizot, Roger Chauveron, and another partner named Maurice. They were, as their names would indicate, from various parts of France; Hounie, for instance, from the Basque country, and Parizot from Burgundy. After a time Hounie and Parizot left and opened their own new restaurant on East 56th Street, between Lexington and Third Avenues, known as Chateaubriand.

The Chateaubriand had the fine French cooking, the expertly chosen wine cellar, and the knowing clientele which had attracted attention to the Chambord. But it did not have the prices which had attracted a different kind of attention, an eyebrow-raised kind, to the Chambord. Chateaubriand was a success from the start, and is still a success, though not in the same 56th Street place. The attractive East 56th Street building, once a museum, fell prey to the wrecker and the builder, so Alex and Roger picked up their skillets and their knives, their martini mixers and their brandy-inhalers, their wines and their sauces and moved two blocks down Manhattan Island to 54th Street between Park and Lexington Avenues, to be precise, to 131 East 54th Street. You'll find them there today.

You'll also find the same dishes which made the original Chambord and the original Chateaubriand famous, and a few additional ones

Roger or Alex picked up on annual trips back to France. Naturally, Chateaubriand cuisine is strictly French, although the menu is quaintly bilingual, reflecting Alex's penchant for waggishness with such items as *Le Roast Canard, Les Scallops Long Island, Le Ice Cream,* and so forth. The accent of Chateaubriand is Burgundian, for Roger, chef and half-owner, was born and raised in Burgundy and received his initiation as a cook in the kitchen of the famous Au Trois Faisans restaurant in Dijon, the Côte d'Or town which is regarded by many as the food capital of the world. Naturally, the Chateaubriand, capital C, features chateaubriand, lower case c, a superb thick cut of richly marbled beef, served for two people, and most happily accompanied by Roger's airy, gently browned, succulent *pommes soufflées,* and a green salad. Duck *à l'orange* is another specialty, generously meated half duck done to a crisp dark brown, with a richly heady dark sauce in which Burgundy wine and shreds of orange assert themselves.

But Chateaubriand food is not all on the side of *haute cuisine.* Roger and Alex are proud of their more gustily plebeian dishes as well, particularly of the authentic Toulon-type bouillabaisse which is served each Friday at luncheon, and the stalwart *cassoulet,* the Languedoc peasant dish of beans and pork, solidly ensconced in thick brown sauce, more fit for lunch to send you back to work in the fields than in an office high above Madison Avenue, but this doesn't seem to deter the executives who find it irresistible each Thursday, when the menu features it.

The Chateaubriand has one of the most exquisitely chosen wine cellars in New York, or in the United States for that matter, and a wine-drinking clientele. Alex is one of the leading figures in the Confrérie des Chevaliers du Tastevin, a Grand Officier, and Roger is a Chevalier in the organization. They feature many of the wines which have received the official accolade of the Confrérie, and which bear its recommendation on the labels.

There is one more extremely pleasant thing about eating at the Chateaubriand; it is quiet, it is unhurried, and while it's always comfortably filled, it never seems crowded. But as with all fine restaurants, it is well to call and reserve your table.

Chez Vous

78 CARMINE STREET

Manager: *Paul Magnano*
Headwaiter: *Renato Belli*
Chef: *Anthony Barbera*

T HIS TINY DOWNTOWN RESTAURANT WAS endowed with a name borrowed from the French which might be broadly translated as "Like Your Own Home." Never were words more true. That is, if your home happens to be small, continually filled with hungry guests, clamorous with laughter and conversation, and richly impregnated with the smell of hearty Mediterranean cooking. Otherwise, its French name is puzzling. For never was a restaurant less French or more Italian. That goes for the food, the atmosphere and the personality of its owners. The entire establishment would fit into the living room of a comfortable home. It has a pocket-size kitchen, tucked away at the rear. The walls of the restaurant proper are almost completely covered with empty wine bottles, neatly arranged in patterns. There are also prominent framed mottoes which urge the guests —as though they needed it—to eat, drink and live it up. Because of the limited space, there is no bar, and of course no spirituous liquors. However, you may have an *Americano,* a *Negrone* or vermouth-on-the-rocks before your meal, and a choice of several excellent wines afterward.

[34]

When Chez Vous is crowded—which is just about all the time—it will hold about forty persons of normal proportions. Located modestly in the remote western outskirts of the Village, it is hard to find and harder still to get into for lunch or dinner. Not because it is a snobbish place, but simply because the comparatively few people who know and love it go there as often as they can. This makes it difficult for strangers, who usually are seated only after the regular patrons are finished, and that may be very late in the evening.

Once you make a reservation for dinner, it is well worth the long taxi ride and the more or less inevitable wait just inside the front door. While you shift from your left to your right foot, the guests at the table you have booked are lingering maddeningly over their black coffee and cigarettes. It is the sort of place that people hate to leave.

The charm of Chez Vous will probably be wasted upon those who, when dining out, insist upon luxurious surroundings, plenty of elbow room, a worldly and extensive menu and a certain slick subservience on the part of the host and his assistants. All this is noticeably lacking at Chez Vous. Instead you will be flattered, scolded and spoiled by Paul, the chief owner, whose enthusiasm and delight in serving his favorite friends are as infectious as the laughter of children.

The staff of Chez Vous are all remarkably energetic, sweet-natured, vital persons. Paul, who possesses the most winning smile to be found in lower Manhattan, tells you what to eat and helps with the service. Maria, his wife, also cooks in the tiny kitchen and enjoys the reputation of making the best ravioli, and white and green noodles, this side of Bologna. Renato, diminutive and a little shy, looks like a quaint character in a neo-realistic Italian movie. He is partner, waiter and co-cook, roaming everywhere at once, loaded to the chin with trays and bottles and full of cheerful small talk, delivered in a unique accent that is just barely understandable. Renato's working costume, day and night, is surprisingly formal for such unassuming surroundings, consisting of black tie and dinner jacket of a rather antique Old World cut.

The food is excellent, ample, well seasoned and occasionally very great. Elegant touches abound. For instance, there is a Florentine fruit-

[35]

bowl of fifteenth-century extravagance, the size of a small bathtub and filled with magnificent fresh fruit, including giant strawberries, nectarines, plums, pineapples and other varieties. Another article of rather surprising size is the perambulating pepper mill, three feet high and proportionately thick.

No more delectable *pasta* can be found anywhere, especially the delicate meat-filled ravioli, Maria's masterpiece. Once a week, there is *Osso Buco* with Mushroom *Risòtto*. For the very fastidious, Paul offers the clean citrus flavor of *Scaloppine Limone,* an ideally light choice after you have surrounded a huge dish of noodles or spaghetti. Paul's pet dessert is *Zabaglione,* a rich, frothy blend of eggs and Marsala wine, whipped up by him at your table. Oddly enough, though, one of the house specialties is Florida Key Lime Pie, which would be regarded with intense suspicion in Italy, but is delicious here, especially when backed by Paul's background chatter and insinuating smile.

When you have been to Chez Vous often enough to be considered a friend of the family, Paul will bestow upon you and your wife and friends the official sign of his special affection. Some evening, when you have just finished a copious dinner and are smiling beatifically over coffee and one of the host's complimentary liqueurs, Paul will approach with a flashlight camera and snap your picture. The next time you come, you'll see the photograph, framed and hung on a wall among hundreds like it, composed of patrons who wear the same beaming smiles, and who are obviously afloat on a gentle tide of red wine.

Believe me, this is no empty honor. It is the final benediction, the visual, incontrovertible proof that you and yours are not only expert judges of fine Italian cooking, but nice people worthy of a permanent welcome at Chez Vous.

Christt Cella

160 EAST 46TH STREET

Owner: *Richard T. Cella*
Headwaiter: *Justo Chiesa (known as "Church")*
Head Chef: *Peter Achino*

F EVER A RESTAURANT EXPRESSED A MAN, IT is this one. Physically, the man was short, rough-hewn and squarely built, like an oaken sea-chest that was built to last forever. His manner was simple and direct to the point of roughness. But behind the craggy exterior— and not too far behind—there was shrewdness, intelligence above the ordinary, a lively sense of humor and a rich love of life. No wonder less gifted mortals were attracted to this man and idolized him.

His name was Christ Cella. He numbered among his friends bankers, Wall Street brokers, newspaper and magazine people, book publishers, advertising agency executives and politicians. Truck drivers, delivery boys and detectives, among other rugged characters, were equally fond of him. All tried their best to court his quick, sardonic grin and were jealous of their right to call him friend.

Every night, in his crowded, rather rickety little restaurant on East 45th Street, Christ Cella held forth. It was an honor to have him visit at your table. If he liked you, he would shepherd you to the bar, late

[37]

in the evening, overwhelm you with free drinks and let loose the while an unceasing stream of talk in which ribald gags, anecdotes about the old country and penetrating good sense were intermingled.

When he was in the mood, which was often, he would lock the doors of his place at ten o'clock of an evening. Then a group of his close friends would sit with him in the kitchen until the pale wobbly hours of the morning. Mrs. Cella, a beautiful woman with a serene disposition, would sometimes join them for a few hours, fascinated as always by the raffish magnetism of her mate. In the center of this crowd Christ would perch on a bar stool, his immensely powerful fingers battering the keys of a glittering accordion. Music and song bounced off the dingy walls of the kitchen and rattled the vessels on the range. This happened during the most dismal period of Prohibition, but all the gentlemen present were primed with excellent whiskey and brimming with backyard red wine that flowed from gallon jugs. Neither the revenue boys nor the local hoodlums ever broke in upon these merry proceedings, for the host had a way with these people, as he did with everybody.

Christ was proud of his family, his house in New Jersey and his restaurant. He was especially proud of Dick, his son. We, who were faithful followers of the great man, watched Dick grow from a small boy to a towering, handsome athlete, captain of the M.I.T. crew, and hero of the famous race with Princeton. After some of these races, Christ gave dinners worthy of Rabelais' wildest imagery. And his generosity was such that he would invite not only his son's crewmates and coach, but the coach and crew of the rival team.

Christ Cella was the closest thing to an innkeeper, in the old true sense of the word, that New York has ever known, and his restaurant became so famous that soon a dozen imitations sprang up along East 45th Street, and Steak Row was born. Today, most of Christ Cella's former waiters and barmen have places of their own—all sub-cella's, as it were. The restaurant is a school which graduates a man with a perfect steak for his diploma.

The steaks in question were—and still are—all that good beef can ever attain at the hands of man. As far as I know, Christ was the first to offer his guests a cut known as the sirloin shell. It was shaped like a miniature bolster and was served charred a crusty black from close contact with flames of blast-furnace intensity. The meat was sliced at the table against the grain in chunks two inches thick on a hot platter anointed with butter, lemon juice, cracked black pepper and salt. Your steak ran freely with red juices and the flavor and texture were what men dream about when they are dog hungry.

Christ Cella's idea of a restaurant was inevitably a simple, strongly masculine conception. He gave you the best steak in the world, a smoking hot mound of hashed brown potatoes or a superb baked and buttered Idaho, fresh green salad if you asked for it, good French bread, slathers of butter, and coffee that was strong and hot. Everything was of superlative quality and freshness. He did his own buying of meat, fish and vegetables, and everything had to be the best. On his own admission, he was the toughest customer the market man had to face each morning, but he was always prepared to pay top prices for what he wanted.

There were other features of the pattern which he set and which is followed religiously today. The waiters are still Italian-Americans of forthright personality, who work in their shirt sleeves and who recite the brief litany of the day's dishes, for no menu has ever been used at Cella's. There are a few wonderful choices for those who are not in the mood for steak. Among them are three-pound broiled Canadian lobsters, triple loin lamb chops, and occasionally grilled sea bass, bluefish or scrod. That about sums it up, except that one usually begins this untrammeled feast with crab meat or shrimps in a good cocktail sauce. At lunch, I often used to order a cut of beef never encountered elsewhere—a rump steak about as big as a first baseman's two fists, that had more flavor than expensive sirloin or porterhouse, and fairly gushed deliciousness when you cut into it.

Even in the depressed early Thirties, a time of fierce competition

[39]

among restaurants, it was a costly matter to dine at Cella's. And it is expensive today, by contemporary standards. But that has not kept the restaurant from selling out, lunch and dinner, for the past twenty-five years. Men are odd about things like that. They will bellow with anger at a suspicious repair entry on a garage bill, or at the price tag on an evening gown, but they're lambs when it comes to paying for great food in congenial surroundings, with an added something which belongs only to Cella's tradition.

Christ Cella died a few years ago, to the deep sorrow of his countless friends. The restaurant is now run by Dick Cella, his son. Dick has kept to the pattern his father created, not because it was the easy thing to do, but because no one could do better. Educated at M.I.T., worldly and suave in his manner and dress, he is as articulate as his father used to be, but wastes no words and indulges in no pretences. When the writer asked him for a few recipes to reprint in this compendium, here is the way he expressed himself:

"As far as giving you recipes goes, I feel that a recipe is like a fountain pen. I hand you a pen and you write with it—then I take the pen and I write with it. Same pen, but the writing's different. I cannot even get two of my own chefs who work side by side to make it come out even, so what's the use? There are a million recipes, and what can one recommend about a thick, juicy steak, except to buy the best, and don't broil it too much."

After occupying the old quarters on East 45th Street for many years, Christ Cella's has at last yielded to pressure and is now at home in new and more commodious surroundings, a short block farther north. There is more elbow room and a newer look to everything, but the basic philosophy is unchanged.

The bar is commodious, and tends more and more to harbor both sexes, instead of men alone or in convivial company. You are apt to see alongside of you a Senator up from Washington, a professional model whose features will be maddeningly familiar, a couple of visiting ballplayers or the couple that lives next door. The evening will slide past, your table will be late in coming, but you won't mind too much. The reason, of course, is that there is almost nothing in life more pleasant than dining out in good company. Especially when the food is the very best of its kind and you are made to feel as comfortable as though you were in your own home—or even more comfortable than that, in quite a few cases.

The Coach House

110 WAVERLY PLACE

Owner: *Leon Lianides*
Chef: *James Bogan*

Y OU CAN'T KEEP THE NEWS ABOUT A GOOD restaurant secret from New Yorkers, even when the place is way downtown and off the beaten track. Take the Coach House, for example, obscurely located on a quiet back street west of Washington Square. It is so good that it has lured to its doors many fastidious diners who rarely venture below 42nd Street except to make out a will or visit their brokers.

The place is further handicapped by giving every exterior indication of being a tea room, which is disquieting to the serious eater. Worse than that, it looks like a tea room that is trying to look like a coach house. The fact is that at one time, it actually *was* a coach house and belonged to one of the old families in this once-distinguished residential section. It still has the exposed beams, the brass lanterns, the hunting prints and other decorative odds and ends of a horsy nature to prove it. To sum it up, the Coach House has everything that would make it irresistibly attractive to gentlewomen of refined taste and small appetite.

[42]

But you will soon discover that there is nothing ladylike about the food you get here. It is Southern cooking of a quality you will be lucky to find in any restaurant in the South itself. The cook is an amiable giant of a colored man from Alabama and the hostess and waitresses are remarkably pleasant and efficient. Skeptical guests may test the kitchen's standards by ordering certain simple dishes which are always a reliable indication of a restaurant's class. One of them might be black bean soup, a staple here. It is unmistakably authentic in its smoky flavor and smooth richness, and totally unlike the insipid purplish liquids we have sampled in far more pretentious surroundings. The triple loin lamb chop and the filet mignon are thick, juicy and of a flavor that wins masculine approval. At frequent intervals, batches of hot corn sticks are brought in from the kitchen and they are the best of their kind I have ever tried. The lump crabmeat in heavy cream au gratin rivals Baltimore's best.

Chicken pot pie is like mother would have made if she had ever learned how. And even that Dixieland cliché, fried chicken with cream gravy, tastes crisp yet succulent, as it used to taste before the war. The Southland's richest dessert, pecan pie, is a house specialty and may be wrapped up to take home for the children, or mailed to your Aunt Jo-Ellen in Atlanta. It is insidiously sweet and crunchy, and highly fattening, and I do not approve of it, but it is hard to resist all the same.

As usual an individual obsessed with perfectionism is responsible for the unexpectedly delightful food and the little human touches of warmth and intimacy. Leon Lianides, the owner, is a serene individual who is gifted in many ways. He is a modest man, and it will probably come as a surprise to some of his regular clients to learn that he is an accomplished gastronome, an expert cook who performs in the culinary idiom of half a dozen civilized countries, a connoisseur of painting and one of the most able restaurateurs it has ever been my pleasure to know. Born on the Isle of Rhodes, he is tall, handsome, dresses carefully and does not resemble in any way the proprietor of what might be mistaken for a tea room but is really one of the best American restaurants around.

[43]

One day, Mr. Lianides is sure to own or direct a great restaurant of international celebrity in the fashionable uptown East Side sector. Until this happens, however, now is a good time to trot or gallop down to the Coach House for a fine meal, good wine and a check that is pleasantly moderate for value received.

The Colony

30 EAST 61ST STREET

Proprietor: *Gene Cavallero*

AT THE TURN OF THE CENTURY, AND through the horse-drawn burgeoning years of the twentieth century, there were a few special and especially elegant restaurants in New York which catered exclusively to what was known as the Carriage Trade. Supreme among these were Delmonico's, at 44th Street and Fifth Avenue, Sherry's at 46th Street and Park Avenue, and Pierre's at 47th Street and Park Avenue. Each had its own building, decorated in the marble-entrance, deep-rug, red-plush-curtain, crystal-chandelier tradition. All are gone, the restaurants and the buildings alike, and where once stood these citadels of gracious living, now squat frowning skyscrapers given over to the grim pursuit of making a buck.

The one restaurant which bridges the era of these epicurean ghosts and today's epicurean shrines is the Colony. It was not their contemporary, as it did not start until the dying days of their glory, but it did precede, by a rather goodly number of years, the present colossi, 21, Le Pavillon, Baroque. And great as are these, the Colony still looks with a bit of condescension upon them, still is the restaurant of the mellow, old New York society, more than of the brightly polished, freshly varnished café society.

It was not always thus with the Colony. Its start was inauspicious, its early life discouraging and even a wee bit sordid. Gene of the noble mien was not its owner, merely a worker there, and the tables that were later to be graced by High Society were occupied by Guys and Dolls.

In the days of its infancy, the Colony shared its now-sacrosanct premises with a gambling joint, small, discreet as such places go, but still a joint. The owner then was Joe Pani, former proprietor of Wood-manston Inn, a nightclub joint, big, noisy, respectable as *such* places go, but still a night club. The Colony even then was a superb restaurant, for it had, in addition to Pani, Ernest Cerutti as its maître d'hôtel, Gene Cavallero as its captain and Alfred Hartmann as its chef. The leading patron was the famous, or infamous gambler, Arnold Rothstein, who had discrimination in his selection of food, but not quite so much in his selection of pals, one of whom ventilated him with several slugs from a .45 because some of the boys felt that Arnold was a little dilatory and ungentlemanly in paying his just and honest gambling debts. But Rothstein's unseemly death left the Colony something less than bereft. In the first place, there were other gamblers who either had the same discrimination (in food) that Rothstein had or who simply believed in following the habits and whims of Mr. Big Shot, and who came in numbers with the current ladies of their fancy. And in the second place, Cerutti and Cavallero, both of whom had long and respectable careers in elevated eating places, were pretty much fed to the ears with their raffish clientele.

Pani was a man of extravagant moods, to the heights today, to the depths tomorrow, and the trio, who now had come to realize that the best hope of the Colony was for them to take over when they honestly and honorably could, pooled their resources and bided their time. Their time came; a black day when Pani saw clearly there was only one way out, to cut his own throat. To him, in his blackest of moods, the boys had conveyed that there were philanthropists ready to free him from his hell, and stay him from his fate. The price he asked, to be thus succored, was $25,000, or almost precisely $7,000 more than the three stalwarts had to their names. But the deficit was quickly provided by Sylvester Haberman who not only liked Ernest, Gene and Alfred, but also disliked the constant habitation of the premises he owned by such characters as Arnold Rothstein and Larry Fay. So the Colony passed into the hands of Ernest Cerutti, Gene Cavallero and Alfred Hartmann. But even then, the Colony did not quickly and gracefully slide into the elegant rendezvous it is today. The Guys and Dolls stubbornly continued to come, and the Ladies and Gentlemen stubbornly continued to stay away. Then, at a period when only the friendship and generosity of suppliers were keeping the Colony alive, there came its Magic Night. Mrs. William K. Vanderbilt came to dinner.

It's impossible to measure the impact of that visitation by comparison with today's standards of society in New York. There is no one comparable to Mrs. Vanderbilt, no one whose influence could make a restaurant overnight. But the Vanderbilts not only were the undisputed leaders of American society, they were also gourmets of considerable and justified repute. Next day the affinitied worlds of New York restaurants and New York society buzzed excitedly. The Vanderbilts returned, and in their wake came other luminaries of New York society; Lord Northcliff, Reginald Vanderbilt, Tommy Hitchcock, Jules Bache, Angier Biddle Duke, the Winston Guests, Mrs. Edward Hutton, the Duke of Marlborough, Alfred P. Sloan, and the Grover Loenings. Today many of the same names and comparable names in society are still on the regular list of Colony customers, and to them have been added highly respected names from the world of the arts: the Lunts and Helen Hayes from the theater; Ludwig Bemelmans, the painter-author; John Steinbeck, S. J. Perelman, the authors; Harold Guinzburg, Bennett Cerf, the publishers.

Today, Gene Cavallero is the only one of the original group left, and is, of course, principal owner. In 1927, Chef Alfred Hartmann sold his share to partners Ernest and Gene, and happily returned to his native Alsace, fairly opulent and highly respected. In 1937, Ernest Cerutti died on the Italian liner *Rex,* on his way back home for his annual vacation. As an indication of how well the partnership had done by that time, Ernest Cerutti left an estate of half a million dollars. That left Gene sole owner, a responsibility he did not embrace too happily, so, two years later he took into partnership George Fiorentino, his solemn, gentle-mannered headwaiter, a partnership which continued to everyone's satisfaction until recently, when George retired.

Today, there is another partner, but still only one name, for the other partner is Gene's son, Gene, Jr., known mostly, simply as Junior. Junior did not blithely walk in to take over the family store. He served a tough apprenticeship abroad where apprenticeship is a meaningful and serious institution. He wrestled with pots and pans in the kitchen of Paris' George V hotel, perfected his French at the switchboard of the Paris Ritz, studied with the *sauciers* at the Suvretta House in St. Moritz, learned the service and dissection of game at the Buffet de la Gare in Zurich, and practiced the care, dispensing and appreciation of wine at the Hotel Ambasciatóre in Rome. Probably the greatest tribute to Junior's absorption in his apprenticeship, and in the years since in the Colony, of the niceties of the restaurant business, is the fact that today he enjoys the professional confidence of both his father and the rest of the Colony crew.

Other important members of the Colony staff have been around a long time, a number of them from, or very nearly from, the beginning. Of the original staff, there remain Felix, the maître d'hôtel, Branchi, the genial captain, Marco, the bartender, and more than a dozen of the waiters. The *chef de cuisine* is Jean Vergneo, who served his apprenticeship in Grenoble, then at the Waldorf, then, nine years ago, as *saucier* at the Colony, and, after three years, as *chef de cuisine*.

Marco Hattem is one of those freakish bartenders who remembers not only what drink you like, but the way you like it; and this he does even if you're an infrequent patron. Marco is a rebel in his attitude toward today's dominant before-dinner drink, the dry martini. He does not believe it should be daintily stirred, but rather that it should have the daylights shaken out of it; and he does not believe that the gin should merely be breathed upon by the vermouth, but rather that the two should be blended in the former classic proportions of about three to one.

A restaurant as fine as the Colony does not indulge in specialties, or perhaps more accurately, indulges in nothing but specialties; caviar, shad and pompano, beef and baby lamb, chicken, squab and ring-necked pheasant, terrapin, all are found here impeccable in quality, cooking and serving. But there is one specialty, not widely heralded, in fact known to only a few old Colony hands. It is, of all things, spaghetti with clam sauce! As this is one of Gene's very favorite dishes, and as he can, not infrequently, be seen eating it on nights away from his own place, in one of his favorite Italian restaurants, it gets affectionate treatment in the Colony kitchen. You'll not find it better anywhere in the world.

Copain

891 FIRST AVENUE

Proprietor: *Edward K. Kern*
Chef: *L. Stone*

EEKMAN PLACE AND SUTTON PLACE, BOTH east of First Avenue, both facing out on the East River, have for many years been amongst the most fashionable sections of New York. Tiny streets both of them, they nevertheless boast some of New York's finest town houses and most famous residences. But they were islands unto themselves, surrounded by cold-water flats, tenements, and tough districts generally.

First Avenue, a short block away from each, was one of New York's seamier avenues, mean and undistinguished, a dreary area of poor flats, dingy streets, rough, beer-sodden saloons. Then, about twenty years ago, a renaissance began in the neighborhood, sleek new apartment buildings began to rise, brownstones and run-down old houses were bought up and rejuvenated, and the whole area, including First Avenue, began to perk up. Smart little shops, particularly craftsmen's shops, began to appear, saloons, notably Billy's gaslit emporium at 56th Street and First Avenue, refurbished themselves and the whole section began to seek the carriage trade which was settling there in increasing numbers.

Then, after the war, gold was really struck when the UN and its appurtenances and personnel moved into the neighborhood at 46th Street and the East River. The rejuvenation of the area was accelerated and still goes on. It is particularly noticeable in the wealth of good restaurants that have come to the neighborhood. There are the Sutton at 58th Street, the Seafare at 57th, Casa Minasso at 52nd, the Diplomat around the corner from the Minasso, the Rendezvous on 48th Street, the Toque Blanche on 50th Street, and the pioneer of them all, the Copain, at 50th Street and First Avenue.

The Copain was opened some years ago by a young man named Ed Kern who had not been a professional restaurateur but did have a feeling for and knowledge of good food, and when he did open it was a courageous move indeed. In fact, had he been a professional restaurant man, his better judgment and experience probably would have restrained him from making the attempt. Fortunately, with the change in the section, his brashness paid off beautifully.

The Copain is small, intimate, quiet and appealing. Its food has a French accent, but the menu is liberally seasoned with American dishes, here and there an Italian dish, and even at least one East Indian specialty. The menu is surprisingly large for such a small place, and frequently has on it such imaginative items as Periwinkles *Provençale, Fonds d'Artichauts au Foie Gras,* Sliced Whale Steak, Turkey Curry-*Rijstafel* and *Boeuf Braisé en Gelée.*

The wine list is surprisingly good. It is not extensive, because there simply isn't room for an extensive cellar, but the choice is excellent.

The Copain is small, almost tiny. The bar is in a cozy separate room right at the entrance from First Avenue. It seats only about a half-dozen people, but somehow manages to stock the ingredients for practically any drink you ask for, including such exotic items as a Gimlet, a Screwdriver, and a *Negrone.*

The main dining room, which is main only in name and not in size, is beyond the bar. The place is usually quiet, without bustle, and the service serene. The prices are not low, but neither are they staggering.

[51]

The clientele is largely neighborhood, Beekman Place, Sutton Place, and the early East Fifties, but for some surprising reason you nearly always run into a couple from Kentucky, or Texas, or Arizona, or some other unlikely spot, who have been told that they simply *must* go to the Copain. I certainly wouldn't say you *must* go, but I do think that if you go, you will enjoy it.

La Côte Basque

5 EAST 55TH STREET

Owner: *Henri Soulé*
Headwaiter: *Albert Spalter*
Chef: *Bernard Valentin*

 HIS BRISK CONTEMPORARY RESTAURANT IS admirably suited to its midtown East Side location and worldly clientele. It was established by Henri Soulé in the former premises occupied by Le Pavillon after that great social and gastronomical institution had moved to new quarters farther uptown. He planned it to be a less resplendent version of the parent restaurant, with à la carte service eliminated and instead a *prix fixe* menu limited to a comparatively few dishes. Obviously, this would reduce much of the waste, risk and high operating cost which are unavoidable in the lofty reaches where the Pavillon glitters.

For the first few months, La Côte Basque was overcrowded with curious New Yorkers who were eager to sample the new creation of the master. The service was hurried and ragged, and unhappy murmurs of disappointment were heard. This was only natural, under the circumstances, for the name and reputation of M. Soulé led most people to expect immediate perfection.

Now that the restaurant is no longer a novelty and has settled down,

I am glad to report that things have changed and all goes well. La Côte Basque has built its own loyal clientele from what is perhaps the most discriminating public in America. At lunch and at dinner, the tables are filled by ladies and gentlemen who have the taste, the experience and the income that qualifies them to appreciate M. Soulé's suave ministrations. The service is now as smooth and as unobtrusive as the fussiest Park Avenue matron could desire. The food, it is almost superfluous to say, is remarkably good, even though it may lack the lavish richness of Le Pavillon's more elaborate cuisine.

The menu is a model of compactness and is made up of comparatively simple dishes. At lunch not long ago, there was a first offering of tempting hors d'oeuvres *à la français,* the chef's own *pâté, oeuf en gelée,* various cold shellfish, a couple of interesting *potages du jour* and ripe melon or other fruit. Afterwards we made a selection from *Moussaka d'Agneau Côte Basque, Rognons Sautés Bercy, Carré de Veau Fermière, Escalope de Ris de Veau Clamart,* Striped Bass *Pré Catalan* and *Filet de Sole Murat,* with an enticing *salade du chef* for the waist-line watchers and an array of *pots de crème au chocolat,* ice creams and delicious assorted pastries for those who live recklessly. There are many fine vintages in the cellar, as may be imagined, but the popular choice seems to be for the lighter and younger wines. At the present time of writing, M. Soulé has announced a new room reserved for men only, where luncheon will be served for seven dollars, exclusive of drinks. A fine idea, we believe, which should be pleasing to everybody, except perhaps the ladies.

Danny's Hide-a-way

151 EAST 45TH STREET

Owner: *Dante Charles Stradella*
Maître d'Hôtel: *Peter Berruti*
Chef: *Nicola Maiocco*

THERE ARE TEN RESTAURANTS ON NEW YORK'S East 45th Street, between Lexington and Second Avenue, where steak is supreme. Perhaps the most famous of them all is Danny's Hide-a-way, owned by the youngest and smallest restaurateur along what has come to be known as Steak Row.

Danny Stradella was once an amateur boxer, a prize-winning Lindy Hop dancer at the Harvest Moon Ball of fragrant memory, an ex-GI who was wounded at Salerno, as well as an aggressive little man who fought his way up from the tough Italian part of Manhattan's West Side to become one of the city's most popular hosts. Danny's success is based solidly on a certain instinct; he knows exactly what his guests like and how to make them feel happy.

Part of this is due to the stern training he received from the late Papa Stradella, who founded a still earlier steak house on this same street, and who put his pint-sized son through every job in the joint, from busboy all the way to manager. The rest is sheer personal charm and hard work. Danny opened his own place when he returned from the war. It had six tables, a tiny bar and was just big enough for the waiter to squeeze through sideways.

Today the Hide-a-way has spread out over three adjacent buildings. The space on three floors is divided into ten rooms, each with a special name and appropriate decorations. These dining areas are always filled and there is usually a line of people waiting for tables. The food is plain, well cooked and about as good an example of solid American he-man fare as may be found the nation over. There are no pretentions to continental suavity, no headwaiters in tail coats, no wine stewards or wine lists. At dinner, there is not even a menu, but Danny will come to your table to recite the house specialties and take your order. He is still young, still a sharp dresser and a sharp manager. He has an instinctive talent for making people of all sorts and degrees want to call him by his nickname and claim his friendship.

At one time or another, everyone eats at Danny's. Some like the food, the cheerful masculine hubbub and the presence of famous people so much that they would like to move in and live *en pension,* if that were possible. There is no better eating place, I would think, for a plain-thinking, plain-eating big business wheel to play host to his most important client from out of town. It is also a favorite of journalists, cartoonists, jovial drinkers, officials of the UN, actors, debutantes with crew-cut escorts and swarms of other people who are just out for a big steak and a gay evening.

In addition to the prime charcoal-broiled beef, Danny is proud of his lobster stuffed with crabmeat and such well-known Italian dishes as Veal Cutlet *Parmigiana,* Lobster *Fra Diavolo,* Veal *Scaloppine* and a purely American version of baked potato which carries this coy printed message on a marker: "You may eat my jacket, I have been rubbed, tubbed and scrubbed." Wines of a somewhat nondescript kind are at hand, but beer and hard spirits are the drinks here. The prices, as they are elsewhere on Steak Row, can add up to an expensive evening, unless you are very careful what you order—but who wants to be careful at Danny's?

Fontana di Trevi

151 WEST 57TH STREET

Owner: *Armando Mei*
Maître d'Hôtel: *Norris D'Alessandris*

IN RECENT YEARS, ROME HAS REPLACED PARIS in the hearts of many Americans who travel abroad. It is not hard to understand why. We are a people who like to be liked. The Italians, without straining too hard at it, captivate us with their friendly ways and Latin warmth. As a city, Rome may not be as light-hearted as Paris, but its ancient sobriety is dappled with sunshine and tempered by unexpected bursts of music and laughter. As for food, the Parisian sort has more distinction, but Italian cooking is full of robust, earthy flavors much to our taste. When it comes to eating ravioli or gnocchi and drinking flagons of red wine, most American tourists find it very pleasant to do as the Romans do.

Under the circumstances, it was only to be expected that some smart restaurant man would open a place in New York with wall-to-wall Roman atmosphere and a kitchen that specialized in the native dishes. Armando Mei, a tall, earnest young Roman endowed with plenty of American drive, was the first to see this opportunity and to act on it.

"Most restaurants have a hard time of it for the first few years,"

[57]

Mr. Mei said to me not long ago. "But we seemed to catch on from the start. People come here and eat and eat, and they ask me, with a sentimental look in their eyes, if the Colosseum is still so beautiful in the moonlight, and whether the old flower-seller still sits in the middle of her flowers at the bottom of the Spanish Steps. Sometimes it makes me homesick for Rome myself."

The Fontana di Trevi, a small, highly colorful *trattoria,* just across 57th Street from Carnegie Hall, comes honestly by its Roman background. It is actually the American branch of the ancient and respected Ristorante Mei, situated on the Giancolo near the American Academy in Rome. It has a menu rich in Roman specialties. Its *Pollo alla Diavola,* a deviled chicken which is the glory of the famous Restaurant Passetto, tasted almost as good to me as the original. The famous entree, *Saltimbocca alla Romano* (literally, "flies in the mouth"), which blends the contrasting flavors of veal, *prosciutto,* sage and red wine, was equally appealing.

Leaving no stone or dollop of papier-maché unturned in his ambition to reproduce his native city's charms, Mr. Mei has filled the narrow little restaurant with familiar scenery. At the rear is the pride of the place, a replica in miniature of the famous fountain which gave the restaurant its name. It is built of glazed terra cotta and spouts water from every conceivable aperture. A spotlight bathes its gleaming surfaces and there is a sound of soft Italian music seeping somewhere from its rear. Patrons toss coins into this fountain, and make a wish, just as they did on their last trip abroad.

No spare foot of space has been neglected by the owner in his effort to pour on the Roman props. One may marvel at an ornately sculptured replica of the Constantine Arch, examine framed sketches of the city's venerable landmarks executed by a local artist, look thirstily at sections of trellis hung with grapevines, and respond thirstily to the invitation of hundreds of assorted wine bottles that cover the walls.

When I dined there not long ago with a party of three other friends, we had a dinner that was chosen by our host, a procedure that

I recommend to others who may patronize the restaurant. Among the good things was Veal *Zingara,* made from a recipe which Mr. Mei said came from the gypsies who wander in and out of the Trastevere quarter as the seasons change. There was an appetizing *Risòtto alla Finanzière* which cunningly combines well-cooked rice with chicken livers, tongue, ham and mushrooms. For me, the high point of dinner was a large heap of steaming hot noodles cooked *al dente,* with a thick russet sauce of mushrooms, tomato purée and smoked ham. Another guest spoke affectionately of the breast of turkey, sautéed in butter with a golden coat of eggs and bread crumbs, almost exactly as it is cooked in the myriad restaurants of Rome.

We drank a Lambrusco wine, with a merry tingle on the tongue, and that laughing Italian favorite, Valpolicella, color of rubies in sunlight. At another time, we had the typical Roman *pasta* called *Spaghetti Matriciana,* with an unusual sauce of onions, olive oil, distinctively flavored Italian bacon called *Pancetta* and fresh tomatoes. A grind of black pepper on this delightful dish, a light snow of Parmesan cheese and a glass of good red wine of the country, all consumed beneath one of Mr. Mei's grape-hung trellises, by itself is the making of a successful evening in New York.

The Forum of the Twelve Caesars

57 WEST 48TH STREET

Owner: *Restaurant Associates*
Director: *Alan Lewis*
Maître d'Hôtel: *Andy Anderson*
Chef: *Fred Ruprecht*

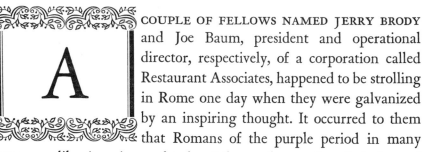 COUPLE OF FELLOWS NAMED JERRY BRODY and Joe Baum, president and operational director, respectively, of a corporation called Restaurant Associates, happened to be strolling in Rome one day when they were galvanized by an inspiring thought. It occurred to them that Romans of the purple period in many ways were like Americans of today. Like us, they preferred the best of everything, and could pay for it. This seemed to fit neatly into a pattern which they were dreaming up for a new restaurant.

Among other aspects of life led by upper-class Romans was a taste for rare wine and foods, usually transported to the imperial capital with great difficulty from far-off places, which of course increased their desirability. The cognoscenti doted on British oysters, gamebirds from Gaul and songbirds from Africa, exotic sea food and shellfish from all the subject seas and rivers. They set an international table of fantastic lavishness and complexity. Their cooking kept up to the boundless larder at their disposal. Roman dishes were of a studied and rococo richness, reeking with curious spices and sparked by condiments as hot as lava.

As the two talented—and strikingly young—associates walked among the ruins and studied the contents of museums and libraries, their imaginations soared. From their daring ideas eventually grew a most unusual and impressive restaurant, utterly unique among New York's many thousands that cater to mass appetites.

The Forum of the Twelve Caesars is a restaurant that lives up to the magnificence of its name. Comparatively new as far as great restaurants go—it was opened in the fall of 1958—today it is firmly established as a favorite eating place of the local epicurean set, as well as a showplace for visiting celebrities from Europe or the West Coast, and one of the required sights for tourists doing the rounds of Rockefeller Center.

A few months after it opened, four of us dined there. It should be recorded that this was a group not easy to please, one which entered the imposing portals of the Forum with a certain skepticism. We had definite premonitions of a letdown. Our feeling was that the food could not possibly live up to the advance build-up, or to the majesty of the setting. We were given a table in the corner of a great square room, done in shades of garnet and ruby, its lofty brocaded walls hung at stately intervals with immense framed portraits of the twelve emperors, the work of a sixteenth-century Italian painter.

The imperial scheme was enriched by such little touches as a barman and assistants wearing the imperial toga, and by accessories like wine buckets in the shape of carved helmets, wine baskets of woven silver wire, ornately embossed copper place plates as big around as a flying saucer, heavy hand-woven linen cloths, and mosaics and statues that might have been plucked from Pompeii at the height of the watering season. On every side of the room, flames leaped from great platters of food that looked like set-pieces at a Neronian weekend orgy.

Where there is showmanship on such a scale, it has been my sad experience to encounter mediocre food. The sort of mind that conceives dining out as essentially an entertainment and a spectacle does not, as a rule, go with a respect for good food and the loving and expert care required by its preparation. We four that evening were impressed by our surroundings. We were struck by the enormous amount of research and imagination—not to say hard cash—that had been poured into this major project. But we fully expected that the drinks would be warm and the food cold, the bread without texture and the sauces without flavor. It is my happy privilege to report that we were delightfully disappointed. The food at the Forum is not only prepared and served with a royal flourish, it is also delicious to eat. We came to this conclusion after three hours of steady attack upon the finest that the management could place before us.

From my notes—stained with purple, incidentally, and growing more and more illegible as they neared the final stirrup-cup downed at the bar just before midnight, or something, struck—I offer a few treasured memories. We began with that delightful ancient Roman apéritif—martinis served in pre-chilled oversize glasses. After this icy jolt to our apprehensive appetites, the parade began. An almost imperceptible signal flashed from the hawk-like eye of our host, Mr. Baum, to his crew of costumed assistants. There was a flurry of robes and sandals and the table was almost instantaneously covered with cold hors d'oeuvres. Here are the names of some of these dishes, exactly as described in the lush rhetoric of the vast menu:

> Artichoke with Strasbourg Livers. The Leeks of Rome, Apician Style. Lentils and Sausages, Sweet and Sour. Smoked Game Fish, Sauce Vitellius. The Great Heather-Smoked Scotch Salmon. Belgic *Pâté* with Wild Boar, Sauce of Damascus Plums. Herring of the Far-off North Sea. Various Hams Served with Delightful Fruits.

The table was cleared and there followed a series of dishes identified as: "MORE PROVOCATIVES—HOT." My notebook records them as follows: "Beef Marrow on Toast, a Lucullus Original. Great Mushrooms Stuffed with Snails. The Great Forum Artichoke, Filled with a Purée of

Oysters. Leek Pie with Hot Sausages. Wild Boar Marinated and Served on the Flaming Short Sword." This last tidbit had a mildly gamy flavor and was brought to us as dramatically as Salome bearing the head of John the Baptist on a platter. The menu, by the way, is a souvenir I shall always cherish. It is an enormous four-page affair, exquisitely printed and bound in a cover tied with purple ribbon and secured by a golden seal. Its literary style has the gusto of Charles Dickens wedded to Suetonius at his most eloquent.

With the early courses, we drank a magical white Château Haut-Brion, chilled in a silver helmet of the Legion filled with ice. It was carried by a wine steward in an appropriate costume, hung with a silver chain and an antique drinking cup.

When the table was cleared, there came another quick succession of individual dishes. Each was a small earthen vessel of antique cast, reposing on a tripod and warmed from below by a flaming container of alcohol. On the menu this course was called: "Roman Ramekins called Minutals, Favorites of the Augustan Court." There were six of them and we decided later that they constituted a high point of excellence on this notable evening. We passed the ramekins around, sampling diligently. Tasting from left to right, they were as follows:

LUCANIAN—Lamb, Sausage, Dill. SYLVAN—Venison, Red Wine, Chestnuts. APICIAN—Egg, Red Wine, Marrow and Leek. LUCRINE —Tiny Scallops and Artichoke Hearts. TARENTINE—Chicken, Mushroom, Truffled Cream. PISCATORIAN—Mousse of Pike, Lobster Sauce.

Our guide and mentor, Mr. Baum, assured us that all were authentically Roman in their conception, recreated after diligent search of Suetonius and Apicius, and after much consultation with learned professors who were specialists in ancient cultures. We had no reason to doubt him. We were bathed in warm good will. The Roman cuisine and stage effects had effected a transformation in our early attitude.

After an hour and a half of feasting, helped along in its middle stages by a couple of bottles of Nuits St. Georges of a notable year,

[63]

we were ready to admit that this was a new experience in the line of gastronomical adventure. With or without atmosphere, authentically Roman or not, this food was equal to the world's best.

Between the early courses and the main event, we were served each a whole fresh truffle, roasted in the ashes by a process described aptly in the menu as Herculanean. If you are curious about the cost of such a rarity, it was quoted on the menu at $7.50 a portion. This was the highest individual price, on the same plane as "Mallard Duck Prepared in the Silver Press," and "Pheasant of the Golden House on a Silver Shield in Gilded Plumage." We had a dim sensation of guilt as we chomped away at the coal-black truffle, delicate in flavor, very crisp in its covering of flaky pastry.

We were offered our choice of the main course from among a dozen or more tempting items. So we chose three different dishes, each of a rather special kind. We sampled them in turn with what we hoped was scientific thoroughness. The first was a small haunch of baby lamb, roasted over charcoal and accompanied by something called "The Sauce of the Two Lively Lillies." The second dish was sirloin of beef, stewed in red wine, with beef marrow and small onions—"A Gallic recipe Julius collected while there on business"—wisecracked the menu-writer. The third *plat principal,* and most impressive of all, really deserved a blare of trumpets and perhaps we actually heard one—it is hard to remember everything at this late date. It was called "Ringneck Pheasant, with Brandied Berries, Baked in Clay Under the Fiery Ashes." A waiter captain first showed us the bird armored in smoking hot gray stone. At a side table, he tapped the casing smartly with a hammer—the only hardware on the premises that didn't look antique. The clay fragments fell in shards and the bird was revealed, wrapped in silver foil which preserved the steaming perfume of the tender flesh.

We did our best to eat more than a few bites of each of these main dishes, but found it impossible to do so. Mr. Baum tempted us at this point with a magnum of Dom Pérignon 1947, a champagne unknown to any of the Caesars and perhaps too good for them, at that. Then,

[64]

purely from pride, he offered several desserts. One was a scalloped blue dish packed with shaved ice in which nestled spears of ripe fruit. There were thin *crêpes* rolled around a stuffing of ice cream and chopped ginger. Prettiest to look at was a whole orange, frozen hard, its top raised like a cap and its interior filled with orange sherbet. We wound up with Coffee *Expressus* and Marc de Bourgogne.

The final half hour was enlivened by the presence at our table of Albert Stockli, chef director for the Restaurant Associates. A large, genial Swiss with a twinkling eye, Mr. Stockli is perhaps one of the few creative master-chefs left in the modern world. Working under the brilliant guidance of Joe Baum, chief genius of the Associates, he invented or adapted most of the dishes on the extraordinary menu. No real lover of the exotic and the unexpected in gastronomy should miss visiting the Forum of the Twelve Caesars. The restaurant must be granted a place with the half dozen or so great ones in this country which rank with the world's best.

The Four Seasons

99 EAST 52ND STREET

Owner: *Restaurant Associates*
Director: *Joseph Baum*
Maître d'Hôtel: *Jacques Casanova*
Chef Director: *Albert Stockli*

WHEN THE FOUR SEASONS OPENED ON THE mezzanine floor of the Seagram Building in the summer of 1959, one of the executives casually remarked to an interviewer that the restaurant had been built at a cost of $4,500,000. After a good look around, even the most confirmed skeptics admitted that this sum was a reasonable estimate. But why all this magnificence? After all, this was an eating place, not a museum or a palace. The official spokesman explained that, to begin with, the owners of the building had insisted upon a restaurant that would be in keeping with its surroundings, regardless of the expense. It had to be elegant, spacious and beautiful, all on a grand scale. Above all, it was to be carried out in the same daring but austerely contemporary architectural style as the building itself.

The bright young men of Restaurant Associates, fresh from their triumphant launching of the Forum of the Twelve Caesars, threw themselves with characteristic devotion into this challenging project. Three eminent architects—Philip Johnson, Miës van der Rohe and Eero Saarinen—were commissioned. William Pahlmann was chosen to create the decorative scheme. Several well-known painters, sculptors, technicians and designers were called upon. Every detail of furnishings, tableware, draperies, lighting and costuming was executed to order by some specialist in his field.

The result of this collaboration is a showplace that now ranks with New York's major attractions for visiting firemen, as well as for the more prosperous segment of the local population. It is also, I am glad to say, a restaurant of undoubted gastronomical importance, the only one of the top dozen in America which is not strictly French or Italian, either in management or in the food it serves. The paintings, carvings, murals, furniture and horticultural marvels have been described in print so often that the story need not be repeated here. After all, what we are most concerned with is food.

In its way, the cuisine of the Four Seasons lives up to the excitement of its architectural setting. It, too, for the most part, expresses its particular time and place. Many of the dishes presented in the exquisitely printed menu are refreshingly different; some are utterly original. A few excellent examples that I have personally investigated are: Lobster Parfait (chunks of lobster meat and creamy pink sauce in a tall conical glass with swirls of whipped sour cream on top); Raw Mushroom Salad with Sauce Malabar; Beef Marrow in Bouillon or Cream; Whole Fresh Truffles Baked in Puff Pastry; Suckling Kid in Lemon and Parmesan Crumbs; *Croustade* of Morels; Quail Stuffed with Mandarins and Nuts; Almond Vichyssoise; Atlantic Bluefish in Flaming Fennel; Turban of Whitefish and Crabmeat Mornay; Crisped Duckling with Calmondin Oranges, *Flambé*; Casserole of Pigeon, Green Almonds and Tomatoes; Amish Ham Steak, Hot Rhubarb; *Poussin* with Wild Thyme; *Sabayon* of Kirsch over Strawberries; Rose Petal Parfait; Frosted Banana-Rum Soufflé.

These dishes were lifted at random from a couple of hundred on the Spring menu. As you probably already know, there are four changes of menu every year, in keeping with seasonal changes in lighting, color scheme, costumes, upholstery and floral arrangements and plantings. The man behind the extraordinary food is Albert Stockli, chef director of the Associates. In our opinion, he is one of the very few genuinely imaginative cooks living. Much of his inspiration in creating original recipes comes from Joseph Baum, executive vice president and managing director of the Four Seasons. It was Mr. Baum who dreamed up several ingratiating features which add to the fun of dining in these elegant surroundings. He believes that vegetables, usually frozen to begin with, are poorly cooked in most American restaurants. And so he subsidized the early crops of certain New Jersey and Long Island truck farms, taking their entire output of new, tender, baby-sized carrots, peas, beans, salad greens, asparagus, and other garden stuff. A basket artistically filled with these midget vegetables is shown to every table for approval and selection.

Another of his genial ideas is the fragrant herb garden that flourishes in a special corner of Albert Stockli's kitchen, handy for use in soups and sauces. Mr. Baum has first call in many remote places for rarities like wild mushrooms, exotic fruits and nuts, *cèpes, chanterelles, morilles,* black truffles from Périgord, white truffles from Piedmont, choice vintage wines from Bordeaux and Burgundy, Channel sole and turbot, Scottish salmon, Colorado trout, Wisconsin goose, Chincoteague oysters, Virginia blue crab and other delicacies.

Not all the clever new dishes live up to the fascinating way they are described on the menu. Some are all garniture and very little flavor. A few are masterpieces of pretentiousness. This sort of thing is bound to disappoint the man who is strictly and solely impressed by the traditional cuisine of France, and who regards all departures as an outrage to good taste. But gourmets who have an adventurous viewpoint approve this striking out in new directions. They have made the Four Seasons a favorite port of call and the list of their names would be flattering to any fine restaurant in the world. The prices here are high, it would seem unnecessary to add—perhaps the highest anywhere, but this is always a controversial matter. The restaurant is flourishing, nevertheless, and was a success from the first day. And this seems to indicate that there are many who bask in its spacious grandeur, who love its food and wines, and are more than pleased to pay for the privilege of enjoying them.

[68]

Gloucester House

37 EAST 50TH STREET

Owner: *Edmund C. Lillys*
Chef: *Dean Anton*

 HERE ARE AT LEAST HALF A DOZEN GOOD sea-food restaurants in Manhattan, but only one that is great. It is called Gloucester House. Like many other top-rated establishments, it is the creation and obsession of one exceptional individual, who dreamed it up in his hard-working younger days, shaped its excellence detail by detail over the years, and now stays strictly on the job to run things with a smiling countenance and a steely grip on the controls.

The man's name is Edmund C. Lillys. He looks and dresses like one of the more conservative members of the Bankers Club, speaks with a cultivated, vaguely foreign accent and knows all there is to know about fish, lobsters, oysters, clams, crabs and shrimp—from baiting a hook to planking a shad. If you ever dine at Mr. Lilly's immaculate and spacious restaurant, with its bone-white scrubbed hardwood tables, non-fishy filtered air, chaste green-and-white New England decor and gracious Negro waiters, you are quite likely to remark, "After all, and with due respect to Soulé and Chauveron, where have I ever eaten better?"

Of course you will react that way only if you are a genuine lover of the edible treasures of sea and stream. Also if you are in the habit of insisting on fish that is freshly caught, its flavor unimpaired by fast-freezing. And if you prefer fish that is cooked simply, without smothering sauces or high seasoning or elaborate complications *à la français*.

The owner of the Gloucester House is a man of firm opinions about the way a restaurant should be run. In order to be sure that he will get the freshest and most succulent sea food, he does the marketing himself and pays stiff prices to get the best. Of all his many talents—and he is a highly cultivated man—he is proudest of his ability as a buyer.

"I was born," he told me, "with the gift of glancing at a row of twenty mackerel and picking out the best fish. As a boy, I lived in a Greek colony on the coast near Constantinople. When the fishing boats came in, the family sent me to do the marketing for that day. I used to hang around the kitchen while the fish were being cooked, and learned how to do it. That started me off in the sea-food restaurant business when I came to this country."

He is dead set against the system of kitchen hierarchy which is a tradition in France and which often makes of one man an arrogant and temperamental virtuoso in a tall white cap, surrounded by resentful underlings. There is no head chef in the Gloucester House kitchen. Each station is run by a specialist—usually a Negro from the South or the West Indies—who cooks nothing but soups, salads, shell-fish, sauces, broiled fish or desserts. All are expert and all are equal. The head man, really, is Mr. Lillys himself. There are no headwaiters in tail coats and no sommeliers in silver chains. This is in keeping with his fondness for plain American ideas. The Negro waiters are mature men with a stately natural dignity and a fatherly manner toward the guests. Some have been with him for twenty years or longer.

Among the dishes worth trying are Guilford soft clam roes, meltingly delicious in their thin coating of buttered crumbs. Or the crab-meat au gratin, which, to the surprise of many who wrongly believe that "au gratin" means "with cheese" (it means "cooked with a brown covering"), is sautéed simply in a copper pan with nothing but the best sweet butter and no seasoning except a squeeze of lemon. The Maine lobsters come in several styles and sizes. The average broiled or steamed lobster weighs about a pound and a half, but there is also a "jumbo" which goes about three and a half pounds and costs $9.25. I assumed that this sweet monster was always served for two, but Mr. Lillys assured me that it was strictly a one-man dish.

"I only sell about eight or so of the big fellows a day," he said. "Sometimes a party of four big eaters from out of town will come in and order one apiece as the main course of their dinner. Texans, usually."

All lobsters are from Maine and the most popular way to cook them is plain broiled. "We broil our lobsters meat side up under a very hot flame, and never turn them. That way we don't loose the juice. We help things along by basting with melted butter. Never any crumbs or stuffing. And no fancy foreign additions like cream, tomatoes or aromatic herbs. A lobster is a great thing in itself. Why spoil it by making it taste like something else?"

Fish are served only in their season and the method of cooking is strictly American, which means broiling, frying or poaching with the minimum of elaboration. Soft-shell crabs are never buried in batter, but sautéed with a light dusting of flour in pure butter. Shrimps are good here, especially when roasted in their shells with a sauce of butter, lemon juice and a ghost of garlic.

The gargantuan eaters from out of town who are often weak with desire for sea food, which is denied them because they live so far from the sea, often run up a bill of twenty dollars or so for two. But they are not as typical among the steady clients as elderly specimens of midtown East Side gentry who totter in often just for a salad and a glass of wine. Everything on the big, handsomely designed menu is à la carte and prices are a good one-third higher than those at the next best sea-food house in this vicinity. But they are justified, in my opinion, for the Gloucester House is the Pavillon or Colony of its kind.

The Golden Horn

122 WEST 49TH STREET

Owner: *Aram Salisian*
Maître d'Hôtel: *Richard Salisian*

THERE IS A WHOLE COVEY OF ARMENIAN restaurants in New York's Armenian section in the East Twenties. But the most famous Armenian restaurant in New York is in the Forties rather than the Twenties, and on the West Side, rather than on the East Side. It is the Golden Horn, at 122 West 49th Street. The Golden Horn is still owned by the man who started it, Aram Salisian, and actively managed by him, his son Richard, and James Graf. Aram was born in Armenia and learned his cooking there. Richard was born in the Armenian area of California and is a graduate of the University of Southern California. His California background has quite a bit to do with the present success of the Golden Horn. He was brought up with, and went to school with, Gene Mako, who was also of Armenian heritage. Gene developed into one of the best tennis players of his day, which was also to be Don Budge's day, and the two teamed as the top American doubles team, leading jazz buffs, and inseparable friends. Their togetherness inevitably brought Don to the Golden Horn, which became his favorite restaurant. When he turned professional in 1938, he went on tour with Ellsworth Vines, who was the professional champion. At the beginning of the tour he fell behind to Vines and in desperation put in a long-distance call to Dick Salisian to come and cook for him his favorite dish, *Ajem Pilaff,* a concoction to which is attributed magic powers. Magic or not, imaginary or not, *Ajem Pilaff* and Budge victories coincided, and his march to the professional championship began. The papers picked the story up, and New Yorkers picked up the Golden Horn. Papa Salisian wired for Dick to hurry home to help take care of the crowd and neither Dick nor the crowd has since left.

Tennis players other than Don Budge list the Golden Horn as their favorite restaurant. Jack Kramer makes it his headquarters when he's in New York, with Pancho Gonzales and Lew Hoad frequently in tow. It's the habitat, too, of entertainment people, of such decorative packages as Lana Turner, Linda Darnell, and Jayne Meadows, and of such varied talents as Steve Allen, Franchot Tone, André Kostelanetz, and the Metropolitan Opera's Nicola Moscova, and Lucine Amara.

The Golden Horn was originally on 51st Street between Fifth and Sixth Avenues, elbow-rubbing with Toots Shor's colonial façaded palace. But the expanding city moved in and the Golden Horn and Toots Shor's moved out, Shor to his own place on West 52nd Street, the Golden Horn to 122 West 49th Street. The new place has three rooms, the Magic Carpet Room with a sixteenth-century zodiacal ceiling, and a legend that any wish made under it will come true; the Mosque Room, a large lounge and bar with red banquettes; and the main, or Gold Room, with murals copied from ancient Persian books, an original Persian painting by Mme. Bouvé, and an inscription which blithely promises that "All those who pass through these portals will be blessed."

The food is Armenian with overtones of Turkish and Greek. The place is famous, appropriately, for Shish Kebab, which the Gourmet Society says is the finest Shish Kebab in America. One specialty of the house is an hors d'oeuvre, cheese rolls called Cheese *Beorek* (blown dough with melted cheese inside). There is a gold menu which describes dishes in such full-blown prose as, *"Ajem Pilaff:* Delectable merger of lamb and rice, served with a sauce as intriguing as an Agatha Christie mystery." There are also succulent lamb dishes, flaky, honey-soaked pastries, stuffed cabbage, herculean coffee and traditional Armenian drinks such as the licorice-flavored Arak, and Armenian resin-flavored wines which you can learn to like if you live long enough. Prices at the Golden Horn are surprisingly reasonable.

Lindy's

1655 BROADWAY

Owners: *Albert Abend and Jack M. Kramer*
Maître d'Hôtel: *Hyman Heller*
Chef: *Heinz Engel*

THE FOUNDER AND HIS WIFE, SADLY ENOUGH, have departed, but Lindy's is still the most colorful, the noisiest, and the most widely publicized restaurant of them all. And yet it is not a great restaurant, as epicures use that adjective. Except for its display of hundreds of autographed photographs and caricatures, its swarming crowds both day and night, and its famous windows crammed with a sea of huge baked apples, giant steaks and hams, delectable fruit-topped cheesecakes and masses of oversized fruits and vegetables in serried ranks, Lindy's looks like any other large, successful Broadway eating emporium. The difference is reflected in the customers. They are today's version of the grifters, the softhearted horseplayers, the cloud-headed eccentrics, the saucy blonde choristers and the wisecracking newspapermen of Damon Runyon's time. There is no other clientele quite like this anywhere in the world.

The same odd characters congregate there, singly and in cozy groups; the same glittering bevy of Broadway beauties, and the same "important personalities" from the theater, the arts, crafts and rackets. If you have a keen ear for dialects, you will hear a dozen of them in a stroll through the packed tables any hour between noon and two A.M.

The corner where the song writers sit is still solidly packed and gives out with the old peculiar humming sound, punctuated by an occasional loud yelp of anger or protest. The comics huddle over *Schnecken* or French crullers and coffee as before, and spear pickles and reputations with the same stabbing ferocity. Respectable gambling gentlemen are scattered through the crowd, behaving themselves, as always. There are sprinklings of small, shapely young ladies whose faces are mantled with fresh make-up and who wear leopard-pattern toreador pants and carry their stage costumes in a purse.

Solidly represented, I am glad to report, are the big eaters, the rotund guys and dolls who devour huge steaks, savory roasts and stews at a rate that often impels the sporting element to make book on their capacity and imminent collapse.

Time will tell whether or not Lindy's will always retain this electric excitement and continue to lure a hungry public that understands the meaning of good food at forbearing prices. From recent visits, I can testify that they still serve the best breakfasts, from late morning to late afternoon, consisting of goblets of orange juice, hot rolls, toasted rye bread, bagels and onion rolls, platters of fried eggs with imported Wiltshire ham, and the finest coffee in a neighborhood where the coffee standard is very high.

Connoisseurs of chopped chicken liver come here as to a shrine. The smoked salmon and sturgeon have become legends. Partly because of sentimental nostalgia, but mainly because of the way it tastes, a great dish here is the boiled spring chicken in soup, with a clear golden color, and a powerful aroma of long-simmered fowl and fresh vegetables. It was Lindy's that launched the Great American Cheesecake, now universally imitated, but still alone in its rich, creamy glory.

But everything tastes good here and that is the real reason why there is a line at the door every midday, at six o'clock and immediately after the theater. The big majority of those waiting come not to see celebrities, or bask in the Runyonesque atmosphere, but to eat, and eat superlatively well in a tradition that is part German, part Jewish and part American. May this be always so. For if Lindy's should ever lower its standards, or pass into alien hands, or drop out entirely, something irreplaceable would go out of the lives of New Yorkers.

Louis and Armand

42 EAST 52ND STREET

Headwaiter: *Victor Berti*
Chef: *Mario Del Boca*

EVERYONE HAS HIS PET RESTAURANT, AND every restaurant has its loyal following. That rather large group of midtown New York executives who have made Louis and Armand their pet restaurant seem to be just about the loyalest of all such loyal groups. Many of them have been wearing the Louis and Armand school tie since its beginning days on West 49th Street, many lunch there every business day, and more than a handful stop back later in the day for cocktails, or cocktails and dinner. Louis and Armand is a real New Yorker's restaurant; what few transients eat there, usually come in tow of New York friends. Because of this sophisticated and rather regular clientele, everything, food, drinks, and service, must be consistently and unfailingly good. Everything is.

Louis and Armand started in life as Louis and Martin, on West 49th Street between Fifth and Sixth Avenues, in the late Twenties. As were all good places to eat those days, it was a speakeasy. Shrewd Martin was the bartender, huge Louis was the chef, and dashing Armand was not yet on the scene. The menu was varied, every dish brought to table was superb, but the place won its early acclaim and following for serving just about the best steak to be had in New York.

This, plus the fact that portions of drink and of food were unusually generous, tended to draw a masculine crowd, a large part of which, for some mysterious reason, consisted of advertising men. In 1930 Martin left to try his hand in a place of his own on East 52nd Street, and Armand came in to be maître d'hôtel and a full-fledged partner, and the name, logically enough, became Louis and Armand. In 1930, they too moved, to 46 East 53rd Street. Here, in these more elegant quarters, Louis emerged from the kitchen and donned a business suit (though he still kept a sharp eye on what went on around the ranges); Armand added to his sartorial meticulousness a fierce upsweeping moustache which became one of the sights of Madison Avenue, and which was to be seen in several advertisements for which Armand modeled; and Victor Berti was brought in from Rumpelmayer's where he had worked both in London and New York, to be captain of waiters, later a head-waiter. Victor jumped ship in 1933 but was lured back in 1937, when Louis and Armand moved to the present stand at 42 East 52nd Street. The Loyal Following were saddened in 1945 by the death of Louis, and again in 1947 by the death of Armand.

Over the years Victor was becoming more and more the dominant force in Louis and Armand and today, with both Louis and Armand gone, Victor *is* Louis and Armand. Legally, the place belongs to the Estates of Louis and Armand, but litigation is now going on, and it is the fervent hope of The Following that Victor and some of the other boys will be made the rightful and sole owners. There is a superb staff, as highly professional as you'll encounter anywhere, most of whom have been with the place for years, and are known to the customers by name, and the customers, in turn, are known to them by name. The atmosphere is very clublike and *gemütlich*.

While the dominant personality at Louis and Armand's, as far as the personnel is concerned, is Italian, and while the Italian dishes are excellent, the cooking is international, which means that it has distinctly French leanings. The steaks, which first attracted attention to the restaurant, are still as good as are to be had in New York. The sea food is also excellent although by no stretch of the imagination could it be called a sea-food restaurant. In summer, the cold buffet is particularly alluring. The buffet wagon is rolled to your table and on it, in an enticing array, are cold duck *Bigarade,* chicken Jeanette, lobster, shrimp, lamb, beef, vegetable salad, and other house specialties. The salads here are also famous, particularly the chef's salad and the sea-food salad. They will also give you a Caesar salad, but protestingly, as they consider it a rather gauche invention of California.

The drinks at Louis and Armand's are particularly good and particularly generous. The wine list is excellent.

The clientele at the restaurant, particularly at luncheon time, is interesting and distinguished. It is still a hangout for advertising executives, also for radio and television people, performers, executives, producers and publicity people, for actors, for publishers, editors and writers.

There is one feature about Louis and Armand that has always appealed greatly to me and which I have found in no other restaurant. When you want something you can ask any waiter, captain or busboy in the place and he will smilingly fill your order. There is none of this business about "This isn't my table" or "I'm not your waiter." It's a nice attitude.

Lüchow's

110 EAST 14TH STREET

Owner: *Jan Mitchell*
Maître d'Hôtel: *Dave*
Chef: *William Hellering*

IT IS SAID THAT HUNDREDS OF SENTIMENTAL persons of both sexes, who live as far away as London or San Francisco, make a supreme effort every year to go to Lüchow's for Christmas dinner, no matter what difficulties the effort may entail. It is not hard to understand why. Since 1882, this great old restaurant has always crowned its year with a warm outpouring of the holiday spirit on a scale that is unique.

An enormous Christmas tree stands in the center of the vast main hall, lifting its twinkling branches, blazing with a thousand lights, to the vaulted ceiling. Around its base, children cluster, fascinated by the glitter. They squat, bemused and enchanted, staring with big eyes at the panorama of the Holy Family and the Three Kings, carved by woodworkers of the Black Forest. According to our favorite waiter captain, this is the largest indoor tree in New York. It looks very much at home in Lüchow's.

On a dais near by, the famous string orchestra plays with dedicated fervor. The music is tinged with nostalgia. They play the lilting waltzes of Strauss, gay tunes from Victor Herbert operettas and, at this season of the year, carols, and old German hymns. A heady aroma permeates the vast, time-darkened rooms. It is the smell of Christmas feasting—a symphonic blend of roast goose, flaming brandy, foaming *Würzburger* and *Kulmbacher* beer, Chanel Number Five and the rich blue smoke from Havana cigars.

Gray-haired men and women are present who speak of Lüchow's as one does of a well-loved uncle or a preferred stock that has never passed a dividend. They were brought here as children and some of them have never missed a Christmas dinner on 14th Street since. The very oldest can remember when the neighborhood was the blazing center of New York's night life, and hansom cabs jostled one another at the gas-lit entrance. Diamond Jim Brady was a steady customer, a living monument to appetite and thirst. With him came often the beauteous Lillian Russell, resplendent in ostrich plumes and bulging lace, demonstrating to her worshipful public that the feminine form divine could still look luscious, even though it tipped the scale at about one hundred and seventy, and was ample enough to surround six prodigious courses and floods of foaming champagne.

The old romantic days are gone forever. But, whether during Christmas week or any week, nothing has changed at Lüchow's, except, as most people think, for the better. Fourteenth Street is now a raffish, noisy street of bargain shops and blackened loft buildings, swarming with shoppers from all the five boroughs and with human flotsam strayed from the nearby seedy purlieus of Union Square. But at its very heart stands *der alte* Lüchow's, unaltered, fabulously prosperous, still attracting famous guests, still one of the nation's finest eating places, perhaps the best known German restaurant in the world.

That it has thus magically retained its robust traditions and its high standards of food and drink and service is due almost entirely to Jan Mitchell, a handsome and youngish man, fastidious in his tastes and habits, who looks like a man-about-town but is actually a shrewd, European-trained restaurateur who is equally at home in a kitchen or an art gallery. Mr. Mitchell took over the ownership seven or eight years ago, at a time when things were on the downgrade and alarmingly close to a fade-out. He restored the cooking to its former glory, groomed the two hundred or so members of the staff to new heights of efficiency, revived the old-time festival celebrations, refurbished the interior without changing its essential character, and made Lüchow's once more a restaurant where old-fashioned hospitality and *gemütlichkeit* reign to the delight of all.

High peaks of the year are the weeks devoted to seasonal festivities. Beginning with Christmas week, there follow sessions celebrating Roast Goose, May Wine, Bock Beer and Venison. During these rollicking parties, the vast dining rooms are filled to their limit with patrons who have reserved tables weeks ahead. The walls and rafters are hung with bunting and greenery. Guests wear paper *Studenten* caps or gay, feather-trimmed Robin Hood hats. A Bavarian band recruited from Yorkville, made up of extroverts dressed in *Lederhosen* and Tyrolean hats, parades relentlessly around the tables, blasting away with all its shining brass. From time to time the musicians sing German drinking and marching songs and sentimental ditties of the 1900's. At the closely packed tables, many occupied by entire families, from *Grossmutter* and *Grossvater* down to the toddling generation, the singing, eating and beer-guzzling reach monster proportions.

But even at ordinary mealtimes the year round, everything is oversize at Lüchow's—the menu, the portions, the heavy beer steins, the thirsts and appetites of the guests and of course the restaurant itself. About a thousand persons can be seated at a time in the downstairs dining halls and the party rooms upstairs. But in spite of this Brobdignagian scheme of things, the staff faithfully carries out Jan Mitchell's edict that every guest in the vast throng must be made to feel at home and happy.

Among the dishes most in demand are game of all kinds in season, especially venison in all its forms, partridge with wine kraut and the famous *Hasenpfeffer,* made from Canadian hare. Other favorite dishes are *Schnitzels* in several different styles, *Sauerbraten* with potato pancakes, homemade *Bratwurst* with sauerkraut, wonderful boiled beef and the tiny smoked pork chops called *Kassler Rippchen.* A famous appetizer is *Schlemmerschnitte,* which is freshly ground raw fillet of beef, garnished with fresh black caviar and chopped onion and served on buttered toast. This was a popular choice long ago of Pavlova and John Barrymore and is eaten a good deal nowadays, especially on Sunday evenings, when people whose names fill the local columns are present and the glitter rivals the time of Caruso, Paderewski and Julia Marlowe.

Perhaps the most characteristic of the many desserts is the famous German Pancake, in size almost as big around as a manhole cover, but incredibly light and tender. This huge, smoking hot *Pfannkuchen* is prepared at table-side, buttered, sprinkled with sugar, cinnamon and lemon juice, covered with *Preiselbeeren* or the filling of your choice, then rolled up and set afire with rum or Kirschwasser.

The formidable leather-bound wine list is studded with many legendary German wines. There is a fabulous Moselle at $26 and several precious Rhine wines at similarly thought-provoking prices. But these are the showpieces. Most of the thirty-odd German wines run considerably less. The selection of French wines and cognacs is surprisingly good and, as may be expected, you will be tempted by a choice of the best beer, domestic or imported, available on this hemisphere. The *Würzburger Hofbrau* and the *Augustiner Brau* are on draught in perfect condition at a dollar a stein, and well worth it. Many a sturdy drinker prefers them to the oldest and most precious bottle in the wine cellar, and who is to say that he is wrong?

For sentimental as well as gastronomical reasons, a visit to New York is not quite complete without at least one evening at Lüchow's. Be sure you wire or write ahead for reservations. And, on the advice of the knowing, be sure to eat and drink lightly or not at all during the hours before you make your pilgrimage to the Valhalla of legendary eaters and drinkers on 14th Street.

Mama Laura's

230 EAST 58TH STREET

Owner: *Laura Albertario*
Maître d'Hôtel: *Carlo Albertario*
Chef: *Ugo Sguanci*

IT DID NOT OCCUR TO ME THAT A RESTAURANT with a name like "Mama Laura's" would be worth patronizing, unless, of course, you happened to be one of those unhappy persons bothered by a compulsive yearning for maternal affection.

And so I dined there the first time rather reluctantly, urged on by a friend who had promised me a surprise. He made good and it turned out to be a lovely evening. The food was authentically North Italian, with a rather unusual mingling of homemade flavor and worldly elegance. As a student of that particular school of cookery, I was not only surprised but delighted. The restaurant, I thought, could stand firmly on the quality of its food alone. It did not need to pretend that Mom was in the kitchen.

Then I made a second and third visit and broke down completely before the warmly enfolding charm of Mrs. Laura Albertario, the well-rounded little woman with curly white hair and eyeglasses who is the owner and guiding spirit. Today I call her "Mama" without self-consciousness, exactly as do hundreds of other clients of this handsome East Side restaurant.

Back in 1939, at the start of its career, the place was known as Maison Mario, after the late accomplished chef and restaurateur, Mario Albertario. His wife, Laura, handed out menus, wrote out the checks and murmured sweetly to the guests in her appealing and slightly comical Italian accent. During the whole of World War II, the restaurant was packed nightly by uniformed men of all ranks and origins. Some of them were in town on leave from flying combat missions overseas; others were spinning out a short and usually tumultuous interlude before being shipped. A warm and almost naïvely trusting soul, the lady of the house hovered over them with a motherly tenderness shadowed by anxiety, for few of these young men knew where they were going or if they would ever return. As might be expected, the *padròna* reminded them of their own mothers back home. They told her so and she adopted them all without exception for the duration. On their last evening at Maison Mario before shipping out, more than a thousand members of the armed forces kissed Mama Laura goodbye and gave her keepsakes in the shape of medals, cap ornaments, lucky dice, flying badges, campaign ribbons and unit insignia. Hundreds of these faded and tarnished souvenirs now hang on a wall near the bar, neatly mounted and framed. They probably mean very little to the regular customers who live in the swanky side streets nearby. But the display is treasured by many out-of-towners who frequented the restaurant during the war and who have returned, graying and paunchy, but still in love with good food and still remembering Mama.

After the death of Mario, Mama bought the brownstone house on East 58th Street and moved the restaurant and her family into it. The chef, Ugo Sguanci, a nephew, got his training at the world-renowned Papagallo's of Bologna, an epicurean center of North Italian cooking. Some of Ugo's best specialties originated in the sacred kitchens of that noble house. A favorite is *Pollo Dorato;* young, tender chicken that has been boned, well seasoned with basil and other herbs, dipped in flour and eggs and lightly sautéed with butter. A dry, white Verdicchio or Soave is the right wine for this delightful dish. Sliced Mignonette of Beef *alla Mama* is from a family recipe that goes back to her native town of Riccione on the Adriatic Coast, where a legendary grandmother ran a small restaurant. If you have a large capacity and an appetite to match, by all means ask for *Fettucini all'Alfredo,* the masterpiece of the late maestro of Rome. A commonplace entrée on Italian menus everywhere, it rarely attains the frothy creaminess and freshness of the original, but it comes very close here. The reason is that the fettucini is not only homemade, but, to quote Mama Laura, it is "handmade." She rolls out the dough for the noodles every morning and cuts them by hand, just as do all conscientious housewives in Italy. Mixed with heavy cream and grated Parmesan cheese, it is whipped up at a warmer at table-side. Some like it so well that they make it the principal course of the meal. Chianti is first choice with this and all other *pasta,* but there are half a dozen other reds almost as good that are at your command.

The dessert called *Bavarese à la Mama* looks like an eruption in a pastry shop and is composed around a center of spongecake enveloped in freshly prepared *zabaglione,* topped with whipped cream tinted in several shades and inundated with a ruby-red liqueur and then frozen. I find this temptation rather easy to renounce. Instead I prefer a wedge of ripe Gorgonzola and a yellow pear or crisp new apple. The co-host, Carlo Albertario, is a handsome and charming young man who shares the direction and marketing with his energetic mother. Altogether, this is a place worth at least one evening of any visitor's stay in New York.

The Mandarin House

133-135 WEST 13TH STREET

Owners: *Ted and Emily Kwoh*
Chef: *Ah-Yee Ma*

 **I**T IS CUSTOMARY AMONG AMATEURS OF THE culinary art to rank Chinese cuisine just below the French. Some experts, indeed, do not hesitate to give it first position. For an American, it is difficult to debate this point, for we are told that true Chinese cooking of the highest order is not available in the United States. What we get in our Chinese restaurants is food that deliberately caters to American tastes. Instead of the endlessly varied and poetically imaginative cuisine of tradition, the mysteriously faceless cook in the kitchen of a typical "chop suey parlor" confines his skill to dishes which have long ago passed the test and are popular with all.

Among these conventional favorites, now so well known that they are included among the recipes of most domestic cookbooks, are: egg rolls, barbecued spare ribs, batter-fried shrimp, sea-food and vegetable combinations, fried rice, eggs Foo Yong, sweet-and-sour pork and, of course, chop suey, which is either unknown in China or regarded contemptuously as a dish invented by foreign devils.

This may have been the true situation up to five or six years ago, but it is so no longer. New Chinese restaurants have sprung up in New York which are brilliantly modern in decor, appointments and service. They have all the old dishes and scores of unfamiliar ones. Not all of them are worth your visit, for behind the façade of glittering atmospheric effects and dismayingly high prices, a good deal of mediocrity exists in the actual flavor of the food.

But there is at least one restaurant in New York which, instead of playing it safe, or resorting to mere showmanship, makes a specialty of what we are assured is authentic "Mandarin cooking," the equivalent in elegant artistry to the *haute cuisine* of France. The restaurant is called, appropriately enough, Mandarin House. It occupies the ground floors of two adjoining brownstone dwellings on the northernmost border of Greenwich Village. It is probably the only Oriental restaurant of the hundreds scattered throughout the metropolis which is owned and managed by a Harvard graduate. Her name is Mrs. Emily Kwoh, a sensitive and cultivated young woman who is personally attractive, highly articulate and a hostess who radiates effortless charm.

"It would be too difficult," she once told the writer, "to describe the difference between Mandarin cooking and, let us say, the Cantonese style which is so well known here. We were brought up on it in my home in Shanghai, before the comrades came. Once it was the food of cultivated Chinese of wealth and position. There are not many cooks, either here or in the East, who can do it justice. But why don't you judge it for yourself?"

And that is exactly what I did at a dinner which I attended a few evenings later. It consisted of ten courses, took three hours to consume, and is known as the Mandarin House Banquet. It is served only to parties, preferably six or more, and reservations must be made well ahead. Here are a few of the more interesting dishes, described as they are in the menu, in Chinese and English.

Shih Chin Len Pan. The Decorative Cold Platter. Roast beef, chicken, roast pork, Mandarin pot roast, cucumbers, Chinese vegetables, shrimp, abalone, sweet and sour spare ribs, sea gelatin, cuts of sea bass marinated in soy sauce then fried and then smoked, Mandarin salad of cabbage, green pepper and carrots.

Soo Chou Hsia Jen. Sou Chou River Shrimp. Tiny shrimp sautéed with bamboo shoots, cubed ham and a bit of red sauce, served with tiny green peas.

Chao San Yang. Hot Striped Sauté. Shredded red beef and shredded white meat of chicken with green vegetable.

Kuo Yue Juo. Pork Tenderloin. Prepared with sautéed Chinese mushrooms, bamboo shoots and cucumbers.

Ha Tao Chi Ting. Pork Kidney. Prepared with sautéed crystal sweet walnut meats.

Tung Kwa Chung. Winter Melon Soup. A clear soup, compounded of chicken, diced ham, port, bamboo shoots, mushrooms, shrimps and tiny green peas, gently simmered, then poured into a winter melon and steamed many hours until the melon flavor is thoroughly blended with the other ingredients.

Pei Ching Ya. Pekin Duck. Duckling, slowly roasted; the skin then carefully removed to be served with delicate Chinese pancakes, scallions and a peppery red jam.

Chi Yung Yu Tsu. Shark's Fin. Shark's fin simmered for 24 hours in chicken broth, blended with chopped white meat of chicken and cooked to the consistency of rich cream.

Soon Hwa Yu. Pine Cone Fish. Carp or sea bass, fried crisply, with a separate sauce of mushrooms, carrots and bamboo shoots.

Mei Jen Tsau Shing. Vegetable Beauty. Balls of chopped shrimp and water chestnut, each decorated with a face; the gowns fashioned from green "psai-tsai" (a vegetable known in the U.S. as the "Chinese vegetable").

Tien Pin. Sweets . . .

Pa Pao Pan. Eight Precious Rice Pudding. A combination of such precious ingredients as: Water Lily Seed, Dragon Eye (like sun-dried lichee fruit) raisins, cherries, red bean jam, Chinese rice, walnuts, almonds, etc.

Pa Sze Ping Kuo. Apples with Spun Honey Sugar. Eighths of cored, peeled, fresh apples are seared in boiling sesame-seed oil, then dropped into honey sugar syrup and cooked till the syrup spins a silken thread; brought to the table piping hot; each morsel is dipped by chopstick into icy water and served—the honey sugar icicle-crisp, the apples blistering hot.

It was a little disconcerting, after a succession of these exotic dishes, to be served the cute ball-shaped item called "Vegetable Beauty," coyly endowed with facial features and a little green gown, exactly like one of the courses at a child's party in Mamaroneck or Carmel. But the rest of the banquet was satisfyingly strange and delectable. Even though I had partaken before of such famous classics as winter melon soup and Pekin duck, they had never tasted quite as good. Oddly enough, this fantastic repast did not produce a feeling of leaden surfeit. I rose from the table light-footed and light-headed, perhaps because I had downed innumerable tiny cups of a dry yellow Chinese wine called *Hwang Chiu,* which was offered on the menu with an alternate choice of French Chablis.

The price of this fantastic feast at the present writing is $8.50 a person. In every way, a genuine bargain. Most of the dishes do not appear on the regular menu, but if you go for dinner some evening, you may still look forward to many unusual and exquisite creations. The chef responsible is too talented to remain anonymous. His name is Ah-Yee Ma, and like the owners, Ted and Emily Kwoh, he is a native of Shanghai and an expert in the field of North China cooking. Before ordering dinner, be sure to consult Mrs. Kwoh or her pretty little Chinese maîtresse d'hôtel. Either of those smiling and friendly ladies will guide you to a gastronomical experience which should remain long among your treasured memories.

Manny Wolf's Chop House

THIS FRIENDLY, COMFORTABLY INFORMAL American restaurant is a next-door neighbor on Third Avenue of the elegant Café Chambord. But no two restaurants could be farther apart in every other respect. The Chambord is all soft footfalls, rich smells of Burgundy and game, the sound of popping corks and the soft flutter of folding money dropping into the palms of the help. Manny's, which for many years used to be a landmark on the Lower East Side, is large and forthright in its policies. It simply gives you enormous portions of boiled beef with cabbage and horse-radish sauce, massive steaks, potato pancakes with pot roast, and there is a steady flow of White Horse or Old Grand Dad on the rocks. Both restaurants serve their particular purpose supremely well. Both are fine restaurants in their genre. If you are well heeled, a bit of a gourmet and well acquainted with the suave side of living, you will prefer the Chambord. If you like to eat and eat well, without putting too fine a point upon it, you will join the crowd at Manny's. It might be added here that one of the Chambord's discreetly cynical waiter captains drops in at Manny's nearly every mid-afternoon for a lunch of a corned-beef sandwich and a glass of good beer, relaxing comfortably in the masculine atmosphere.

Bill Borst, headwaiter for twelve years, looks like a graying instructor of literature, but of course is far more learned in the ways of fast-moving Third Avenue and the sophisticated East Side. According to Bill, the restaurant attracts hearty eaters by serving the largest helpings in town. Looking around the room, it was plain to see that he did not exaggerate. Waiters were serving plates filled to the rim with meat and vegetables. Steaks and lamb chops are king size here. The portion of boiled beef, cabbage and potatoes would satisfy a hungry coal miner. Butter is served in triple blocks, bread and rolls are piled high, cocktails are big enough even for the neurotic thirst of the coterie from Madison Avenue.

It is not surprising that at lunch there is always a wall-bulging crowd, nearly all men. The big room and commodious bar reverberate to the baritone growl of solidly constructed business leaders, important "wheels" from the skyscraper office buildings along Park Avenue, and visitors from the hinterland who are hungry for red meat. At dinner the crowd is entirely different. It is made up mostly of comfortable married couples and chummy parties of six to ten people whose idea of dinner is four substantial courses, usually along the lines of a shrimp cocktail to start, chicken noodle soup, a large hummock of sirloin or porterhouse steak and a thick-cut wedge of apple pie crowned with vanilla ice cream. Mom's Chicken-in-the-Pot is one of Manny's most honored creations, and a full meal in itself. The cooks wear impressively tall white hats and do their stuff in a kitchen with big glass windows, immaculately furnished with shining copper and aluminum vessels hanging from hooks along the top of the range. On a day when your hunger is razor-sharp and nothing but big helpings of simple, well-cooked food will do, Manny's is the place to go. Considering the contentment which usually ensues, the cost of lunch or dinner is always a pleasant surprise to the uninitiated.

Maria

141 EAST 52ND STREET

Owner: *Maria Seletti*
Chef: *Pelligrino Lenni*

HOSEN FROM AMONG THE THOUSANDS OF other Italian restaurants in the big city because of the excellent food and the engaging Mediterranean friendliness of the owner and her staff, mostly relatives or clansmen. A tiny but always well-filled box of a place, Maria's confines itself to a few dishes and makes no attempt to impress its clients by decor or entertainment. But everything is prepared with "heart," as the French say, and the food has an honest goodness and a character of its own.

At the rear of the restaurant, there is an open kitchen, about the size and with the compact organization of a galley on a merchant vessel or a destroyer. The kitchen, the whole place, in fact, used to be even more compact. It was one of New York's tiniest restaurants, a real two-by-four affair. The regular clientele managed somehow, content to sit at small tables put close together, or jam along the living-room-size bar, over which Maria, cigarette dangling, presided. But the clientele of a place with the charm of Maria's refuses to stay small, and as it grew, Maria grumpily agreed to enlarge the place. The enlargement was little more than a boost from two by four to three by five, but it relieved the congestion a bit, at least for a while. The open kitchen, or galley, is the domain of a shirt-sleeved, swarthy male cook who works with incredible rapidity and a skill that reflects his nautical background. His daily performance is dramatically fascinating to any observer who is interested in culinary techniques. How does he assemble the stews, the grilled meats, the salads so quickly and with such ease? It is all a matter of experience, with the added lift of magical deftness of hand and a certain native bravura.

Among the specialties of the house are hot hors d'oeuvres, Shrimps *Vino Bianco* and Breast of Chicken *Parmigiana*. According to Maria, all recipes of the house are carefully guarded secrets. So, if you want them, you will have to sit up close to the performing chef, and try to memorize the ingredients and the inner significance of his sleight-of-hand.

A while back, Maria was quite sick and took a prolonged rest. Then she returned on a limited schedule, which has increased somewhat, but is still less than the fantastic stint she did in the early days. Running the place very ably indeed in her absence are her adopted son, Val Fanfoni, and her niece, Bianca Tonetti. Both worked in the place before, Bianca as hatcheck girl and Val as an informal headwaiter. And both love Maria and are determined that she'll be proud of them and remain proud of her baby. She now comes in frequently, and any evening she doesn't put in a personal appearance she phones to have a long chat with Val and Bianca and any of her pet customers who happen to be around.

Maria's has a surprisingly smart custom. Nearly everyone who comes is a New Yorker, and the majority of them New Yorkers of considerable accomplishment—society people, artists, writers, photographers, stage people, and so forth. It's one of the few excellent, but chummy, New York restaurants open on Sunday, a blessing to those New Yorkers who would rather have a delicatessen sandwich at home than go to the usual open-on-Sunday restaurant.

There are many pleasant things about Maria's, not the least of which are prices quite fantastically low.

Mercurio

53 WEST 53RD STREET
Owner: *Marcel Massolo*

FOOD IS OF THE UTMOST IMPORTANCE HERE— Northern Italian food that requires careful preparation and the lightest of touches. Such modern assets of the restaurant impresario as showmanship, a gift for publicity and a way with celebrities are missing in the owner, who is a staid man with a great respect for the palates of his guests. There are no dazzling decorations here, no flamboyant works of art, no schmalzy beat of canned music flowing from hidden apertures. Nothing, in other words, to take a man's mind off his enjoyment of a smoking mound of spaghetti *al dente* bathed in parsley-flecked clam sauce, or a succulent dish of grilled shrimps. The waiters never dash about with dangerously overladen trays, voices are never raised, everything moves and meshes with smooth, serene efficiency.

This may not be the town's greatest Italian restaurant, as some maintain, but it is comfortably up with the first five or six. It looks, sounds and even smells like a good eating place in Milan or Florence. Those who love Italy and the best in Italian food will feel at home in one of its comfortable banquettes, a bottle of Chianti poised in a cradle, the subtle perfume of garlic blending with that of bubbling butter as the waiter compounds some delicate dish.

Mr. Massolo, who looks like a bank official, calls the cooking predominately *Piémontaise*. He adds, however, that the kitchen is ready and eager to prepare any regional Italian dish of merit on a moment's notice. For instance, the chef is acquainted with at least a hundred different ways of cooking veal. One of these, and perhaps the simplest of all, is Veal Cutlet *Milanese,* just an ordinary veal cutlet, but a dish which knowing gastronomes often single out to test the ability of the Italian cook. Mercurio's chef deserves full marks, as proven on frequent visits. His finished product is not at all like the thick, furry chop we are used to in most American restaurants. The bone is removed except for an inch or two at the tip. The meat is flattened out to the thinness of a fine Swiss watch, dipped in eggs and crumbs and seasoning, sautéed to a crisp golden brown in oil and butter, with a wisp of garlic and a squeeze of lemon. A glass of light-bodied Bardolino or Valpolicella brings out the delicate savor of the meat.

Mercurio is equally proud of Veal *Ucceletti,* comprised of thin slivers of the filet, sautéed on a fast fire, with a bouquet of Italian herbs, and, just before serving, a splash of Soave wine from Verona. *Bocconcini dei Prete* is contrived from veal, chicken and beef, rolled and stuffed with a *farce* of meat, cheese and herbs. A delectably light sauce is made with a base of the stuffing.

Osso Buco Cremolata is an ancestral dish, common to all parts of Italy, but prepared with a special flourish here. Americans have learned to cherish this ample dish, in which shin of veal is braised and simmered in a sauce of dried wild mushrooms, grated white Italian truffles and filets of plum tomatoes. It is served nestled on a saffron-tinted *risòtto,* or if preferred, a bouquet of *tortellini. Pasta* is mostly homemade, with about a dozen kinds listed, with *Fettucini all'Alfredo* a great favorite. This is mixed at a side table with cream, the yolk of an egg and Parmesan, resulting in a concoction of noodles that transforms this homeliest of materials into something worthy of heaven's banquet ball.

Le Moal

942 THIRD AVENUE

Owner: *Rosine Le Moal and sons*
Maître d'Hôtel: *Andrew*
Chef: *Jacques de Chanteloup*

THERE IS NOTHING STRIKINGLY BEAUTIFUL, extravagant or original about the otherwise first-rate Third Avenue restaurant called Le Moal. In that very lack of the spectacular, perhaps, lies its charm to the great majority of diners, ever on the hunt for reliable cooking, competent service and a low dinner check.

To regular customers, who live nearby and lunch or dine there several times a week, it comes close to being home. To appreciative strangers, it evokes nostalgic memories of those legendary "inexpensive little French bistros" which no returned tourist ever stops lying about.

As is almost obligatory with restaurants which do a good job these days at fairly modest cost, this is a family affair. Rosine Le Moal and her two strong sons, Andrew and Robert, keep a sharp eye on details, work harder than any six salaried outsiders, and are passionately absorbed in each of the moment's duties, whether it be pouring a wine, balancing the books, or soothing the chef in a moment of crisis.

But, be reassured; this is not the sort of restaurant family that attempts to adopt its clients or enfold them in a warm and sticky blanket of intimacy. The Le Moals are of Breton background. These are people who are sincerely friendly if they like you, but who will not thrust themselves upon you, and do not expect you to share their personal woes and triumphs. To me, at least, this is a refreshing change from the manners of some restaurateurs I know, who may drive their best guests away by very excess of love.

I have noted that there is nothing visually overwhelming about this place. It follows that its success must be due to the food served there. I find this a not unimportant detail in the career of a restaurant.

Behind good food there must inevitably lurk a superior cook. In this case, it is a chef with a name so melodiously French that its very sound awakens the appetite—Jacques de Chanteloup, formerly *saucier* under the savage eye of Henri Soulé at Le Pavillon.

On M. Chanteloup's menu there are always at least twelve regular dishes and two specialties of the day. A Thursday special, at this writing, is *Civet de Lapin,* a noble and ancient dish of rabbit which is prepared according to the laws of that respected school of French cookery known as *La Cuisine Mijotée,* which requires long and loving simmering over a slow fire, with a consequent flowering of the flavor of rich juices and essences that quicker or less patient methods cannot bring forth. This stew is made with the best rabbit or hare on the market. It is carefully cut up into pieces, browned with onion and bubbling fat, and cooked in an earthenware vessel with herbs, garlic, more onions, a few thick slices of salt pork, and some heavenly moisture contributed by rich stock and a sound red wine. During the final period, the liver, giblets and blood of the rabbit are added and the simmering goes on for another half hour. At Le Moal, you will not be regarded askance if you vigorously mop up the dark brown gravy of this dish with the crusty bread which is served for that very purpose, but of course there is nothing obligatory about this.

Another accomplishment of the kitchen and a favorite specialty is *Poulet Maître Jacques,* which is savory and quite unlike the roasted chicken of the usual table d'hôte, but which the chef refuses to describe in detail, in spite of all my blandishments and even threats. After all, a man must have one or two secrets to himself, if he would be considered worthy of his tall white bonnet. *Canard Bigarade,* a more familiar dish, is roasted young Long Island duck, crisp and brown, perfumed by the juice and flesh of oranges and perhaps a drop or two of fragrant liqueur. M. Chanteloup is proud of his *Tripes à la Mode de Caen,* which once won a second Grand Prize at a national contest for chefs held at the New York Coliseum. This dish, unlike the better known Norman version, has a pronounced sunset coloring due to the admixture of fresh tomatoes. A few purists will be troubled by this ruddy hue, like New Englanders when they are confronted by a tomato-fied clam chowder, Manhattan style. But the chef of Le Moal, being Breton, swears that this is the way tripes are done in his native province, and all the other kinds are misguided imitations.

Many of the conventional dishes of provincial French cooking are available, like onion soup, frog's legs, a generous *plateau* of hors d'oeuvres, snails as they are tricked out in Burgundy, and an excellent minute steak sautéed in shallot butter. Among the desserts, I recommend to the ladies the *Poire Hélène,* made of pears, ice cream, chocolate sauce, and a thin outer coating of crunchy toasted almonds. There is also *Mousse au Chocolat,* served in individual cups, with the full, true flavor of chocolate, light and creamy and happily lacking in cloying sweetness.

A pleasant place to eat, this, decorated and furnished without ostentation. Le Moal has a handsome mahogany bar in the front portion, bathed in soft rose-pink lighting. Near this is a small glass-enclosed dining section with yellow leather banquettes, also a main dining room which manages to seem comfortably spacious by some trick of optical illusion. The only attempt at decoration is expressed by a few nicely framed wall paintings and a family of authentically costumed dolls from Brittany, seated coquettishly atop the wine rack and smiling roguishly at some colorful travel posters on the opposite side of the room.

Andrew, the older brother, is manager and maître d'hôtel. Bob presides at the bar, following in the footsteps of his sainted father, "Papa" Le Moal, now enjoying his nocturnal Vermouth-Cassis in a better world. A cousin, Joe Douphours, handles the cash. And Rosine Le Moal, prim, sweet-faced and reserved, is the unobtrusive mistress of all. She would prefer to live quietly in the country, she told me, tending her garden and a few chickens, than be mixed up in this demanding and precarious business of feeding the fussy gourmet-inclined apartment dwellers of the midtown East Side. But I am sure that she really loves every moment of it, and was born for it. If you are in the mood for sound and simple French food and are in the neighborhood of 57th and Third Avenue, I hope she will be there to greet you and make you welcome.

Moskowitz and Lupowitz

40 SECOND AVENUE

Owners: *Max and Hy Anzelowitz*
Maître d'Hôtel: *Nat Green*
Chef: *Frank Strika*

I N NEW YORK, YOU DON'T HAVE TO EAT WHAT is good for you, or what the average citizen prefers. When the mood hits you, it is possible to get far, far away from conventional food, whether French, Italian or Stouffian—and that means as far as the corner of 2nd Street and Second Avenue, on the lower East Side. Here the honorable house of Moscowitz and Lupowitz for fifty years has dispensed Roumanian-Jewish cooking of an authentic kind.

The flavors of the food are as exotic as the names of the dishes. In one generous meal of five courses, your palate will taste in turn appetizers that are sour and winey, an unctuous soup, meat that blazes with the flames of pepper and garlic, intensely spicy vegetables or cereals, and desserts sweeter than honey.

Here are a few of the more familiar items: chopped liver with radish and chicken fat; *schmaltz* herring; *knubble* carp; stuffed *derma;* chopped eggplant; consommé with *kasha* or *kreplach;* roast goose with browned *kasha; mamaliga* with *brindza;* potato pancakes; potato *knishes;* goose *pastrama* (in season, whenever that might be). Many come to this famous old place for the famous charcoal "broilings," which arrive spitting hot and spiced with oriental mysteries—planked steak, *mushk* steak, *carnatzle,* Roumanian tenderloin, sweetbreads, baby lamb, goose livers and steer liver. Seductive side attractions are the pickled cucumbers, tomatoes and sauerkraut served as appetizers.

The gaiety here bursts spontaneously into flower. Occasionally the waiters sing loudly in an unknown tongue and there is a scattering background music of tambourines and cymbals (or perhaps it is only a phonograph record). The two sprightly young owners, Max and Hy Anzelowitz, are full of good nature and more than willing to help you order if you are baffled by the menu. The place fairly bounces with humanity at its most expressively emotional level. Prices can be a bit on the stiff side if you let your curiosity get the best of your sense of caution. Drink bourbon or Scotch with dinner, if you would do what the Roumanians do, or Malaga wine and seltzer from a *spritz* bottle, or cold celery tonic, and be sure to top it off with a fiery draught of Slivowitz, a plum brandy which makes an ordinary orchestra sound like gypsy music.

Le Pavillon

III EAST 57TH STREET

Owner: *Henri Soulé*
Maître d'Hôtel: *Martin Decré*
Chef: *Clement René Grangier*

WHEN GOURMETS GET TOGETHER, THEY ARE inclined to talk about very little except food and wine and cooking and restaurants; and their conversation frequently degenerates into argument. They never seem able to agree on just what is the authentic recipe for bouillabaisse, or whether Bordeaux wine is superior to Burgundy, or if maybe Moselle isn't better than either, whether it is more fun to eat in Italy than in France, was 1934 Dom Pérignon superior to 1947 Dom Pérignon, is sole taken from the English half of the Channel really better than that taken from the French half, is Nova Scotian salmon comparable to Scottish salmon, and so on, and so on. But there is one statement that can be made in almost any group of gourmets in the United States, certainly in New York, that never seems to be disputed. That is the statement . . . "The Pavillon is the best restaurant in the United States."

Come to think of it, there are *two* statements which are never challenged. The second is . . . "Henri Soulé is the best restaurateur in the United States." The great and famous of the world, people of wealth and standing, actors, artists and writers, patronize his restaurant; but the principal reason why they assemble there is not that they are rich, or famous, or talented, but that their knowledge of food and wine is beyond that of most other people. Even your own favorite restaurant owner, when his customers have departed and you are sitting around having a glass of wine with him, and the talk inevitably turns to food, will grant the superiority of Soulé and Le Pavillon. Perhaps he has worked for Soulé, as many restaurant men around New York have; and left, likely, in something of a huff, as many have; but still he will speak of Soulé with awe in his voice, and praise him and his restaurant unstintingly. But with the awe there will be a note of affection, despite the fact that, likely, he left in a huff, for Soulé is an extremely likable man; it is just that he is so excruciatingly exacting, and can't understand that the zeal for perfection that is white hot and consuming in him doesn't burn quite so brightly in all others.

Le Pavillon is supreme in its food, in the careful selection of its wines, in its elegance and in its service. And perhaps, in fact almost certainly, in its prices.

Henri Soulé came to the United States in 1938, as an official representative of the French Government, to run the restaurant at the lovely French Pavilion at the New York's World's Fair. There were many excellent restaurants at the Fair as many countries strove to put their best food forward; Russia, Roumania, Switzerland, Italy, others. But the Pavilion stole the show. It became an overnight sensation, and New York's most knowing gourmets, blasé enough so that they actually would have been willing to pay for the privilege of staying away from the Fair's other attractions, eagerly made the trek to Flushing Meadows to eat at the French Pavilion. So great was its success that a grateful France gave to its entrepreneur, Monsieur Soulé, the cherished red ribbon and cross of the Legion of Honor.

World War II came and M. Soulé was unable to get back to his beloved and stricken France. It would be heartless and false to say that the gourmets who had come regularly to the French Pavilion, and in doing so had become his friends, were pleased with this development, but let's say they would have been pleased, and elated, if it had happened for less tragic reasons. They persuaded and helped him to open his own restaurant in New York, on 55th Street, opposite the St. Regis Hotel; and what more logical, indeed inevitable, than that it be named Le Pavillon. It held forth there honorably until 1957, when the building was sold and plans were made to tear it down. The plans did not materialize, but the Pavillon nevertheless was forced to move up two blocks to 57th Street, to the Ritz Tower, where it is now. And there, a miracle took place. When old friends walked into the new Pavillon for the first time, apprehensively, they looked around, gasped with unbelief, sighed with relief, smiled with sheer happiness; some even vented tears. For they were standing in the same Pavillon; the coatroom immediately on the left, the long narrow dining room directly ahead, flowering into a larger room in some forty feet, the bar on the left, the tables in the bar in precisely the same positions, the same people behind the bar and in front of the bar, the same deep-red satin brocade on the walls, the same smiling Martin, the same cherubic, shining Soulé. The world, they decided, was not altogether lost.

It's difficult, and even a bit foolish, to single out special dishes at Le Pavillon. Everything it does, it does superbly. Caviar lovers think it has the best caviar in the United States. Chateaubriand, and steak *poivre,* and filet of beef aficionados insist these are unsurpassable. They're probably right. Soulé goes to the market himself, scrutinizes the suspended carcasses as an art connoisseur would examine canvases, and spots unerringly the sides and shells he wants. Game lovers find grouse, partridge, duck, and pheasant in season, done in their manifold ways, at their unique best.

The best cooking of France is supposedly in Paris. But many prefer regional cooking, and would put at the top the cooking of Lyons. Then there is the cooking of Bordeaux, and the Loire Valley, and Provence. It's probably correct to say that Le Pavillon marches in the stately manner of the better Parisian restaurants, serving the classic dishes of the better food regions. But it also injects a rustic note here and there, a truly Provençal dish, complete with tomatoes, olives, garlic and robust sauce, that is a delight for lunch, particularly on a cold or a surly day.

Pavillon food is really more to be eaten than written about. But the only way to know it is to go there, not for a dinner *before* something else, but for a dinner that will also be your evening, to ponder over the menu, and consult and be guided by Henri or Martin, or Fred, Martin's younger brother, or any other of the knowing captains.

The selection of wines, too, should be put into their hands. M. Soulé does not have the largest wine cellar in New York. But very likely he has the best. It is a *cave* of Collector's Items. M. Soulé knows wines as do few other restaurateurs in New York, or anywhere. He leans toward champagnes and Burgundies. He especially favors Dom Pérignon, the Moët-Chandon which, in a really special year, is awarded the sobriquet of Dom Pérignon, the monk who invented the method of making champagne. In the Pavillon cellars are representatives of the few Dom Pérignon vintages left in this world today, 1943, 1947, 1949, 1952. There also are a few, a very few, of the famous and exquisite 1934 Dom Pérignon, but these are so rare that they are not even on the wine list, are served only to someone who understands them thoroughly, and who realizes that the chances are that they have seen the best years of their lives. The classic Bordeaux are there at their best, as are the classic Burgundies.

There has to be a footnote to this essay on Le Pavillon, dealing with the historic Pavillon uprising of March, 1960. The first intimation of trouble in this paradise came when we called friend Soulé for reservations. Le Pavillon was closing! For adjustments in the kitchen! Knowing the perfection of that Pavillon kitchen, we were reasonably certain that any physical or mechanical adjustment could only be superfluous; and assumed that the changes must be human. The next day's New York *Times* splashed the story; Proprietor Henri Soulé and Chef Pierre Franey, after some twenty more-or-less blissful years of association, had parted in a huff—over how many hours a week the kitchen help should work. "He is stingy," said Chef Franey. "He is a fresh young man," said Proprietor Soulé. "This is awful," moaned New York's *haute monde*. Then, on March 14, the announcement was made that Le Pavillon had a new chef, and would open for dinner the next night, March 15.

The new high bonnet is Clement René Grangier, formerly of the Faisan d'Or in Bordeaux, formerly of the Claridge in Paris, formerly of the S.S. *Normandie* on the high seas, formerly of the Plaza Hotel in New York, formerly of the Greenbrier Hotel in White Sulphur Springs, formerly of the Ambassador Hotel in New York. Le Pavillon is open again, all's right with the world.

Hotel Pierre

FIFTH AVENUE AT 61ST STREET

Proprietor: *William R. Ebersol*
Chef: *Manuel Orta*

**I**F YOU HAD TO NAME THE HOTELS IN NEW York which serve food equal to that served in the best restaurants, you would need only one breath; for, as far as cuisine goes, the only hotel that can be mentioned in the same breath with the St. Regis is the Pierre.

The Pierre was a gargantuan child of the boom-time Twenties, a huge edifice underwritten by loaded Wall Street financiers for their friend and favorite restaurateur Charles Pierre, whose restaurant at 47th Street and Park Avenue shared with Delmonicos and Sherry's the carriage trade of New York. Being a restaurant man, Pierre felt strongly that the heart of a hotel is its kitchen; so in addition to giving that heart his personal attention, he managed the great coup of bringing out of retirement, from France, his old friend Escoffier, indisputably the greatest chef of modern times. With these two immortals in charge, no place to dine could possibly have a more blest start in life.

Pierre is dead. Escoffier is dead. Frank Paget who stepped into Pierre's shoes is dead. But carrying on in the kitchen the tradition of Escoffier, Pierre and Paget is Chef Manuel Orta. And under his aegis, the luster of the Pierre's reputation as a place of fine food goes on undiminished.

The Pierre is a considerably larger hostelry than the St. Regis, so Chef Orta has to spread himself a bit thinner than does his good friend Chef Castaybert of the St. Regis. But not too thin, and his touch, the magic touch of the true *maître,* is evident whether you eat alone in your room, or along with 499 other diners at a banquet in the large and elegant Main Ballroom.

The gayest and most dignified of the three public dining rooms in the Pierre is the Cotillion Room, open for luncheon, dinner and supper. Despite the fact that there is entertainment and dancing, the food is superb. Some of the specialties of the Cotillion Room are Marinated Iceland Brook Trout, Turban of Shrimp and Bananas Singapore, *Vol au Vent Régence,* and Nectarine *Glacé* Pierre.

The grill is more informal, more relaxed, and pays particular attention to luncheon. The menu is a complete one, with the offbeat addition of a variety of East Indian dishes, such as chicken curry and sea-food curry.

The Café Pierre is for good, solid, relaxed eating, blessedly devoid of dance bands and sheath-enclosed female singers. Here you'll find your roast beef, rack of spring lamb, breast of duckling, roast Vermont turkey, steak and chops and lobsters and other old favorites, old friends, all exquisitely done.

The Pierre has one of the best wine cellars in the United States, wide in its choice and expertly selected.

Polonaise

230 EAST 51ST STREET

Owner: *Paul Pawlowski*

OR SOME REASON OR OTHER, THERE ARE very few Polish restaurants among New York's 20,000 dining places. And even the Polonaise, excellent though it be, makes only a half-hearted attempt at presenting food in the true Polish style. It may be because the native cooking is northern and has a peasant heaviness, while the Polonaise prides itself on being a smart restaurant, with a clientele which prefers lighter fare, with wines and conversation to match.

However, if you make a point of asking for them, the kitchen can do you some appetizing Polish specialties, much like the finest Russian cooking of Imperial days, but marked by an extra heartiness and less subtle flavor. There is a first-rate borscht, for example, with a base either of beets or cabbage and tasting quite different from versions encountered in New York's Russian or Jewish restaurants. *Bitki Polonaise* is a juicy cut of pork tenderloin, sautéed with mushrooms in cream. One of the more countrified items is Polish sausage, or *kolbasz,* heavily scented and served with sauerkraut and potatoes—a genuine threat to delicate digestions, but just a tasty morsel to those who have been working in the fields, or hunting the stag.

Golombki is stuffed cabbage, massive, strongly flavored and bathed in sour cream. There is, of course, the inevitable *shashlik* or Shish Kebab, but this, too, differs in flavor from the common variety. It is made with choice filet of lamb, cut in chunks, marinated in red wine and onions, strung on skewers with green peppers and tomatoes and served with raw onion and rice. Polish *zrazi,* something like the Italian *rollatini,* has a stuffing of eggs, mushrooms and onions and is eaten with a side helping of steamed buckwheat groats.

Mr. Pawlowski, who fulfils all the romantic specifications of the European host with a class background, is handsome, convivial and has a warm following among New York's night-blooming East Side set. To most of his guests, he is known as "Uncle Paul," which will give you an idea. He is the one to consult if you are in the mood to experiment with Polish food and drink.

On the wine list, there is an impressive roster of French, Italian, American, Chilean and German wines and the range of prices—from $3 for a New York State "claret" to $14 for Mumm's Cordon Rouge Brut—is wide enough to accommodate all tastes and incomes. Mr. Pawlowski can be counted on to produce a bottle of that oddly hay-scented vodka known as Zubrovka, which should be taken cold, straight, and at a single gulp.

La Potinière du Soir

47 WEST 55TH STREET

Owners: *Pierre Bezin and Albert Forgelle*
Maître d'Hôtel: *Raymond Guihèneuf*
Chef: *Ambroise Vaillant*

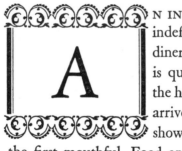 N INTIMATE, CHEERFUL PLACE, WITH THAT indefinable air that signifies good food to the diner who knows his way around. The hunch is quickly verified. Service is swift and silent, the hot food is hot and the cold food cold; wines arrive at the proper temperature and the waiter shows you the bottle and requests you to sample the first mouthful. Food and drink are respected here and so is the value of the client's hard-won money.

This close resemblance to a serious Parisian restaurant is due, I am convinced, to the presence of one of the most quietly accomplished restaurant managers I know. His name is Raymond Guihèneuf and he is employed by the owners of a sister-restaurant across the way, which is known simply as La Potinière, and is also very good, but much larger and not possessed of the same polished perfection, or at least that is my opinion.

I will match Raymond Guihèneuf's courtesy, knowledge and skill with the carving knife, chafing dish or *crêpe* pan against the work of any other expert in the field. If you want to enjoy an unforgettable dinner, put yourself in his hands with perfect confidence. He may suggest, as an appetizer, *Moules Ravigotes* and *Champignons à la Grecque* from the resplendent panoply of hors d'oeuvres. Then *Truite de Rivière Amandine,* to be followed by an *entrecôte* cooked with butter and shallots, or, if you have the capacity, an authentic *Cassoulet Toulousain* of white beans, goose, sausage and herbs. The house makes a specialty, in the trend of today's Parisian restaurants, of the lighter and lesser known wines, which are usually fragrant, joyous and very kind to the pocketbook. Listed on the menu are Muscadet, Quincy, Château de Selle rosé, Pouilly-Fumé and the flowery white wines of Alsace.

The dessert wagon is a monumental temptation, from the suave, velvety chocolate mousse, brimming in its silver bowl, to the *gâteau maison,* usually a layer cake piled high with whipped cream and stuffed with delicious mysteries of the pastry chef's devising. The house can offer several distinguished cognacs, a sound marc and the usual assortment of French liqueurs.

At a gala dinner for six that was held on the wedding anniversary of two friends, Raymond spoiled us in masterly fashion. He started us with a game *pâté,* then ladled out *crème cressonière* and to add the proper note of celebration, brought us an entire rack of lamb, browned to crisp perfection, and flanked with tiny roasted potatoes and garden peas. Our host, who prided himself on his ability as an amateur chef, asked for a green salad, adding *sotto voce* that this was the supreme test. Raymond turned it out at the table in a twinkling; a poem of verdant tenderness, classically scented with garlic, crisp, fresh, exactly as one dreamed a salad should be.

The waiters here are young Frenchmen who are quiet and grave in their manner, and who go about their duties with a minimum of noise or confusion. When I once asked one of these perfectly trained persons whether there was a ripe Camembert or Pont l'Evêque to be had, he did not reply by bringing me a tray of elderly assorted cheeses. Instead, he considered the question for a long moment, and said, "I cannot recommend the Camembert or the Pont l'Evêque to monsieur. Both have been too long in the refrigerator. But we have just received a Brie from France which is not at all bad." And so it turned out to be. The unfailingly excellent food and the intelligent service prompts me to put La Potinière du Soir at the head of my list of outstanding but reasonably priced French restaurants, perhaps a little above or below Le Veau d'Or, according to the time of year and the conditions existing in the kitchen. Again it should be emphatically stated that it is the man who makes the restaurant. If you should want to put this to the test, be sure to ask for Raymond by name and abandon yourself completely to his competence.

Les Pyrénées

234 WEST 48TH STREET

Owners: *The Pujols*
Maître d'Hôtel: *Louis Daniel*
Chef: *Roger Bonnet*

 ALF THE FUN OF GOING OUT TO DINE IN New York is making pleasant discoveries in some unfamiliar part of town. Good hunting and many surprises are waiting in that turbulent midtown section that lies west of Fifth Avenue, especially on those crowded side streets that project from either flank of Times Square. Here the roving dinner guest may take his pick from hundreds and hundreds of intimate and colorful restaurants, where the specialties of at least thirty-five different foreign nationalities are served. Judging by their number, which mounts continually, Italian, French and Chinese restaurants are first in favor with New Yorkers, as well as with the millions of out-of-town visitors who pour in constantly from everywhere.

Among the swarms of restaurants of all sorts, one of the best and certainly the most ambitious is Les Pyrénées, located on a dark, rather grim street in a spot about as close to the honky-tonk heart of Broadway as you can get without actually being trampled.

If you are nostalgic for France, this restaurant will do much to assuage your yearning. It has no pretensions to the lordly cuisine of the wealthy, but whatever it serves is cooked with honesty, intimate knowledge and love. The onion soup will remind you of the steaming, hearty soups you may have enjoyed in the *brasseries* of Paris or some provincial city like Lyons. The *terrines de lapin* or *canard* have a wholesome country flavor and are delightfully mated with the crusty French bread and good butter. The *coq au vin,* the *tripes* and the snails prepared with shallots, butter, wine and garlic, in the Burgundian manner, all have the unctuous and fragrant character you associate with the best French cooking.

Roger Bonnet, *chef de cuisine,* is round-faced, wears an ample mustache and comes from Beaune, in the center of one of the great wine and food districts of France. He excels with such time-honored native dishes as *Boeuf Braisé Beaunoise,* which is short ribs of beef, browned slowly and then simmered until the meat is ready to fall from the bone, with red wine, small white onions and vegetables. As far as my own experience goes, his *Jambon Persillé* will be found on no other restaurant menu in New York. Having made this statement, I am fully prepared to receive violent contradictions and full documentation. The town's complexity, in the matter of restaurants, is such that it is impossible to come close to knowing its full resources. M. Bonnet, a modest man, actually blushed when I told him that this famous Burgundian specialty tasted just as delicious as the large helping I had eaten not long ago at the great Hôtel de la Poste in Avallon, where it was made with the succulent *jambon de Morvan,* a local product, and costs the tourist about the same amount as the complete table d'hôte dinner at the Pyrénées.

In such an out of the way place as this, it is an unexpected delight to be served imported turbot, poached gently in a *court bouillon* and accompanied by a hollandaise sauce that could not be smoother or more piquant if prepared by a *saucier* at La Méditerranée in Paris. Or *Jarret de Veau Comme Chez Soi,* or *Poulet à l'Estragon,* the latter a whole young chicken stuffed with butter and fresh tarragon, then roasted to that crisp brown state which seems to be the secret of the French country kitchen. Best of all, there is no effort at the Pyrénées to appear smarter or more *mondaine* than is actually the case. The dining room sprawls comfortably without any special architectural design and is gaily and, some think, garishly decorated with "hand-painted" murals of a lively nature. The prices are gratifyingly moderate. Because many dine here before going to the theater, the service is swift, unless you direct otherwise. Among the regulars are many knowing lovers of good cooking who live in the plushy East Side of town and are accustomed to paying the towering tariffs common in the elegant caravansaries of that section. They do not patronize the Pyrénées because of the prices, but because they have a weakness for fine French food, without ostentation or pretense.

One evening not long before this was written, I dined there with a friend, simply, but with such agreeable results that the menu seems worth recording. We were greeted at the door by René Pujol, a brother of Jean Pujol, and member of a closely knit clan that owns three restaurants on 48th Street, and is related to half the French restaurateurs in the city. All the Pujols speak with the rich, rumbling accent of their native Ercé, a small town in the Pyrénées. All of them have a smiling friendliness that warms the heart.

It was Louis Daniel, maître d'hôtel and still another partner of the Pujols, who helped us choose our dinner. Louis, a dark, sharp-featured man who talks, as he moves, with rapidity and energy, is a Breton from Rennes. More or less on his advice, we shared a first course of baked stuffed oysters and a thick slice from the *terrine de lapin.* Next we were given a noble chateaubriand, fresh from the broiler in that condition between *bleu* and *saignant* at which I hold beef to be at its best. With it came *sauce béarnaise* and *pommes soufflées,* insubstantial as bubbles but much more appetizing. Louis plunged deeply into the cellar and came up triumphantly with a Musigny 1937, which to me was the high point of the occasion. To crown the dinner, we had a *soufflé chocolat,* with mocha cream sauce, that was perfection. Black coffee and cognac followed, and with it a comfortable hour of gossip with *la famille* Pujol.

We learned that among the frequent diners were Air France pilots, men of the maritime service, and many people of the theater. René remembered an exciting evening when they were honored by the presence of Jean Pierre Aumont and Grace Kelly, in the days when she was a beautiful commoner. Charles Laughton is a good friend of the house. Theatrical performers drop in often after the show for a snack and a drink in the bar, which is a dimly lit room with a slightly conspiratorial air, and stays open until four o'clock every morning. After their own restaurants close, the chefs and assistant cooks of many French eating places are in the habit of sitting at the little tables until closing time. "What do they talk about?" I asked M. Pujol. "Food," he said, "*naturellement*! They talk angrily about how one should make the proper bouillabaisse, or the best way with a *cassoulet,* or the trick in making puff paste or *quenelles* of pike. Sometimes I am forced to ask them to lower their voices and make peace. But they are all really good fellows. Never have I had to resort to force."

Most clients of the Pyrénées rarely meet one whom I consider the very heart and soul of this charming restaurant. This is none other than Odette, wife of Jean Pujol, a lady who keeps the books, deals with the suppliers and, like many of her countrywomen, is endowed with the practical shrewdness which keeps the establishment out of the *rouge* and well into the *noir.*

No doubt I am prejudiced, but I find Odette to be a gentle person of rare quality, with a quiet sweetness and poise that is as enchanting as her pretty face. She comes from Dijon, that heaven of cultivated gluttony, and was born into the atmosphere of superlative food and wine. But she leaves the cooking, the wine cellar and the daily menus to professional experts like Roger Bonnet and Louis Daniel, for these are men's jobs and they are better at it. If you are ever in the mood for the Pyrénées some evening, mention the authors of this compendium to Odette, *en passant,* as it were, and I think she will take special pains to make you glad you came.

Quo Vadis

26 EAST 63RD STREET

Directors: *Bruno Caravaggi and Gino Robusti*
Maître d'Hôtel: *Paul Perolini*
Chef: *Marcel Grange*

RUNO CARAVAGGI AND HIS ASSOCIATE, GINO Robusti, are two charming gentlemen who are living support of my contention that a restaurant is only as good as the person or persons at the head of it. When I first visited the Quo Vadis one evening long ago, it was Bruno who greeted me just inside the door. A small immaculate man with a dazzling smile, he seemed to sum up in his gracious personality the many reasons why this restaurant has attracted a good segment of New York's "best people," most of them highly articulate in their loyalty.

A consummate host like Bruno makes the act of dining out, no matter how often it is repeated, as pleasant as a party. At the Quo Vadis, they not only satisfy your hunger in various subtle and elegant ways, but soothe and remold your ego after a hard day at the mines. And these ministrations are accomplished with a light touch, unspoiled by obsequiousness or condescension.

Unlike some other fashionable caravansaries in the same sector of the Gold Coast, the Quo Vadis does not encourage discriminatory treatment of its guests. There are no zones, corners or cramped little rooms where the socially exalted or the conspicuously wealthy are sequestered. There are no "good" tables or "bad" ones. On your first visit as on your latest, you will be seated in a good light, where you will enjoy a clear view of the surroundings.

You will be made to feel welcome and at home from the moment of your coming. But neither Bruno nor Gino share the peculiar urge of some New York restaurant owners to enter intimately into the lives and careers of their patrons. They are cordial and far from stuffy, but they never depart from the realities which govern the relationship between customer and host.

As for the food, it is good enough for the most fastidious tastes, without actually attaining greatness—a word, incidentally, that I reserve for no more than two or three restaurants in the entire nation. Other top-rated establishments, however, may well envy the Quo Vadis for its most precious quality, a certain sunny atmosphere that is reflected in the smiling faces of all the help, from the lowliest *piccolo* to starchy-bosomed Paul, the maître d'hôtel. Perhaps this is because the majority of the people here are Italian and, even though trained to a high international polish, still retain much of their native warmth. The cuisine is entirely French, though, with a splash of Belgian richness here and there. I was enlightened on this point by Bruno.

"People who come here for the first time," he said, "usually ask for Italian dishes. This is because of the name. But I point out to them that 'Quo Vadis?' is Latin, and they should remember it from their school days. The Belgian flavor you recognize is because both Gino and I were trained in the restaurants and hotels of Brussels when we were very young." As a matter of fact, Bruno was one of the best known head waiters in town when he officiated at the resplendent Brussels restaurant which occupied these very premises, thirteen years ago. And Gino performed similar duties at the Colony. Both made innumerable friends among the wealthy and celebrated who formed the nucleus of their present clientele.

The chef, Marcel Grange, is celebrated in his profession for his mastery of all kinds of game. He will also provide, on short notice, most of the classical preparations of *la haute cuisine française*. But if you prefer to eat more simply, you will find his touch just as sure. He has a fine hand with broiled steaks and chops, turns out a sumptuous luncheon dish of Eggs Benedict, broils a chicken or baby turkey to just the right turn and will seduce you with his artistically composed mixed grill *à l'anglais*.

The point is that these dishes will not only arrive piping hot, perfectly cooked and subtly seasoned, but that your waiter will not infer by his manner that you have committed a *gaucherie* by ordering them instead of something more elaborate and costly. In my own memory book—a vast as yet unwritten volume in which are recorded the treasures garnered during a lifetime of passionate eating and drinking—there are several dishes which I associate with meals I have had at the Quo Vadis. For one, I recall a *Petite Marmite Henri IV,* as good as you might get at Sunday dinner in a prosperous provincial household in Béarn. It was clear, pure and strong and it steamed gently, sending a delightful perfume to my nostrils. There were tender bits of chicken, beef and fresh vegetables in its fragrant golden depths.

This is a classic soup and it demonstrates the quality of the kitchen at the Quo Vadis as well as anything else might. Its flavor was what Curnonski, prince of gastronomes, meant when he said: "The best cooking should taste of what it contains." Fondly remembered, also, was a small rack of lamb, served for two and carved at a side table by a waiter captain, working with great speed so that the juices would not lose their savor. This lamb had true springtime flavor, strangely difficult to encounter in most American restaurants. The chops were small and succulent, pink at the heart, crisply brown outside and lightly ennobled with garlic. My notes on a recent dinner also celebrate a delicate appetizer course of smoked fillets of brook trout, the color of cream faintly flushed with rose. The taste of this delicacy mated well with a cold and very dry Pouilly-Fuissé.

Another house specialty is filet of beef sealed in a pastry crust, the meat meltingly tender and the dark, winy sauce enriched with *foie gras* and truffles. There are the usual extravagances of a menu of this class

—caviar at $7 a spoonful, superb Scottish salmon and grouse in season, Dover sole in three or four styles, soufflés of impressive altitude—"in all the perfumes." For dessert, one might also try the house version of *crêpes* Suzette. It is as good, almost, as going to the play, for Paul prepares the precious pancakes amidst soaring flames, with a dramatic flourish that Barrymore himself might have envied.

There are good wines in the cellar but the management does not make a fetish of ancient, cobwebbed rarities. Instead it prefers to offer the robust, lively wines of fairly recent vintage. However, Mario, the cheerfully rotund sommelier who is known to his friends as "the Baron," is proud of the Château Lafite 1934, at $16, and the magnums of château-bottled Bordeaux of the great years, at $26 the magnum.

The restaurant is spacious and looks rather like a fine old New York mansion on a night of festive celebration. There is an intimate bar and cocktail room up front and this opens into two large adjoining rooms decorated in cream and dark red, with lofty ceilings and many ornately framed paintings.

Lucius Beebe, a shrewd judge of life's more lush and rococo aspects, once rated the Quo Vadis for all-around satisfaction just below two other famous French restaurants which shall be nameless here. I am inclined to agree with his opinion. Certainly, there is no more agreeable place in town to spend a long, mellow evening. There are no rough surfaces or sharp corners about the Quo Vadis. No shouts are heard, no dish-laden trays dropped, and nobody ever causes a scene about the check. You get the impression that if such crudities should ever occur, Bruno would drown himself in a Nebuchadnezzar of the best champagne.

All things considered, I recommend the Quo Vadis for very special occasions, like the entertainment of a valuable client, or an important but undecided prospect, or a rich uncle from Seattle. It even rates high enough for an intimate dinner consisting of you and your wife, or you and your oldest and most discriminating friend. Beyond that, I should not care to go in recommending any restaurant.

Ritz Restaurants

 N ITS DAY, THERE PROBABLY WAS NO MORE beloved eating place in New York than the Ritz, or the Old Ritz, as it now is affectionately called. It was not *a* restaurant, but *several* restaurants and each had its devoted patrons and followers. There was the Men's Bar on the street floor of the hotel, with its own Madison Avenue entrance, through whose portals no woman, ever, was allowed to pass. The Men's Bar had an aggressively loyal clientele of prosperous, well-fed males who came for martinis a bit after twelve, stayed for lunch after martinis, and frequently came back for martinis before dinner, or just stayed on, pleasantly enveloped in the comforting atmosphere of the Ritz. The emphasis on martinis is because Dick, the bartender at the Men's Bar, was considered the master of the martini. We can report he still is. The Ritz is gone, dismembered, demolished, but Dick flourishes today as the bartender at the National Golf Links in Southampton. The martinis: superb.

The Ritz Grill was a lovely, fairly small room downstairs from the lobby. Its golden hour was noon, at lunch. The Grill drew an exceptional group of people each day, people mostly from the business world, but the kind of business that tumbled over into the arts: book publishers, authors' agents and their clients, magazine editors, play producers, an occasional actor or actress. The food was excellent. Always on Friday there were New England clam chowder, white and creamy and heavy with clams, and the true small Long Island scallops from Mecox Bay, a rarity even on eastern Long Island and practically unknown in New York.

The greatest of the Ritz restaurants was the Oak Room on the main floor up a small flight of stairs, elegant and haughty, irreverently known to the more raffish denizens of the Men's Bar and the Grill as the Dowager's Delight. It did have a fair representation of dowagers and it was a delight, so perhaps the name was not out of line. In the summer, the Oak Room had an adjunct called the Japanese Gardens, a sort of courtyard with fountains, pools and plants. It was before the days of air-conditioning, but the fountains and pools and plants did have a cooling and salutary effect.

The Ritz gave way to what is known in New York, often ironically, as progress. It was battered into rubble, and on its site at Madison Avenue and 46th Street arose an undistinguished box of a building dedicated to advertising.

But the Ritz did not die. Its spirit moved northward, in a straight line, up Madison Avenue, where it settled at 61st Street, in the place now known as the Carlton House. Many of the accoutrements, much of the personnel, and a great deal of the soul of the place, moved up with it, and now, accustomed to the ambience, are flourishing, and restoring to the dedicated, the feeling of good living that was to be enjoyed only at the Ritz. The main dining room is there, and so is the Men's Bar. They're not altogether the same, but they're close enough to make life worth living.

There is probably only one man in the United States who could have brought this off: Gaston Lauryssen. Gaston is a consummate hotelier and restaurateur. After impressive apprenticeship in hotels in Europe (he's a Belgian by birth) he served in New York as manager of the Tuscany (the best small hotel in this country), and the St. Regis, in

Beverly Hills as manager of the lovely Bel Air, and in Florida as manager of the opulent Boca Raton. He was made manager of the Carlton House at its start and determined that it would mirror and echo the Old Ritz. It took considerable doing; he once asked a writer and editor not to write up the Carlton because it wasn't quite ready. But he feels it's ready now and so do we.

There are two restaurants in Carlton House, the Ritz Bar and the Ritz Dining Room, in both of which you will find pleasant reminders of the Old Ritz, some human, some inanimate. For quite a few of the old hands made the move from 46th Street to 61st Street and so did fixtures, chairs, decorations and even china, crystal, and silver. Steve Terzano, the maître d'hôtel, who had been with the Ritz since 1908, and who brought his faithful legion up the Avenue to the New Ritz, died on Easter Sunday morning of 1959. But Grandi, the little white-haired busboy, and Camillo, the waiter, and Janos, the captain, still hold forth, along with a dozen or so Old Ritz waiters.

Armand Kauffman moved up from 46th Street, where he was *chef saucier,* to 61st Street, where he became *chef de cuisine.* Armand retired in 1955, at which time head-man Lauryssen lured back from France, Gaston Martin, who had been chef at New York's famous Lafayette Hotel down on Irving Place. Gaston still rules the kitchen.

Many of the dishes which appeared on the menu of the Old Ritz live on on the menu of the new. Now, as always, the most popular dish in the dining room is Chicken Hash, a dish noble in character though plebeian in name; and the most popular in the men's grill is Hamburger. This, too, has a grandeur not indicated by the name. It is of really prime beef, ground in the Ritz kitchen, and enriched by a special Ritz sauce. The Ritz was always famed for its sea food and, in season, you will find, done superbly well, such delicacies and rarities as Shad Roe *Véronique,* Sole *Véronique,* Scallops *Amandine,* Smelts *Meunière,* Brook Trout, and exquisite, seldom to be found on menus anywhere: Whitebait and Oyster Crabs. Game is on hand when available, and Chef Martin has brought with him from the Lafayette all the secret ways that wonderful restaurant had of bringing the very best out of lamb. Gaston's selection of wines is impeccable.

Romeo Salta

39 WEST 56TH STREET

Owner: *Romeo Salta*
Maître d'Hôtel: *Mario Cossentini*
Chef: *John Raicovich*

AMERICAN VISITORS TO ITALY ARE OFTEN delighted to discover that North Italian cooking has a light and subtle refinement that rivals the best French cuisine. The most memorable examples are to be found in the inns and restaurants of Bologna, Milan, Florence and Genoa. Here in America, the best North Italian cookery flourishes mainly in New York and perhaps half a dozen outlying cities. Among the finest is Romeo Salta's, formerly a renowned Hollywood spot, now an established success in New York.

When you visit this small but elegantly appointed rendezvous of the fastidious, be prepared for three things—remarkable food, exceptional wines and a check that can easily touch high altitudes. A portion of spaghetti, macaroni or egg noodles with a simple dressing of butter and cheese costs $3.50. *Spaghettini* with white or red clam sauce is the same. In fact, $3.50 seems to be the uniform charge for the twenty or so varieties of *pasta* on the menu, including such intriguing ones as meat-stuffed *cannelloni,* chicken-filled *tortellini* and baked *gnocchi* tastefully embellished with spinach, Parmesan cheese and Sauce Bolognese.

Despite their familiar sound, these dishes take on a special glamour at Salta's. Not only are they seasoned and cooked to perfection, but their service is surrounded with a ceremony that would flatter the most pampered of gastronomes. Signor Salta himself presides as a rule, assisted by several flunkies at a side table. *Pasta* is served in huge covered silver platters with a baronial look, kept warm on a *réchaude*. The *patron* blends the sauce with a dramatic flourish, adds a drift of cheese with a gesture like a benediction and tosses the creamy strands heavenwards with the same passionate abandon that marked the performance of the king of noodle-tossers, Alfredo of Rome.

But *pasta,* while indispensable to the true lover of Italian food, is only a preliminary course at Romeo Salta's. There are dozens of other early temptations, like broiled *scampi* of giant size, clams in half a dozen manifestations and wonderful imported raw-cured ham, *mortadella* and salami. Soups number about fifteen kinds and there is a big choice of meat dishes, one more seductive than the next. The *patron* will probably recommend one of his specialties, like *Piccata* of Veal *al Funghi, Scaloppine "Zingarella," Saltimbocca alla Romana,* or, if you radiate an air of affluence, a thick beefsteak grilled over coals in the Florentine style.

The menu here is the most ample of any Italian restaurant in New York. Among wines not often encountered are a dry white Fazi Battaglia Verdicchio, a white or red Frascati, dry red Grignolino, sparkling red Reciotte and a couple of festive Italian-type champagnes which gush merrily but are too fruity and sweet for the cultivated taste.

Russian Tea Room

150 WEST 57TH STREET

Owner: *Sidney J. Kaye*
Maître d'Hôtel: *Anatole*

HE NAME OF THIS RESTAURANT IS SOMEWHAT misleading. Russian it may be, but certainly it does not resemble the sort of tea room we are familiar with. Oceans of tea are imbibed here, but it is served exotically, in a tall glass set into a metal holder to protect the fingers from second-degree burns. And the tea is usually spiked with rum or flavored with lemon. As for the food, it stays strictly away from pecan pie, yams in a marshmallow setting or chicken croquettes with cream sauce.

Borscht is a staple here. Ruby-red borscht in a deep plate, served hot or cold according to the season, and heavily endowed with sour cream, tomatoes, shredded beets, diced cucumbers and sprigs of dill. Next to borscht, the Tea Room is famous for being a neighbor of Carnegie Hall, but it is the food which attracts most people. Very popular is *Karsky Shashlik* which is tender cubes of spicy lamb, spitted and grilled with onions, tomatoes and mushrooms. Classic favorites are such Russian staples as *kasha* and mushrooms, *Blinchiki* with cheese and sour cream, *Côtelette à la Kiev,* buckwheat pancakes with sour cream and caviar, and a tart jellied dessert called Cranberry *Kissel*.

The food ranges from good to exceptional and prices are relatively modest. But these facts alone would not account for the restaurant's unique reputation. What goes on there comes closer to European café-life than anything we have this side of the ocean, and it is this lively foreign air that attracts the majority. From noon till midnight, the big room is crowded and hums and buzzes with animation. There is a rich veining of colorful and eccentric personalities, for this is where the worlds of music, ballet, theater, concert hall and *couture* mingle in relaxed communion. Most of the customers are professionals, from the studios, rehearsal halls, schools and auditoriums that line 57th Street. The first skin-fitting leotards and matador pants showed up here long before they became generally fashionable. Long hair, violin cases plastered with foreign labels, ballet slippers, Renaissance beards and even sarongs are fairly commonplace symbols of the constantly shifting throng, which fills the place right through the day and evening.

Besides the stimulating presence of artists and their entourage, there are always plenty of nice ordinary people who come to watch, to bask in the cultural warmth or merely to eat a good Russian meal at moderate cost, without benefit of sword-dancers, balalaikas or gypsy violinists. One loyal customer I know has no connection with the arts, but patronizes the Tea Room regularly because of his weakness for the rough black peasant bread and sweet butter, the hot meat-stuffed pastry pillows called *pirojok,* the creamy chopped chicken livers and, above all, the borscht, which has no equal. Also, I suspect, he is very fond of his favorite waitress, an elderly white-haired Russian lady who looks like a gentle version of Gertrude Stein and who caters to his gastronomical whims with great understanding and good humor.

Sid Kaye, the owner, is slender, dynamic and dismayingly articulate about life, art and the restaurant business. He is a fast man with an anecdote or gossipy bit of enlightenment gleaned from his contact with the famous. At the time he bought the restaurant, a dozen or more years ago, it was already old and established. He had the good sense not to change a thing, except to condense the menu and apply a few touches of shrewd modern management where they would do the most good. The same chef still prepares the same classic dishes. There is the same price scale, except for a recent understandable revision that does not soar too high, considering the times.

When I asked Sid Kaye to drop a few names of his more celebrated customers, he said that they would fill a book. "But you might mention my friend Marlon Brando, if you want to—he loves us. Or Paddy Chayevsky. And Jan Peerce, Marian Anderson, Rubinstein, Horowitz, Milstein—the great artists. José Ferrer is a buddy of mine. Kim Stanley, Yul Brynner, Helen Hayes, Sol Hurok, Lennie Bernstein, Dimitri Mitropolous—you name them, you can't go wrong!"

Not long ago, it was announced that Carnegie Hall next door would be torn down—golden memories, legendary acoustics and all—to be replaced by the usual steel-sinewed multi-storied monster. Sid Kaye clung to the hope that his cherished restaurant would not have to go. But before him always was the premonition of uprooting and change. However, he is a man of restless energy and dauntless imagination and he is also as sentimental about his place of business as the oldest and most crotchety customer. "As long as I am alive," he told me, beating his breast, "there will be a Russian Tea Room. Maybe somewhere else. Maybe looking a little different. But still the same food, and the same nice people." But the good news, as of this writing, is that Carnegie Hall is saved! The city fathers have decreed that it will stay where it is. And so, I hope for many years, will the Russian Tea Room.

St. Regis Hotel

2 EAST 55TH STREET

Manager: *Pierre Bultinck*
Maître d'Hôtel: *Lawrence Rozzo*
Chef: *Joseph Castaybert*

 N OUR PARENTS' DAY, JUST ABOUT THE BEST place to eat in any city was in the leading hotel or hotels . . . the Waldorf and the Plaza in New York, the Parker House and Ritz in Boston, the Bellevue-Stratford in Philadelphia, the Sherman in Chicago, the Palace in San Francisco, the Jefferson in Richmond. Alas, this is no longer true. The heavy commercial hands of Hilton and Sheraton and Statler and Manger have fallen on the land, the heavy clink of the Chain has fallen on the hotel.

But here and there across the country individual enterprise raises its frightened little head and personal ownership of a hotel fights valiantly for its lovely life. The most outstanding and encouraging example of this is the St. Regis Hotel in New York, which still stands proudly on the southeast corner of 55th Street and Fifth Avenue. It's a noble address, one of the choicest and most fashionable in the whole world. It should be. It was originally the home address of the famous Astor family and it still was until recently, for the St. Regis Hotel was owned, until he died in 1958, by Vincent Astor, then, until early 1960, by his estate. Not only the location, but parts of the building itself, the stone and the marble and the plumbing, are descended from the original Astor mansion. So is the concern with perfect food and wine and the perfect service of these essentials of life. Here, in the heart of the heart of New York, is a last vestige, a last warm reminder that innkeeping is an art, an art being sustained now by Colonel Serge Obolensky (an Astor in-law) and Pierre Bultinck. In doing this, they and Vincent Astor before them have established one of the very finest kitchens and wine cellars to be found in New York, in the United States, in the world.

Of course, any hotel must live under the irrefutable law of cooking that the quality of food lessens as the number of diners increases. But in the case of the St. Regis, this means not that the meals go from fine to inferior as numbers increase, but rather from exquisite to superb to fine. Despite the law, the St. Regis can serve a superb banquet for a hundred or so people, as it has proven rather consistently in the succession of dinners it has done for the Confrérie des Chevaliers du Tastevin (with the Pierre, the St. Regis shares the honor of being the favorite meeting place of the Confrérie). One Tastevin dinner of hallowed memory, at the St. Regis, had, as its menu:

RÉCEPTION
Caviar—Fois Gras—Gougère

PREMIÈRE ASSIETTE:
Le Consommé Double au Fumet de Céleri
avec Paillette au Parmesan

DEUXIÈME ASSIETTE:
La Mousse du Cardinal des Mers
avec sa Garniture et Diamants du Périgord

TROISIÈME ASSIETTE:
Le Filet de Charolais Rôti Maître de Chais
La Courgette Florentine
La Pomme Nanette

QUATRIÈME ASSIETTE:
Le Granité au Vieux Marc

POUR SE RAFRAÎCHIR:
L'Aiguillette de Caneton
en Gelée Bigarade
Les Feuilles Vertes aux Herbes Fines

ISSUE DE TABLE:
Le Fromage de Brie

BOUTEHORS:
Le Soufflé Glacé Framboise
avec La Pêche Flambée Feu du Diable
Le Chariot Vendangeur des Côtes de Beaune

Le Café Noir

The wines and liqueurs which accompanied this meal were:

Bollinger Brut 1953 en magnum
Nuits St. Georges Blanc, Clos de l'Arlot 1955
Clos des Cortons 1937, Domaine J. Faiveley
La Tache 1955, Domaine de la Romanée-Conti
Richebourg 1934, Jules Belin
Dom Pérignon 1949
Clos de Vougeot 1947, Confrérie des Chevaliers du Tastevin

Cognac Hine Impérial
Marc de la Cloche
Benedictine D.O.M.
Chartreuse

Such a dinner naturally is not an ordinary occasion. It is planned well in advance, is rehearsed thoroughly (the entire dinner prepared, eaten, and criticized by the Dinner Committee once, twice, or even three times before the actual performance). Then, too, it doesn't hurt any that Pierre Bultinck, the manager, and Joseph Castaybert, the *chef de cuisine,* are Chevaliers. But the chances are unlikely that you'll be giving banquets at the St. Regis. Instead you will probably be eating in the public rooms. The Maisonette has outstanding food but it also has dancing and entertainment which, to this particular glutton, are an abomination with a fine meal. The St. Regis Roof is the summer version of the Maisonette. The King Cole Bar is strictly for men at lunch, with a masculine menu and outsize martinis. The Oak Room is the true dining room of the St. Regis, an elegant setting for elegant dining. If, though, you wish to savor the art of M. Castaybert at its most exquisite, give a small lunch or dinner, (six, eight, ten or twelve) in one of the beautiful St. Regis private suites. Consult with M. Castaybert or with Louis Pages, the banquet manager, well in advance, preferably at least a week. Be on time. And don't be faced with a two o'clock conference at the office or an 8:30 curtain!

There are many specialties at the St. Regis, but here are three they themselves select:

Billi-Bi is a superb soup which is served either cold or hot. It's subtle and a bit mysterious and makes an excellent "Guess what's in it?" conversation piece. The recipe is in the recipe section, as are the recipes of the dishes below.

Crab Remick is an excellent appetizer, and Chicken Kiev is one of the classic masterpieces of culinary art. I personally prefer Chicken *Sauté Béarnaise,* a simple dish of boiled chicken, white wine, onions. So does M. Castaybert. It was the favorite recipe of his mother, and the dish she first taught him to cook.

But no dish is too great a challenge for M. Castaybert and his kitchen, and no dish is so simple as to incur their disdain. Indeed, they consider the simple dishes somewhat more of a challenge than the grand ones.

In any event, expose yourself to the outstanding food of the St. Regis, and do so quickly because time seems to be running out. For the St. Regis has been sold, not to a dedicated individual, but to a corporation whose favorite shade of green is not that of spinach soufflé, or a mixed green salad, or a bottle containing a classic Rhine wine or Moselle, but that exquisite shade of green found in the paper currency of the United States. The man behind the corporation is William Zeckendorf, a gourmet of considerable stature. If he had his own way, and if his forebears had thoughtfully provided him with a legacy of $100,000,000 or so as did Vincent Astor's, he would probably have the desire, and certainly have the knowledge, to continue this as one of New York's finest hotels, and one of New York's finest places to eat. But corporations have to feed the greediness of stockholders as well as the palates of epicures, and must resist the relentless pressure of competition. The St. Regis is on solid ground geologically but shaky ground economically. Its corner of 55th Street and Fifth Avenue is one of the most valuable in the world. It's size and construction are such that it is very difficult to run it, in the St. Regis manner, at a suitable profit. Its days are numbered. So hurry and visit it. Eat there. Give a luncheon or dinner in one of its small private suites. Prospect in its wine cellars. Send your compliments to Chef Castaybert. For before too long, these pleasures undoubtedly will be but a memory.

San Marino

236 EAST 53RD STREET

Proprietor: *Tony Gugnoni*
Maître d'Hôtel: *Serge Barberini*
Chef: *John Torti*

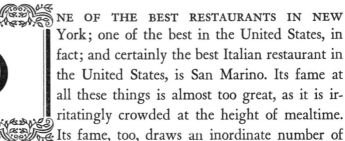NE OF THE BEST RESTAURANTS IN NEW York; one of the best in the United States, in fact; and certainly the best Italian restaurant in the United States, is San Marino. Its fame at all these things is almost too great, as it is irritatingly crowded at the height of mealtime. Its fame, too, draws an inordinate number of celebrities and one of its charms is the almost totally oblivious attitude its owner and his family and the staff have toward celebrities. They greet them graciously but they seem blissfully unaware that they deserve any special attention.

One night a number of years ago I went into San Marino and Tony, the owner, greeted me and said "Oh, you just missed that musician you like so much."

Liking and admiring musicians happening to be habitual, I inquired, "Well, which one, Tony? Who was it?"

"You know, the Italian musician."

"*All* Italians are musicians, Tony. Which one do you mean?"

"The famous Italian musician, the one, he conducts."

A light dawned. "You don't mean *Toscanini?*"

Gestures and smiles. "Toscanini! Yes, yes!"

A little while ago, just after Clifton Daniel and Margaret Truman had been married in a considerable outburst of publicity and fanfare, they came into San Marino. They were greeted politely and warmly but apparently without any recognition of who they were or what they were. They were told there was no table but if they would like to wait for a bit, Tony would do his best to take care of them. They quietly sat down and chatted and in about twenty or thirty minutes were given a table, no extra attention, but obviously were delighted not only with each other but with the food and wine they ordered.

At another time, at two tables across the room, the President of Italy and his wife were immersed in fine Italian dishes and Frank Costello and his bodyguard were likewise immersed. Despite the slight variance in their morals and methods of attaining eminence, they did share Italian parentage and devotion to good Italian food. The President, incidentally, considered San Marino the best Italian restaurant he had encountered in the United States and hinted, although he could not for political reasons say so openly, that it was the best Italian restaurant anywhere.

Tony has had a full half century of experience as a restaurateur. After the customary apprenticeship as kitchen slavey, cook, waiter and captain, he emerged as headwaiter at Zucca's on New York's West 46th Street, then undoubtedly the most famous and ornate of New York's many Italian restaurants. When Prohibition laid its blight upon the old established eating places, the cognoscenti of New York's restaurant world went underground into the murky habitat of the speakeasy. Tony and three of his confreres opened a superb little speakeasy at 5 East 12th Street in New York. It prospered, as did its owners, so that by the time Repeal slayed the dragon Prohibition, the partners were ready to open the rather sumptuous Sixty-eight, logically at Number 68 Fifth Avenue. Their success impressed everyone, but none quite so much as a greedy landlord. He kept raising the rent until they were obliged to move, to a building they were lucky enough to find across the street. The name Sixty-eight was retained, but it was now *il*logically located at 59 Fifth Avenue. Wartime difficulties, scarcities, and controls made the business terribly nerve-racking, relations between the partners began to corrode, and they finally decided to sell out. Tony stayed on for a while as maître d'hôtel of Sixty-eight, then decided to start his own place which is San Marino.

Tony is a consummate restaurateur, at home in the kitchen, on the floor, or behind the bar. He loves to invent, he loves to cook, he loves to eat, he gets an almost beatific look when someone lights up at the first taste of one of his beloved dishes.

Tony has such an enveloping interest in food that his specialties incline to change. Old standbys are his Green Noodles, Clams Tony, Mussels Tony, Veal *Piccato*. He's also extremely proud of his Ravioli and *Cappelletti,* Minestrone (hot or cold), Bean Salad, and *Osso Buco*. San Marino has found it impossible to make reservations during rush hours so your best chance is to go early (6:30) or late (9:30). And you might as well know it, the old guard of San Marino customers would quite frankly say to you, "Please don't come at all. We're selfish enough to want it to ourselves."

There's a rather sad corollary to this success story. When Tony made the decision to leave Sixty-eight he told his intimates, "Pepita [his lovely wife] and I open a little place, do all the cooking, just a few tables for our friends. We take it easy. We got enough now. . . ." Enough, they do have, enough money, enough work, enough worry. And lovely Pepita died, suddenly, at the top of their success.

The Stage Delicatessen

834 SEVENTH AVENUE

Owner: *Max Asna*

A FAVORITE EATING PLACE NOT ONLY OF people of the theater, but of touts, bookies, wrestlers, con men, prize fighters and their managers, hackies, musicians, ladies of the chorus and many distinguished citizens of the city and the nation, including the Mayor, the Fire Commissioner, Senators, Congressmen, journalists and at least one novelist who is bearded, jovial and likes hot corned-beef sandwiches on rye.

Between noon and early morning, the place is usually filled, and at regular mealtimes hungry people often line up on the street outside, almost visibly drooling as they sniff the lovely smells that waft through the doorway. Just what is the charm of this cramped and boisterous restaurant, where the food is mostly snackish, the public violently mixed and mixed up, and the service can be described as swift but on the slap-happy side?

Some think it is the presence of the owner, Max Asna, a small, plump, voluble man who has been called a character among characters. Here is a man of a thousand quips, some of them unexpectedly funny. He delivers his observations on humankind ceaselessly, like beer from an open spigot, in a dialect that sounds like Sanskrit to the uninitiated.

Others think—and I approximate their spoken opinion barely—"Max? Whoever hoid of him? It's the pastrami on rye I come for."

To a student of New York's teeming humanity, the Stage is a fine place to observe its more colorful aspects. Surprises abound. The last time I went there to feast on Yankee bean soup and a thick segment of cherry cheesecake, a man at the next table leaned over and slapped me on the knee (the tables are folksily close together at Max's) and greeted me effusively by name. He looked vaguely familiar but he was dressed in a bright plaid sport coat and I didn't recognize him as my barber until he followed up the greeting by remarking that I needed a trim. New York is a democratic town when it comes to food that is special. In addition to meeting my barber, I have recognized among other guests at the Stage people like Leonard Bernstein, Tennessee Williams, two Yankee outfielders, Steve Allen, Sidney Kaye of the Russian Tea Room and the leading lady of the starchiest English play on Broadway.

There is an endless procession of sandwiches, salads and main dishes of a hearty nature, like superlative kosher calf's liver, tender pot roast with crisp potato pancakes and excellent T-bone steaks. But what lures most regulars are the quick-and-easy choices—bologna or salami with eggs pancake style; marinated herring; chopped chicken livers; turkey leg or breast with cranberry sauce and coleslaw and so on. The joint stays open from the first scrambled eggs and smoked whitefish to the last lox-and-cream-cheese on a bagel devoured by a hungry grifter in the virginal light of morning peeping out from behind the Coca-Cola sign. All of this often wonderful food is quite inexpensive and most of it is well worth any man's investigation.

21

21 WEST 52ND STREET

Maîtres d'Hôtel: *Philip, Emil, and assorted Kriendlers and Bernses*

I F YOU WERE FORCED TO NAME THE BEST known restaurant in the United States, and probably the one American restaurant almost literally known all over the world, you would have to settle on 21. Known also as the 21 Club, known also as Jack and Charlie's, 21 comes by its name logically—it is located at 21 West 52nd Street in New York City. It is a large sandstone building, twice as large as it used to be, because it had to be-twin itself in order to accommodate or attempt to accommodate the large number of people who assailed its doors. This doubling of size naturally started the wags to calling it 42. There is an iron gate outside the entrance door at 21, and the restaurant itself is known sometimes as the Iron Gate, and its products as the Iron Gate Products, which has perhaps unfortunately enhanced its reputation as a tough bastion to storm.

Aside from its exclusivity, its implications of wealth, its social position and its professional prestige, 21 is still a restaurant second to none in New York, New Orleans or San Francisco and on a par with the best in Paris. Like other great restaurants in other places, and other times in history, 21's reputation is founded primarily and unequivocally on food. While it's axiomatic in the restaurant business that fame is achieved

[143]

by the kitchen but that profits accrue from the bar, 21 is burstingly proud of the fact that it sells twice as much food as liquor.

But is this a fortress impenetrable to the uninitiated? Is this a place almost impossible to get in? Are the doortenders monsters of unfriendliness? Are the owners likewise monsters of impenetrability? The answer most definitely is no.

What's the truth about this impenetrability? "The fact is," says Jerry Berns, one of the owners, "21 is filled at all times by regular customers. With most tables reserved and bar space in urgent requisition by old friends, we just do not have the room for many people we do not know."

In the first place, practically everyone you come in contact with at 21 is an owner. The doormen are relatives of the owner, and part owners themselves. The person who greets you whether you go into the bar on the first floor or whether you go upstairs to the second floor is probably a relative, and that means a partial owner. The original owners (and their original restaurant was on West 49th Street rather than on West 52nd Street as it is today) were Jack Kriendler and Charles Berns, hence the Jack and Charlie's. They moved from West 49th Street to 21 West 52nd Street in 1930. 21 was then a speakeasy, as the place on West 49th Street had been a speakeasy. It was perhaps— and maybe we shouldn't say perhaps—the best speakeasy in New York. It attracted the most remarkable crowd of what were then known as celebrities—and would today be known as celebrities—movie people, writers, editors, artists, society people, financiers, Army and Navy brass, and so forth. It operated on the basis of the old English inn or pub. The proprietors and the customers became very good friends indeed and remain so to this day—those of them who are alive—unfortunately many of the most important ones are dead. During the bank holiday, for instance, 21 advanced cash, of which it had a surplus, to its best customers so they could continue to live in the rather lush manner to which they had been accustomed. The owners of 21 had their own criteria and standards of what constituted celebrities. To them, celebrities were not necessarily taken out of Who's Who, or the Social Register, or Dun and Bradstreet. Actually, the books they vastly preferred over these just named were the books that their steady customers and best friends themselves wrote. The revered customers, and the best friends, at 21 were people like Harold Ross, editor of *The New Yorker,* John O'Hara, Ernest Hemingway, John Steinbeck, Budd Schulberg, Dick Simon of Simon and Schuster, Bennett Cerf, Helen Hayes, Faye Emerson, the late and great Bob Benchley and his son Nat Benchley, Charles Addams, and other people of that kind.

21 is one of the very few buildings left in New York that is solely and wholly a restaurant, on the order of old time, now sadly demised, places such as Sherry's, Delmonico's and Martin's. The basement is given over to the vaulted wine cellars (latest census 250,000 bottles) specially designed refrigerated storerooms groaning with the raw products of goodness, and various kitchen accoutrements. The main or street floor contains the entrance, cloak room, waiting room (women are not permitted to enter the bar unaccompanied so must wait outside for tardy escorts; they can, however, be served drinks there), the cigar stand which contains probably the best collection of cigars in New York City, also the most recent books of the many authors who are 21 regulars, a bar and the three-partitioned downstairs dining room and beyond the inevitable swinging doors, the immaculate and efficient kitchen. The second floor has two more formal and elegant dining rooms, the front room, which is preferred, and the back room, which is Siberia (and to be banished to it is living death for the New Yorkers who feel that one's reputation can be enhanced or besmirched by the seat one is given in a restaurant). There is also a private dining room, the Puncheon Room, with its own bar. The third floor has the large Hunt Room, which is devoted to outsize and staggeringly expensive private parties. This, too, has its own bar. The fourth floor has, in addition to a barber shop, a private dining room which used to be owner Jack's apartment, and another smaller private room with built-in bar. In its public rooms 21 has space to seat 320 people at one time; at almost every lunch and almost every dinner, these 320 seats are completely occupied not once, but two or three times. The bar is fifty-three feet long, which will permit some twenty-six people to stand at it elbow

to elbow. Actually, though, in the busy hours, many more than twenty-six people are served there as they stand two, three or four deep. The busy hours are from 12:30 to 2:00 and from 6:00 to 9:00. After 9:00 there is a bit of a breather but around 11:15 when theaters disgorge, there is another flurry of customers which lasts until about one o'clock when there are polite suggestions that everyone get the hell out.

You would think that with this surge of humanity it would be impossible to prepare and properly serve really exquisite food. You would be wrong.

In the first place, the raw material of gastronomy that comes fresh each day into the kitchens of 21 is the very best the world has to offer. It is no secret that the choicest items from everywhere do come to New York because it is the greatest market in the United States for the best food, in many cases the only market. Delicacies which are not available in even the most exclusive markets are flown direct to 21—grouse in season, plover's eggs, Dungeness crab, Canadian salt oysters, venison and bear, antelope and buffalo meat, Mexican quail, Delaware terrapin. 21 (and a few other places) get the pick of these good things, for the simple reason that there is no true democracy in the world of good eating; distribution of the wealth of good food simply does not exist. The choicest of the choice goes to a few privileged distributors (privileged because of their prestige, knowledge, and willingness to pay premium prices); and is passed along by them to a few privileged purveyors, retail stores and restaurants. You won't always find all these delicacies; 21 believes in serving food in its natural season, and has no truck with the off-season stunt type of offering that freezing makes possible.

Getting the best raw materials is the battle only one-third won in the restaurant business. There are still two campaigns to wage and win before victory is achieved: the preparation and the serving. The preparation of the food is in the hands of the *chef de cuisine,* Yves Louis Ploneis, a practitioner of his art at the Greenbrier at White Sulphur Springs and the French Pavilion at the New York World's Fair before donning the tall white hat of chef at 21. Under M. Ploneis is Ernest Del

[1 4 6]

Maestro, as night chef, André Canezin and Guido Rota as *sauciers,* and under this eminent triumvirate are forty-nine helpers. In addition to its people in the kitchen, 21 has ingeniously drafted into culinary service the black-coated, black-tied captains on the floor. Each of these talented and experienced gentlemen has been trained in the niceties of chafing-dish cookery, so that many of the simpler dishes can be, and are, cooked directly at your table: such dishes as Steak Diane, scrambled eggs with sausage, bacon, etc. This table-side cookery has a number of advantages; it relieves the kitchen of considerable detail, permitting it to concentrate on its more complicated assignments: it provides something of a spectacle, or at least a diversion, for the diners: it gives to certain dishes which are at their best piping hot, the immediacy of fire. As it must be in all restaurants, the predominant accent in 21 food is French. But there is also solid respect for American cooking as expressed in such well-liked 21 specialties as boiled beef with horse-radish sauce, corned beef and cabbage, hamburger steak (really freshly chopped, prime sirloin), scrambled eggs with sausage—and there are Jewish echoes of the owners' apprenticeship at Aunt Jennie Grossinger's in smoked lox and herring.

The service at 21 is exquisite. Philip Caselli, previous to 21 at the Central Park Casino, rules the staff of some ninety captains, waiters, and busboys. A more accomplished restaurateur could not be found in the United States. Emil Bernasconi, formerly of the Ritz-Carlton, but almost always of 21, is head bartender.

So, it seems, 21 has triumphed in the three phases of every restaurant: procurement, preparation, and serving; and has achieved the victory which places it in the very front rank among the great restaurants of the world.

Veau d'Or

129 EAST 60TH STREET

Owners: *Georges Baratin and Henri Guiguet*

THIS MAY BE THE ONLY RESTAURANT IN NEW York where French is actually spoken more often than English. True, a good part of the French heard at the Veau d'Or is marked by the various accents of Minnesota, Georgia or Brooklyn. But one is also aware of the rapid-fire crackle and singing cadence of authentic Parisian speech. For this lively little restaurant attracts not only the fervent Francophile and the nostalgic ex-expatriate but also swarms of native-born French, both resident and *en passage*.

Whether they turn out to be the genuine overseas article or not, the people who overflow the capacity of the Veau d'Or, daytime and evening, are unquestionably the most joyously and unashamedly articulate of any restaurant public this side of the Faubourg St. Honoré. At the height of an evening's noise and confusion, the tiny bar is four-deep in standees, the air clamorous with conversation and richly scented with the lusty aroma of provincial cooking. By some secret formula known only to the management, the small room is made to hold about twice what it should. But nobody seems to complain, except those, of course, who are turned away. The tables are so closely packed that you will usually wind up actively imbedded in the conversation of your neighbors. As an old patron who loves the generous food, the sound wines and the Gallic gaiety of the place, I have found myself exchanging not only visiting cards but swapping experimental gulps of wine with the charming blonde at the next table, or the bald-headed bilingual gentleman with the rosette of the Legion of Honor and gallant manner.

Fundamentally, of course, it is the quality and honesty of the food and the reasonable prices which have made the Veau d'Or what it is today—perhaps the most successful small French restaurant in America. One eats and drinks heartily and never wearies of a menu which stays about the same except for seasonal emendations. The portions are almost embarrassingly large. Perhaps the favorite of all is the plump squab chicken, served one to a portion. It is roasted to a crusty brown succulence and flanked with country-style sliced potatoes and green vegetables, exactly as you would get it in an *auberge* in Normandy or an enlightened bistro like La Grille in Paris.

On certain days of the week, there is *gigot d'agneau*—roast leg of lamb carved in thick, pink-hearted slices, kissed lightly with garlic and cooked with all the juices, an exclusively French accomplishment. White beans are the classic accompaniment, followed by a fresh green salad. Among the recommended first courses is a *terrine* of rabbit with a mildly gamey flavor, celery root in a creamy mustard dressing and an unusual preparation of cold mussels in a delectable *sauce ravigote*. Georges and Henri are especially proud of another specialty, a fat country sausage, highly spiced, dished up hot in a thin crust of flaky pastry.

There is no wine list and no chi-chi about ordering or drinking wine. At the Veau d'Or, wine is as familiar and as popular as bread. They expect you to drink wine instead of water, reasonably enough. After all, if you happen to dislike wine, why did you take the trouble to come? There are vintage wines cached somewhere in the backstage area, but they are rarely requested. Most patrons order a *vin rosé,* either a Tavel or a sturdy specimen from Provence. Red Beaujolais is also much in demand, and white Sancerre or Muscadet—all wines that go down easily, require no ceremony or reverence in the drinking, and are refreshingly inexpensive.

Your enjoyment of the Veau d'Or will be enhanced if you go often enough to gain recognition and a friendly "*Ça va?*" from Henri or Georges, the owners. These two are old friends and business associates, yet despite their obvious compatibility, they are as sharply unlike as can be. Georges is short, plump, with a ruddy lunar countenance that beams with simple kindliness and good humor. In reality, behind the beam, he is a stern and tireless taskmaster, a serious family man of bourgeois principle, born into the restaurant business and single-mindedly devoted to his work. Henri, in contrast, is mercurial, sharp-featured and cynically humorous in his outlook. He is a favorite with those of his clients who are quick-witted Parisians, actors, artists and people of the fashion world, with whom he exchanges brisk repartee interlarded with the latest argot of the *faubourgs*.

Both go about their work with amazing energy and purpose. But their over-all scheme of management is an enlightened one. Except during the Christmas holidays, they take turns running the restaurant and each takes two long vacations every year. Henri goes off to Canada, Mexico or the Rockies to hunt or fish. Georges takes his family to Florida in the winter and spends two months every summer at Les Pléiades, the celebrated inn at the edge of the Barbizon Forest, outside Paris, which is run by his sister-in-law and is a haven abroad for all genuine devotees of the Veau d'Or.

The average check for two at this lively and unpretentious little segment of France in America should come to around twelve dollars, including wine and a couple of cocktails. The *prix-fixe* dinner involves four solid servings that are calculated to stay the pangs of a large man who has fasted for at least ten hours. Reservations will not do you much good, because the cramped quarters and insistent horde makes them difficult to hold. Best thing is to arrive late in the evening, beween 9 and 10, anchor yourself to the bar and hope for an early break. Most people who love the Veau d'Or think it is worth the trouble.

Restaurant Voisin

575 PARK AVENUE

Proprietor: *Hy Uchitel*
Maître d'Hôtel: *Michele*
Chef: *Richard Clark*

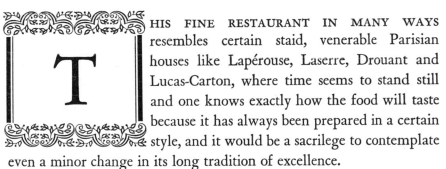

THIS FINE RESTAURANT IN MANY WAYS resembles certain staid, venerable Parisian houses like Lapérouse, Laserre, Drouant and Lucas-Carton, where time seems to stand still and one knows exactly how the food will taste because it has always been prepared in a certain style, and it would be a sacrilege to contemplate even a minor change in its long tradition of excellence.

But, in New York, the element of change has become the one certainty of life, as the city marches with giant steps into the future. Not too long ago, the loyal clients of Voisin were shaken to learn that their beloved restaurant was forced to vacate its apparently eternal premises at the corner of Park Avenue and 53rd Street, to make way for a vast building project. Where would Voisin go? And what would happen to the sublimely restful calm of the old rooms, the charm of the little bar, the soundless dexterity of the veteran staff of waiters, the classic international cuisine? Finally the restaurant moved to new quarters farther up the avenue. Today, where it used to be now stands the soaring, austerely beautiful Seagram Building, a square block in size and a mile high.

Now a couple of years have passed, and the understandable trepidation of the Voisin's friends is forgotten. For nothing was lost along the route from 53rd to 63rd Street. The only change has been in owner-ship. The new owner, praise be, is as devoted to the old ideals and prin-ciples as the most demanding customer, for he himself was a customer and has no inclination to change what had originally attracted him.

The typical guest of the Voisin could be described, with a certain amount of literary license, as mature or elderly, rather conscious of social position, widely traveled, fond of luxury and more interested in the left than the right side of the listings in the *carte du jour*.

The polished, Old World character of the restaurant is as perfectly suited to this sort of person as dry white wine to fish, or old cognac to strong black coffee. The waiters, the several captains and the maître d'hôtel all have personalities that blend smoothly with the surroundings and the carefully nourished traditions. There is not one exciting feature about Voisin—no outsize menus written in flamboyantly embroidered language, no flaming culinary displays except when the recipe demands it, and no decor that overwhelms by its magnificence the actual reason for coming here, which is to eat and drink beautifully. All the restau-rant has is perfection of an old-fashioned kind, admired by the few who can afford such things.

The chef, Mr. Richard T. Clark, an Englishman who trained under Escoffier, at this writing has presided over the kitchen for thirty-four years. He is master of a dozen different types of cuisines, all on the highest plane of quality. Among his better known creations is a glori-fied version of chicken pie, heavy with rich chunks of chicken breast, in a succulent sauce of cream and butter and a top crust of delicate puff paste. Terrapin Maryland, the preparation of which has become almost a lost art, is another of his dazzling specialties.

If you cherish American cooking of the authentic kind, try the Long Island duckling with orange sauce, or creamed chicken hash, or the boneless shad and roe in season. Voisin buys the finest oysters, clams, lobsters and crabs, and sea food in general, without regard for cost. In the foreign field, Voisin will cook your favorite dish, whether French, German, Italian or Central European, with scrupulous regard for the true ingredients and accepted techniques. You might try testing the chef's skill by ordering such disparate preparations as *Filet de Sole Marguery, Ragoût à la Deutsch,* roast beef with Yorkshire pudding, sautéed chicken livers with apples and onions, *Fruits de Mer au Gratin* or Viennese *Rostbraten.*

Prices? Well, nobody ever selects Voisin for dinner who is living on a budget. This is both a showplace of the wealthy and a temple of the gastronome, where formal dress is not obligatory but seems more right than not. If you dote on caviar, it will cost you about seven dollars for a rounded tablespoonful. But if your taste in food is less extravagant, you could start off a perfect dinner instead with *Foie Gras Frais de Strasbourg,* flown in by jet airliner, at $4.25 a portion. Crabmeat avocado, or lobster cocktail are somewhat lower in price. From there, a good selection might be *Consommé de Quenelles,* then grilled English sole, squab chicken *Polonaise,* fresh peas or asparagus in season, a fragrant almond soufflé, and a final benediction of black coffee and cognac.

Such a dinner would come to about $25 a person, including wine, but not tips. Voisin's wine cellar yields such treasures as a Grand Montrachet of 1952, Château Haut-Brion 1950, Chambolle-Musigny Les Amoureuses 1937 and historic vintages of Rhine and Moselle wines.

My feeling about this grand old restaurant is perhaps cloudy with sentiment. For several years it has been the place where I go with my wife and two old and dear friends to celebrate our respective birthdays. If these old bones hang together until February next, an old custom will be maintained. I cannot think of any spot more suitable to the occasion.

Whyte's Restaurant

145 FULTON STREET
and
344 WEST 57TH STREET

Owner: *Ray Hopper*

T SEEMS TO ME THAT THE HARDEST THING to find in New York is a restaurant that serves plain, delicious American food, of the kind a man remembers wistfully from his boyhood. But there is always Whyte's, a bustling landmark in the downtown business district for the past fifty years. Its opulent prosperity is based solidly on the fine American food for which it is famous. And, like all unusual restaurants, it is the lengthened shadow of a single man. Ray Hopper, the owner and active manager, knows his business because he grew up in it, and because he is himself an eater and drinker of prodigious discernment.

When he was a youngster in Hoboken, New Jersey, where he was born, he put in a few hours before school every morning as a helper on a horse-drawn wagon that made a daily trip to Manhattan by way of the Lackawanna Ferry, bound eventually for Gansevoort and Washington food markets. Mr. Hopper was brought up in a world of market produce piled mountain-high, of eggs by the hundred dozen, cold rooms hung with meat and poultry, silvery fish and sea food fresh from Gloucester and Nova Scotian ships tied up to the downtown piers.

[154]

Like most restaurant perfectionists, he learned to cook by watching and helping his mother in the family kitchen. This profound knowledge of food led to the job of Food Purchasing Agent for the Hamburg American and North German Lloyd steamship lines, when he was still in his twenties. In 1940, he was appointed to a similar position by the Whyte family at the huge restaurant with the Old English façade which has been a familiar sight on Fulton Street for so many years. With the passing of the original owners, Ray Hopper bought the place. Five years ago he opened an uptown branch on West 57th Street which is now a lusty success.

Certain old-fashioned American ideas of quality are still the law at Whyte's, thanks to Ray Hopper's devotion to traditions established by the founders. He has no criticism to make of frozen foods in general, but does not use them except for two or three fruits and vegetables which are available when their fresh counterparts are out of season.

Men of robust appetite flock to this huge restaurant as to a club and tables are at a premium from noon onward. Whyte's is renowned for the freshness of its fish, perhaps because it is but a skip and a slide from its delivery entrance to Fulton Market. The steamed Maine lobster, Maine lobster stew and sautéed jumbo shrimp are wonderful, and so are the chowders and farm-style thick soups. One of the few places where finnan haddie is cooked decently outside of England is Whyte's. Cotuit oysters of a special quality are reserved for this restaurant, and are offered not only on the half-shell but in half a dozen tempting styles. The immaculate charcoal grill turns out broiled shad and shad roe in season, prime sirloin steak and juicy ribs of beef. The double rib lamb chops and the calf's liver steak and bacon are solid dishes that satisfy masculine appetites. East Indian curries are great favorites and Ray has assured me, with great solemnity, that the original recipes were introduced long ago by a young Hindu prince, who worked as a cook for private reasons which he never revealed.

Whyte's bakes all its rolls, cakes and pies in ancient brick ovens behind the kitchens on the Fulton Street premises. A motherly, bespectacled lady with a light hand is responsible for the luscious pies which male patrons devour with nostalgic appreciation. I have never lunched at the old Whyte's downtown when the two enormous dining rooms were not completely occupied by happy, talkative groups, mostly composed of businessmen of that quarter. A few white-haired elders have been regulars since the place opened fifty years ago. Two who were introduced to me are Roy Howard of the Scripps-Howard newspapers and Harry Hirschfield, the perennial jokesmith and toastmaster. Judges, lawyers, brokers, newspaper editors and sports writers eat here every day because they love American home-style cooking. Whyte's is one of the last places in New York which can satisfy their hunger. It should be noted that the uptown branch uses the same menu and employs the same principles as the one downtown. George Macris, the host there, is an officer in the firm and a charmer and accomplished restaurateur in his own right.

Some
Remarks
on
Wine

MAN HAS WRITTEN AND SPOKEN MORE nonsense about wine than about any subject with which he deals, with the possible exception of love. It's a pity, too, because the nonsense aura surrounding wine has made many people approach it with a false and constrained attitude and many others to stay away from it altogether.

Wine is an agricultural product as are potatoes and rice, bananas and cherries. It comes from grapes, which are crushed, and their juice then allowed to sit and invite the bacilli which cause fermentation as they do to milk or apples and other living things left to die. Men apply their hands and wiles to a few wines such as champagne and port, but for the most part wine is a simple and inevitable manifestation of nature. So why make such a fuss about it? Why surround the serving and drinking of wine with rote and rigmarole, why talk of it in a jargon of self-conscious words and phrases when common-usage words, both English and French, will suffice and simplify? It is perfectly all right to make a hobby of wine, of learning as much as you can about wine, just as it is to make a hobby of ceramics or stamps; and to trot forth that knowledge when in the company of other wine-hobbyists.

But to inflict it on all guests and fellow diners is an act of unconscionable intellectual snobbery. There's no particular cultural significance to knowing a lot about wines, any more than there is in studying and learning the batting averages of big leaguers. And one unfortunate result of this snobbism of wine is that it has made a number of people who could and would enjoy it say "To hell with it." A good deal of it is a pose anyway. There are very few people in the world who can sip a glass of wine, blindly, and tell you its year and its vineyard, and almost all of these are professionals. Some few people have taste-bud memories as some have photographic memories, but these are not intellectual or cultural achievements, but rather physical endowments or even physical freakeries.

The wisest way to select wine for your cellar and table, or to choose it in a restaurant, is to take advantage of the knowledge and endowments of the professional experts. The good wine growers here in the United States, the good wine importers, the good wine retailers, and the good restaurants have experts at work for you from the vine to the glass. If you want to live happily in the paradisial world of wine, learn who the experts are and whom they work for, and give these places your custom. If people like Frank Schoonmaker, Fred Wildman, Michel Dreyfus, Tom Marvel, and organizations like La Confrérie des Chevaliers du Tastevin endorse a wine you can be sure it's not only an honest wine but an outstanding one of its kind. And if a retail store or restaurant carries such wines you know it's a safe place to buy or eat in as far as wine is concerned.

Practically every country in the world, except the northern countries such as Scotland, Ireland, Canada, Norway, Sweden, and Denmark, grow wine of a sort. France, Germany, Italy, and Spain grow the most, the best, and the best known. North Africa grows a great deal of wine, in fact much of the *vin ordinaire* that is used in France. Russia grows some rather sickeningly sweet wine in its southern area. Hungary has its Tokay. The national wine of Greece, retsina, has resin in it, which gives it a violin-bow taste; you can get used to it, but it might take a lifetime. Even England grows a wine, using barley as its base instead of grapes. But England imports most of its wine, port and sherry from the English-controlled wineries of Spain and Portugal; clarets, Burgundies and champagnes from France (claret is a completely English designation for Bordeaux), hock from Germany (another English term), and Chianti, Orvieto, Barolo and Soave from Italy. Recently England has been bringing in more and more of the excellent wines of South Africa and Australia, as Commonwealth wine is free of the taxes which add so considerably to the cost of the wines brought in from foreign countries. South America has its wines, the best of which are grown in Chile. And on the more exotic side are the sake wines of China and Japan, made from rice, and the Chinese rose wine which tastes not as if it were made with the soft gentle petals of the rose, but with undissolved rose thorns. It is pleasant to be able to say, unequivocally, that the United States stands well near the top, in quality, quantity; honesty of bottling and labeling; in this torrential worldwide flood of wine. The American wine industry has flowered and matured since Repeal, and is a national asset to be proud of.

Despite the fact that a number of people indulge in an excess of chi-chi where wine is concerned, and that a lot of pompous nonsense has been written about wine, there are certain traditions which have grown around the serving and drinking of wine and as long as they stay within the boundaries of common sense, as most of them do, they are worth embracing.

1. White wine goes best with fish and fowl.
2. Red wines go best with meat, game and muscular cheeses.
3. White wines should be served chilled, red wines at room temperature, or, more simply stated, unchilled.
4. The wines should progress in excellence as the courses of the meal march forward, the lowliest served first, the most regal with the last (other than dessert) course, preferably the cheese.
5. A sweet wine should never be served with a meal, but be reserved for the dessert.
6. Cocktails or other hard drinks should never precede wine.

That's about it. There are a few esoteric rules and a few rather fussy refinements of these. Let's look at these, and analyze them. And let's start with an additional rule, made to apply to the drinking of wine and all other activities of a good and normal life. It is this: There exists no rule that can't, and shouldn't, at times be broken.

RULE 1. *White wine goes best with fish and fowl.*

Yes. Well, yes and no. White is a light wine and fish is a light edible. More than the colors are amenable, the textures are, too. This is true of highly domesticated fowl, too, of creamy-white chicken and hand-raised partridge, for instance, the delicate flesh of which, like the delicate flesh of sole or crab, finds affinity with the delicate body of a white wine. But when you get to more robust fowl, to turkey, and pigeon, and duck, white wine, if a sturdy one such as one of the Montrachets, yes; but a less formidable white wine might very well find itself over-shadowed, and you would do better with a rosé or a light red wine, a Beaujolais, or a lighter Bordeaux. In fact, it would be our definite recommendation to go away from white wines (again, excepting Montrachet or perhaps Haut-Brion Blanc) with sturdier fowl. And with duck or game birds there is no question, go to the reds.

RULE 2. *Red wines go best with meat, game, and muscular cheeses.*

It's difficult to find any chink in the armor with this rule. Red wines *do* go best with meat, game, and muscular cheeses. Where a chunk of good rare beef would completely dominate a white wine, it meets its hearty, gusty equal in a good red wine. The same is true of an assertive cheese, and of game—duck, goose, venison, boar.

RULE 3. *White wines should be served chilled, red wines at room temperature, or, more simply stated, unchilled.*

That's a good enough rule as rules go. But remember, coldness is an enemy of flavor; you can chill the exquisite taste completely out of a fine white wine, which is, of course, a pity. At home, a white wine can be put in the refrigerator (not the freezing compartment) several hours in advance, and taken out and uncorked say a half-hour before serving. In a restaurant, it's a good idea to let the bottle stay in the cooler until

the wine waiter serves the first glass, then ask that the bottle be removed from the cooler. Don't ever take the lethal shortcut of putting ice in the wine itself. Two cooling and consoling wine drinks, champagne cocktail and *Spritzer* (Rhine wine and soda) are properly made with ice, but as it is assumed that they will be made with the most ordinary of champagne and Rhine wine, there is no barbarism in destroying qualities which don't exist. Red wines should be served unchilled, for the simple reason that they taste better that way. The books say "at room temperature," a beautifully meaningless phrase. The rooms in English baronial mansions, and in French châteaux, in the days when the "room temperature" rule was first promulgated, were previews of Antarctica. The rooms in American apartments and hotels today resemble the Finnish sauna. In fact, American homes are so grossly overheated today that people have been known to bring a bottle of wine in from outdoors, grow alarmed at the chill feeling of the bottle, and apply heat. This is as appalling as injecting ice. Just try to have a bottle of good red wine in the room where it will be served, upright and uncorked, thirty minutes to an hour before serving time. Don't subject it to any artificial temperature devices of any kind.

Rule 4. *The wines should progress in excellence as the courses of the meal march forward; the lowliest served first, the most regal with the last (other than dessert) course, preferably the cheese.*

This is a perfectly sound rule for a dinner where courses march but few tables today are gustatory parade grounds, and the custom is pretty much to have one-wine meals. This is a good trend; habitual several-course, several-wine meals are an unfailing prescription for diminishing fitness and expanding figures. At an informal dinner for two or four persons, even when there are three or fewer courses, it seems a bit pretentious to go into the business of multiple wines. The epic meal, like all other of life's grandiloquent occasions, should be an occasional triumph, not a regular event. Then the rule of serving wines of progressing stature is a good and rewarding one.

Rule 5. *A sweet wine should never be served with a meal, but be reserved for the dessert.*

[164]

This is as obvious as not sprinkling sugar on your roast; unless, of course, you happen to *like* sugar on your roast. A particularly cherished friend, who happens to have an advanced case of saccharine tooth, likes nothing better than a thick, succulent, juicy steak with a bottle of Château d'Yquem, thus, at one sitting smashing hell out of several of the most hallowed wine rules. White wine with red beef, the sweetest of all natural wines with the body of the meal, and a whole bottle of Château d'Yquem for one person at one time! But he likes it that way so, bless him, let him have it. The rule is a good one though, so save that bottle of Château d'Yquem for dessert time and then be content with one glass of it.

RULE 6. *Cocktails or other hard drinks should never precede wine.*

Objection! This simply is not true, furthermore it demeans that great and noble American Institution, the dry martini, and moreover it is un-American as it's a rule devised and promulgated by the French, who know nothing whatsoever about cocktails and even less about the dry martini. There is a great deal to be said for serving a white wine, a good Chablis, for instance, or champagne as an apéritif. But if your soul pines for a martini, do not deny it this balm. A heavier, or a sweeter drink: a whiskey sour or old-fashioned, or daiquiri, should be pondered a little longer, but if you're going to be unhappy without it, by all means indulge yourself. One or two authoritative drinks will not spoil your taste for either the food or wines that will follow.

Practically all the wine groups and eating groups have a rule the members meticulously observe at their dinner and usually in their homes as well. This rule is abstinence from smoking at any time during the drinking of apéritifs, and during the meal until its ending is pronounced by the serving of coffee. This is a rule which should be enacted into a natural law with death by torture the penalty for its infraction. Cigarette smoke and cigarette offal are an abomination wherever food is being served and eaten, and are fatal to the enjoyment of wine. Even when the coffee appears, cigarettes should be barred. The proper thing to smoke at the end of a good meal is a good cigar. Even some of our more enlightened lady diners are beginning to join the menfolk in lighting up a cigar when coffee and cognac time comes (in Scandinavia this is the custom).

It's encouraging to see, these days, a growing knowledge of the proper effect of time upon wine. Age has, for the most part, been excessively regarded amongst the virtues a wine can possess. Some people had the quaint notion that "the older the better" was almost literally true, and would ooh-and-aah over a dust-shrouded bottle and faded label when actually the wine within had long since seen its most robust days and had sunk into old age and senility, well on its way to death, not the honorable death of consumption, but the death of waste which must come to all living things. Age always changes wine, and up to a certain period in a healthy wine's life, improves it. But there comes the time the wine should be drunk, for thereafter it starts inevitably on the long sad road of deterioration. White Burgundies generally are ready in four or five years, in full bloom in seven or eight years, and likely to be on the way down after that. A few years can be added for red Burgundies. Bordeaux wines live longer and a good vintage of a good growth can and will live half a century or more. At that age, it will be a delight and a nostalgic experience, but it was a better wine earlier in its life.

The Northeast

Ambassador Inn

EAST QUOGUE, LONG ISLAND
NEW YORK

Owner: *Lorenzo (Larry) Lercari*
Chef: *Mario Colombo*

HOSE OF US WHO HAVE HOMES IN THE Hamptons of Long Island are peculiarly blest with good places to eat. Probably in no other place in the United States, outside a few of the larger cities, can there be found so many excellent restaurants in such a comparatively small area. If we're feeling out-of-this-worldish, there is the Out-of-This-World, at Wainscott, with its eerie decor and its spareribs, chops, steaks, and other robustly good dishes. If we feel like fine food in a jolly, even raffish, setting, we submit ourselves to the Character in the White Jacket, Herb McCarthy, at his Bowden Square in Southampton. If we're inclined to be lured by a surpassingly good buffet and an incomparable view from high sandy hills which overlook Shinnecock Bay, and the Atlantic beyond, there are Scotch Mist Inn and Tucker Mill Inn. And if we feel like an excellent meal, in homelike surroundings, amongst old friends, we head for the Villa Paul in Hampton Bays, or the Patio in Westhampton, or the Ambassador Inn in East Quogue.

Back in the days of Prohibition, the Ambassador was a roadhouse-speakeasy, grim and almost sinister, hardly the place for the family's Sunday dinner. The bar was gloomy and uninviting, the main dining room was gaudy, done in the taste of the times and the owners, and the food, if you wanted to be really charitable, was so-so.

Some time after Repeal, the Ambassador was taken over by Paul Villa and his wife Marie, with Paul in the dining room and behind the bar, and Marie exerting her considerable talents in the kitchen. The place was redecorated, refurbished, rejuvenated, rehabilitated—and rewarded with warm acceptance by the entire Hampton community. In fact, the acceptance was so overwhelming, the success so spectacular, that after several years of herculean effort, both Paul and Marie were faced with seriously corroded health; and at the firm insistence of their doctor retired, and went back to their little home town in Italy, high above the Mediterranean. The Ambassador was sold to Paul's cousin Lorenzo, and his partner Antoine.

After a few years, Antoine left to open Café de France on West 46th Street in New York, and Lorenzo stayed on as owner, entrepreneur, maître d'hôtel, bartender, sommelier, and master of the kitchen. All these tasks he performs efficiently and with almost unbelievable good cheer. After all, his long experience includes years on the Italian Line, a spell at Le Pavillon, with Soulé, and several years in the best hotels. So there really isn't much that could come up in a restaurant that would disturb or baffle him.

Lorenzo (Larry in Americanized form, Renzo to his Italian-speaking friends) is particularly proud of his local specialties: crisp-cooked Long Island duckling from a farm within quacking distance; clams from the nearby waters of Peconic and Shinnecock bays; mussels from his own mussel bed in Shinnecock, about a half-mile from the restaurant. The mussels, plump, succulent, immaculately clean of sand, with gleaming black shells, cooked delicately with just a touch of olive oil, a sprinkling of parsley, and a whisper of garlic, are a particular treat. The Ambassador also serves an excellent lobster, but that is from Maine, not from Montauk as it was once upon a time. The Italian dishes, spaghetti (especially with clam sauce), veal *scaloppine* or *piccato,* ravioli, and minestrone, are also good.

The Ambassador is open about ten months of the year, closing only in the dead of winter, when Renzo swaps kitchen and bar implements for paint and scrubbing brushes to give the place a thorough face-lift.

The Barclay

RITTENHOUSE SQUARE EAST
PHILADELPHIA, PENNSYLVANIA

Catering Manager: *Cesar Innocenti*
Maître d'Hôtel: *Mario Salvatore*
Chef: *Philip De Carlo*

HERE WAS A TIME, AND NOT TOO FAR IN THE musty past, when Rittenhouse Square was the very heart and essence of all that was fashionable in Philadelphia, its name capable of conjuring up the same visions of elegance and good living as did the names of New York's Gramercy Park and London's Berkeley Square. It was a park, or square, of a mere six acres, around the borders of which stood the buxom, rococo brick and sandstone manses of Philadelphia's snootiest families, the Biddles, and the Livingstons, and the Strawbridges, and the Willings, and the Barleys, and the Warburtons, and the Clothiers. Here, until World War I, life was lived as well and as elegantly as it was any place in the United States. In ample, beautifully appointed private dining rooms napery was snowy white, silver gleamed, crystal shot shafts of fire, boards groaned, wine flowed.

Alas, no more. The six acres of park remain, with the crisscross walks, the grass and shrubs and trees, the desultory fountain in the middle, the nursemaids and children, the poodles, the Flower Festival in May (for charity, of course) and the amateur Art Exhibition in October (for charity, naturally). But all else of what made Rittenhouse

Square an awesome name to socially conscious people is gone. The brick and sandstone private homes have either fallen under the wrecker's sledge, or been converted to such odd-sounding share-the-culture projects as Theosophists Union and English-Speaking World. The gaps have been filled by monstrous edifices, apartment houses, U.S. Signal Corps (née The Pennsylvania Athletic Club) and hotels.

One of the hotels, the Barclay, is the subject of this essay. For the Barclay tries valiantly to retain a shred of the former character of Rittenhouse Square, a bit of the elegance and satisfaction that were to be found in Rittenhouse Square's private dining rooms. In fact, and this, regrettably, is not lavish praise, its food is probably the best available in Philadelphia today.

There are no overwhelming specialties at the Barclay, it's just that all the traditional things are done superbly, and served in such elegant, quiet, and tasteful surroundings. As in the dining rooms of the Rittenhouse Square of memory, the napery is snowy white, the silver gleams, the crystal shoots shafts of fire, the board groans, and the wine flows.

The wine flows, but not the way it should. This is just one more depressing corollary of the really foul idea of all wines and liquor being bought and sold by the State Liquor Authority. The law forbids all advertising of any kind, all promotion, explanation of, or educational material about wine or liquor. As a consequence, there is little feeling, or demand, for wine in Philadelphia. But the Barclay does have wines, and good ones, and will be happy to bring them forth if you ask your waiter or captain about them.

Among the better dishes at the Barclay are the Hot Canapé of Shrimps, Crabmeat and Mushrooms Philip, Broiled Boneless Shad in season, Snapper Soup Baltimore and *Filet de Boeuf Sauté Richelieu*. On the American side, there are such hearty specialties as Spring Lamb Stew with Vegetables, a thick cut of Roast Prime Ribs of Beef, Roast Maryland Turkey with Cauliflower Mornay and Candied Sweet Potatoes, Steak Minute O'Brien and a cluster of about twenty different desserts headed by Pineapple Chiffon Pie and Rice Soufflé Pudding.

Very good, anywhere. Tremendous, for Philadelphia!

Beau Séjour

BETHPAGE, LONG ISLAND
NEW YORK

Owners: *Edward and Paul Wilson*
Headwaiter: *Siegfried Kohlhagen*

A PORT OF CALL SINCE 1908 FOR NEW YORK'S more indefatigable gourmets, this serenely elegant Long Island restaurant is housed in the midst of gardens in a lovely mansion of the period. Driving out to Bethpage from town takes about an hour. Sporting citizens of an earlier generation used to make it in dusters and goggles over the old Vanderbilt Motor Parkway. In its time the place has known many distinguished visitors and the owners make special reference to Enrico Caruso, Arturo Toscanini, David W. Griffith, Harry Truman, Captain Amundsen, General George Marshall. It is also held in fond esteem by most of the landed gentry who own estates along the North Shore.

A family affair for fifty years, the restaurant was founded by Bernard Pouchan, an uncle of the present owners. M. Pouchan had been chef of New York's famous Café Martin and, according to current testimony, was a true martinet in his stern allegiance to the traditions of *la véritable grande cuisine*. But in his new surroundings he had the good sense to utilize native foods as American as green corn, Blue Point oysters, Peconic Bay clams, Long Island duck, local asparagus and broccoli, sea bass, crabmeat and Montauk lobster.

One of the most celebrated of his culinary inventions is the dish called Soft Clams Sauté on Toast, listed as an hors d'oeuvre, but so rich as to take a deep tuck in any but the most gargantuan appetite. The recipe sounds simple enough, but no imitation ever seems to capture the luscious richness and sea-swept flavor of the original. Perhaps this is because it is not easy to find soft clams of the size and quality which the Beau Séjour obtains from a private source.

The kitchen is also prepared to pamper you with roast duck of a crispness and brownness that is the despair of most housewives and all cooks of lesser degree. Vegetables are served in their vernal state of seasonal freshness. The sauces, the butter, the bread, the service of wines and the impeccable whiteness of the table linen—all signs of the superior restaurant—are to be found here at their best. Pursuing the menu further, there is a delightful casserole of chicken in red wine and another of guinea hen with a brandy sauce. Lobster is broiled with regal lavishness, as in the days of Jack's and Rector's. Steaks of languishing tenderness may be had with the sound masculine accompaniments of hashed brown, au gratin or creamed potatoes, each done to perfection.

Indomitable eaters might care to top this sort of food with a pet dessert of the house called Almond Rum Layer Cake. The recipe, in all its intimidating intricacy, is offered at the end of the book. It makes a difficult, perhaps insuperable, problem for even the best of cooks, but offers pleasant reading on a purely literary basis.

We've heard rather distressing things about Beau Séjour recently and are afraid they may be true; that both quality and service have slipped, and that the owners no longer have the determination necessary to keep it a really fine restaurant. We've heard also that they're aware of this and have pledged to redeem its hallowed name and reputation. It would be a genuine pity if this were not the real truth.

Blue Spruce Inn

ROSLYN, LONG ISLAND
NEW YORK

Owner: *Carl W. Werner*
Maître d'Hôtel: *Hans Weigel*
Chef: *Walter G. Wurl*

N THE GREEN, WARM MONTE CARLO SPRING of 1933, Carl Werner was the bartender at George's English Grille (George was a Hungarian, Carl was a Bavarian, Monte Carlo was Monacan, but it was George's English Grille, nevertheless), an excellent bistro down the hill from the Casino and the Hotel de Paris, down toward the harbor. In that same spring, the authors were in Monte Carlo with their wives, playing tennis each day, and nearly every night being administered to by George's quite wonderful Hungarian food, and Carl's quite wonderful martinis, wines and liqueurs. It was all very pleasant, and under the civilizing and warming influence of the Hungarian food, the martinis, wines and liqueurs, a genuine friendship with George and Carl burgeoned. Carl had been in the United States for a short time, working at the Longchamps which was then at 47th Street and Madison Avenue in New York, and spoke quite passable English. We urged him to return, in a sincere but vague sort of way.

In the gray, chill winter of 1933, the blight of Prohibition was lifted in the United States and New York celebrated Repeal and the return of legal drinking. The authors and their wives were in New York on Repeal Day, eating at the now-demolished and mourned Ritz-Carlton at 46th Street and Madison Avenue. After lunch they went to the Oval Room for coffee and brandy. They were waited on—by Carl Werner!

From here on, this account gets a bit involved. With the prospect of Repeal, a group, including the authors, had decided to open a restaurant. Ludwig Bemelmans, writer, artist, connoisseur of wine, food, and women, was the central figure in the group. The restaurant was, and is, known as Hapsburg House, although the originators and original owners are long since out.

After greeting Carl Werner on that December day in 1933, we suggested to him that he go up to Hapsburg House, and talk to Bem about a job as sommelier. He did; he was hired; and he became the first authentic sommelier in the United States, complete and replete with a chain of keys to the cellar around his neck, a silver *tastevin* cup, a short jacket, and long black apron. The Hapsburg, at that time, had probably the best wine cellar in the country, and Carl presided over it knowingly and affectionately. He graduated from that job to the managership of the restaurant; from there to the managership of the larger Stockholm restaurant at 313 East 57th Street; and from there to the ownership of his own fine restaurant, the Blue Spruce Inn, in Roslyn, Long Island.

It can be said, categorically, that Blue Spruce is one of the best inns in the United States. Carl has put into it all the knowledge of food, of wine, of innkeeping, of hosting, of decor, that he learned from his association with Longchamps, George's Hungarian Café, the Ritz, Bemelmans, the Hapsburg, the Stockholm, and the various associates and customers who are his good friends.

Roslyn is one of the more fashionable suburbs of New York City. Blue Spruce draws its clientele from Roslyn and the surrounding horsy countryside, also from New Yorkers sophisticated in food and wine.

Blue Spruce has a fine bar, appropriately called the Polo Bar (being near Meadowbrook and Syosset, it is in the heart of the polo-playing territory of the country). It specializes in Bavarian and Viennese food—*Szigeti* Goulash, *Backhändl,* schnitzels, *Palatschinken,* strudels; and fine Rhine and Moselle wines. But it also can set before you, in perfect form, the glorious sea food of Long Island, American steaks and chops, and the classic French dishes. The authors are proud to have had a hand in making Carl a solid American businessman and to number him among their good friends.

Bookbinder's

125 WALNUT STREET
PHILADELPHIA, PENNSYLVANIA

President: *John M. Taxin*
Maître d'Hôtel: *Albert R. Taxin*
Chef: *John Croxton*

P HILADELPHIA IS POOR IN RESTAURANTS, BUT rich in having two original Bookbinder's. There's no question about it, Bookbinder's was once one of the greatest sea-food restaurants in the United States. It ranked, in the eastern United States (and that's where the greatest sea food is), with Harvey's and Hogate's in Washington, and with Billy the Oysterman in New York. Billy had the riches of the Atlantic and the Long Island bays on which to draw; Harvey's, Hogate's and Bookbinder's had Chesapeake Bay. Of course, they, too, went to the Atlantic for lobster and fish, but the two sections had their specialties.

Alas, all of them came upon hard days. The product of the sea was still good, but the health of the owners and their successors was not, and the health of the product suffered coincidentally. Someone has taken over Harvey's and it's not a very good restaurant. Hogate's is fair. But rather mysterious things have happened to Bookbinder's.

One offshoot moved off and uptown to Philadelphia's 15th Street and proclaimed itself "The only restaurant owned by the original

Bookbinder family." The other stayed downtown at 125 Walnut Street and clarioned itself as "The Old Original Bookbinder's."

Which is heir to the throne? Which is the True, the Old, the Original, the *Only* Bookbinder's?

Who cares?

I would cast an unconvinced vote for the downtown, the 125 Walnut Street version, because it occupies the premises, and because, in my opinion, it most sincerely tries to emulate the original. It is a good restaurant. It leads you right into the section that was Ben Franklin's and Betsy Ross's, and where the Declaration of Independence was unveiled and where the Liberty Bell rang its sweet song, then became silent forever.

Bowden Square

SOUTHAMPTON, LONG ISLAND
NEW YORK

Owner: *Herb McCarthy*
Maître d'Hôtel: *Philip Lugris*
Chef: *Speros Vassilakos*

FOR THREE MONTHS OF EACH YEAR HERB McCarthy's Bowden Square Inn is located in the heart of one of the richest and most sophisticated communities in the United States, Southampton. At the end of these three months, the summer residents who make it rich and sophisticated depart and the restaurant must then for nine months draw on the solid, prosperous, year-round business and professional people.

Herb McCarthy is one of the few restaurateurs in the entire eastern end of Long Island who have learned how to please and win the custom of both the summer people and the year-long people. In fact, most of the other good restaurants in the area (Ambassador Inn, Sea Spray Inn, Dune Deck, and Yardarm) silently fold their tents and take it on the lam. Only the Patio in Westhampton, Tradewinds in Watermill and Bowden Square in Southampton, among the really good restaurants, brave the winter winds which bring the shutters to so many well-heeled homes. And of these, Bowden Square appeals to the most people. In fact, in our opinion, it is a much more pleasant place in the winter than in the summer, because it is just *too* popular in the summer. On Saturday nights particularly it is jam-packed into the early hours of the morning, the bar is overrun, tables are too few, the dancers tread on each other's toes and the noise is a din. But in off-season even Saturday nights are comfortable and pleasant with plenty of room at the bar, the dancing room closed and pleasantly silent, tables for everyone, and a cheerful, friendly fireplace blazing in the middle of the room.

Herb McCarthy himself is a genial and waggish host. He studied law at Fordham and graduated, but decided to follow in the family business of innkeeping rather than the more austere profession of law. Bowden Square is nearly thirty years old, and all those years in its present location at the corner of Bowden Square and North Sea Road in Southampton, and for all those nearly thirty years Herb McCarthy has been its sole owner and its manager.

When Bowden Square started, Southampton was a quiet, almost dreamy, tree-shaded village. The social and the wealthy hardly knew of its existence. Then they began coming in ever-increasing numbers, they are still coming, and they have transformed the once-dreamy village, in the summer at least, into a bustling, traffic-ridden, party-giving town. In season, the main street is as busy a retail strip as you are likely to see outside New York's Fifth Avenue. Immensely smart (and expensive) shops line both sides of the street.

In the summer, the same people who keep these shops glittering and prosperous keep Bowden Square glittering and prosperous. They come there for lunch, for dinner, for supper and dancing, and they give parties there. It is all very gay, in the large main dining room, in the smaller bar, on the awning-covered porch, and in the flower-filled garden with its parasol-covered tables.

The food at Bowden Square is American with a French accent. The steaks and chops are of outstanding quality. The oysters are, in our opinion, the best in the United States. Herb has his own bed out in Peconic Bay, a few miles from the restaurant, off the little island of Fireplace, and the oysters themselves are known as Fireplace oysters. The Indians used to build little brick fireplaces on the beach and bake and roast their oysters there, oysters from the same bed which now supplies Bowden Square. The surrounding waters also supply the place with marvelous clams, mussels, and the incomparable Peconic and Mecox Bay scallops, tiny succulent balls of deliciousness which are, for the most part, available only in this area of Long Island, as they are so prized that they are eaten almost entirely by the local people, and very few find their way into the outside world. In fact, they are frequently hard to get even on the shores of the bays where they are caught, and you almost literally have to know one of the scallop fishermen in order to be assured a regular supply in season. Long Island duck and locally raised and pampered chickens are also specialties. Lobster is popular here too, although the Montauk lobster supply has just about disappeared and Bowden Square lobsters come from Maine, as do most self-respecting lobsters these days.

The wines selected by Herb are especially good and varied. He has made a serious study of wine, which has entailed several trips to the wine countries in France and Germany, and has sought expert advice in addition to his own considerable knowledge. While he is an irreverent host, calling most guests by their first names and always ready with a quip or gentle insult, he is a hard and knowledgeable worker in the kitchen and the wine cellar and the dining room, and severely proud of his place. It is decidedly worth a visit if you are ever in that delightful part of the country.

Chesapeake
Restaurant

1707 NORTH CHARLES STREET
BALTIMORE, MARYLAND

Proprietor: *Sidney Friedman*
Chef: *Edward Sullivan*

IT WOULD BE STRANGE AND INAPPROPRIATE if Baltimore, washed by the salt air from Chesapeake Bay, and having first call on its bounty of glorious sea food, didn't have more than one good sea food restaurant. It does. In addition to Miller Brothers, there is another excellent sea-food place called, with great appropriateness, the Chesapeake. Some people like it better than they do Miller Brothers, but the fair thing is to say that they are both very good.

Naturally, their menus are not too dissimilar. On the Chesapeake menu you will find Chesapeake Bay crabmeat in all the forms to which it lends itself, deviled, baked, lump, cake, au gratin, salad, cocktail, and so forth. Lobster also goes in for great variety. The lobster, incidentally, is not from the Chesapeake but from the cold waters off Maine. There are also Chesapeake Bay flounder and scallops, and game in season when the birds from Canada head south along the eastern flyway. For those demented souls who can't stay away from meat even

[184]

in a fine sea-food restaurant, there is excellent steak, roast beef, and lamb chops. There is even that old favorite, planked steak, charcoal-broiled and surrounded with endless vegetables. There is one very refreshing note on the Chesapeake menu. It is this: "Not responsible for 'well-done' steaks. Please do not ask us to broil our beautiful steaks well-done." Bravo!

The Chesapeake selection of wine is not sensational but it is quite varied and intelligently chosen. And for those who feel that good beer is a lovely companion to sea food (it is) and even to steaks and chops (again, it is) there is an alluring variety of beer and ale, draught, domestic and imported.

Coventry Forge Inn

COVENTRYVILLE, PENNSYLVANIA
(Mailing address: R. D. 2, Pottstown, Pennsylvania)

Proprietor: *Wallis Callahan*

YOU LEAVE PHILADELPHIA, DRIVE THROUGH Fairmount Park, onto the wide concrete sweep of the Pennsylvania Turnpike, past Manayunk, past Conshohocken, past Valley Forge. Along about here, you keep your eyes open because you're to turn off at Route 100. You turn onto a narrow hard-top road, though with plenty of room for two cars to pass unless both happen to be Cadillacs, in which case it's better to slow down a bit. Seven miles through this gently rolling bucolic Pennsylvania country you come to a still narrower road, and after a mile of this you make a sudden dizzying, sharp right upturn, and in a minute you're at the back door of a charming old Pennsylvania farmhouse, warmly lighted. This is Coventry Forge Inn, thirty-six miles from the center of Philadelphia, already of some repute even though in existence only since 1954. But thirty-six miles! Is it worth it? We'll see.

You enter, and almost immediately a bit of the grumpiness over the long drive begins to chip off. You can take in most of this ground floor at a quick glance, a room with tables on the left, a room with tables on the right, and a room dead ahead with what looks like some sort of bar arrangement at its end, a hopeful and encouraging sight.

Aside from the necessary multiplicity of tables and chairs, the place is attractively and appealingly furnished, not with preciously transplanted antiques, but with what look like (and turn out to be) the authentic furnishings of the old homestead, which goes back to 1717.

It is a matter of only a few minutes before you are approached by a small, wiry, dapper young man who greets you pleasantly and introduces himself as Dick Callahan. He explains that his brother Wallis is busy in the kitchen but if you'd like to have a drink, Wally will be out presently to talk about dinner. You follow Dick to the back room where there's a big, broad table with benches on one side and one end and chairs on the other side and the other end. Bookshelves form the walls behind it. The thing that looked like a bar from the entrance turns out, encouragingly, to be a bar. It's not a stand-up or sit-down bar, but rather a working bar, a long board with the gadgetry of drink-making, with an ice container beneath, and a deep sink on the side. Dick mixes martinis all around. Midway in the second martini, Wally emerges from the kitchen and is, at first, almost a comical sight. He's shorter than Dick, huskier, bald, and has one of the most monumental mustaches ever grown by man, a huge bushy affair in which grouse could nest, long and dashingly upswept at the ends.

His mien is serious and you haven't talked to him long before you realize that he knows and loves cooking. He came upon the art as a GI in France and his life was there and then ordained. When he and Dick returned from the service, they decided a restaurant was what they had to have, and their mother, Claire Callahan, a celebrated character actress in the early part of the century and until 1950 or so, provided the housing for their dream in the old home she owned in Coventry Forge. Hence, Coventry Forge Inn.

As Wally studied at the Cordon Bleu Ecole de Cuisine in Paris, he leans toward the aristocratic, rather than peasant, school of French cooking. But he's also given to experimentation, as are all conscientious graduates of the Cordon Bleu. The first example of his wedding of the classic with the experimental you will face will be his Cheese Soup; he'll be hurt if you don't order it and crushed if you don't praise it.

This might be followed by Frog's Legs *Provençal,* Game Hen with Wild Rice or a chateaubriand; a Tossed Salad *Fines Herbes,* and for dessert, Peach Melba, *Baba au Rhum,* or *Crêpes Suzette,* or a selection of fine imported cheese. The owner proudly said recently, "We have not had to serve broiled chopped sirloin in almost a year."

The Callahans know good wines as well as good food and have stocked such impressive items as Romanée Conti, Chambertin, and La Tache, Pouilly-Fuissé and Bâtard-Montrachet, and Meursault "Les Perriers." From Bordeaux, there is a Château Olivier, from the Rhone, Châteauneuf-du-Pape, and from Anjou a delicate Vouvray. There are also selections of superb Rhines, Moselles and champagnes and a proper assortment of Italian and American wines. The liquors and liqueurs are the best available and intelligently varied. The cellar is particularly to be commended, as Pennsylvania's State Liquor Control cares nothing about quality, so to get the best it is necessary to go to considerable effort which, sadly, few places in Pennsylvania bother to do.

After eating well, and drinking well, and relaxing comfortably, the trip back to Philadelphia is a breeze; in fact, when you get back pleasantly short of midnight, you find yourself feeling smugly superior to the people who stayed put and ate less well.

Prices at Coventry Forge are reasonable. It's worth a trip if you're in the area, but don't go without first calling the inn's number, HOmestead 9-6222.

La Crémaillère
à la Campagne

BANKSVILLE, NEW YORK
(Mailing address: R.F.D. 1, Greenwich, Connecticut)

Owner: *Antoine Gilly*
Maître d'Hôtel: *Pierre Troadec*
Chef: *Georges Moriaz*

NTOINE GILLY ONCE OWNED ONE OF THE best and most fashionable restaurants in New York. It was genuinely French, as was its proprietor. If it never became nationally known, it was only because its owner didn't want it that way. He preferred to serve his patrons on an intimate, personal basis. Nevertheless, it was known to the most discerning kind of New Yorker, and highly respected as well.

Then, one day, the small building in which La Crémaillère was housed went the way of most small buildings, to be replaced by the huge building which today is the Carlton House. Viewing the wreckage, and pondering on the hectic and pressuring life of New York, M. Gilly said "To hell with it all," or Gallic words to that effect, and turned his eyes countryward. He chose a lovely old building a mile or so off the Merritt Parkway, in Banksville, New York, which is a next-door neighbor to Greenwich, Connecticut. There he runs a restaurant which has few peers in the United States, and very few indeed outside New York City.

La Crémaillère has a chef, Georges Moriaz, who is great at his art, but the presence and proprietorship of Antoine Gilly means that it has two chefs who are great at their art. For M. Gilly is primarily of the kitchen. The food naturally is distinctly French in its accent. The hors d'oeuvres feature such French-inspired dishes as Fresh *Moules Rémoulade, Saucisson de Morteau, Escargots de Bourgogne, Terrine de Faisan* and Celery *Rémoulade;* the soups include Vichyssoise, Boula-Boula, *Petite Marmite,* and the omnipresent Onion Soup au Gratin. The entrée list is long and again French-inspired: *Quenelles de Brochet Armoricaine, Poularde Rôtie à la Paysanne, Coq au Vin Crémaillère, Tripes à la Mode de Caen, Tête de Veau Vinaigrette, Emincé de Boeuf à l'Estragon, Rognons de Veau Sautés à la Bourguignonne, Choucroute Garnie Strasbourgeoise.* Desserts include *Poire Hélène, Meringue Glacée Chantilly, Pot de Crême, Coupe aux Marrons,* soufflés and *Crêpes Suzette.* There are, of course, many more items, in both French and English, on the menu, but this should give you an idea.

M. Gilly, who is a Commandeur of the Chevaliers du Tastevin, has, as you would suspect, a beautiful collection of wines. But in addition to the imposing, formal wine list, there is featured each day on the menu an interesting selection of *Vins du Jour* in which you will find such unusual French wines as Mercurey, Quincy, Sancerre, Muscadet, Vin Gris d'Arbois, Anjou Rosé, Vouvray. These are regional and delicate wines, supposedly allergic to travel, but actually with today's fast transport they do travel perfectly well, and are at their best when quite young. If you prefer to order a grander wine, there is the large wine list replete with bottles, heroic both in the origin and year of birth.

La Crémaillère is expensive, but its prices are surprisingly modest if compared to the prices of food of similar quality in New York. After all, there is a difference in cost of doing business in the most expensive city in the world and one of its more remote suburbs.

Ho-Ho-Kus Inn

HO-HO-KUS, NEW JERSEY

Owners: *Gordon L. Butler and Helen L. Wilson*
Headwaiter: *Edward Meek*
Chef: *William Heinrich*

WHEN WE WERE KIDS, IN THE FLEDGLING years of Prohibition, there was a creepy little place in northern New Jersey called the Ho-Ho-Kus Inn. It was shadowy, off by itself, reached over country roads, run by questionable characters straight out of a Chicago gangster movie. It was a speakeasy, so we didn't take our girls there, or even the other fellow's girl, but it was an adventuresome and heady thing for the fellows to drop in for an applejack highball or a spot of needled beer.

The Ho-Ho-Kus Inn is still there, in the same old colonial building, serving food and serving drinks. But how it has come up in the world! It is now as fine a restaurant as there is in New Jersey, and one of the notable places of New York's entire suburban area.

The country roads are gone, having succumbed to broad concrete highways lined on both sides with garish supermarkets, super-stores, super-neonned bazaars. And the isolation has gone. Ho-Ho-Kus Inn is now in a crowded, built-up area. But it still has its 1790 façade of colonial sandstone and is still restful with the charm of an earlier century.

The hosts are Gordon Butler and his sister, Mrs. Helen Wilson. Gordon is a refugee from the huckster channels of Madison Avenue, where he slaved as a copywriter in the immaculate halls of J. Walter Thompson. His escape to Ho-Ho-Kus Inn is a saga comparable to that of Edmond Dantes, the Count of Monte Cristo. He and his sister learned in mysterious fashion that the place might be for sale, investigated, fell in love with it, and, after numerous complications and moments of high drama, managed to buy it.

It then was in a sorry state of repair, but with the help of friends both knowing and affluent, they were able to restore and redecorate it, and open it as an attractive, and authentic, country inn. Happily, they have done well.

The Inn has, on its ground floor, a bar, a tap room, and two dining rooms. The bar is attractive, of good length, and presided over by a most amiable and knowledgeable colored chap. As your eye roams the back bar, you will see every kind of liquor and liqueur you ever heard of, and a few which will be strangers to you. The Tap Room is in the old tap-room tradition, with early American chairs and tables, a crock of cheese on each table, and good beer and ale. There's also piano music there over weekends.

The place has a generous menu, with a specialty each day (Monday, Veal Paprika; Tuesday, closed; Wednesday, *Sauerbraten;* Thursday, Plantation-Style Capon; Friday, New England Clam Pie; Saturday, *Coq au Vin;* every day, Ragout of Beef, Huntsman style). But the dishes they're most proud of, day in and day out, are the Veal Paprika, *Sauerbraten,* Capon, Clam Pie, and *Coq au Vin.* The wine cellar is excellent and the prices are not unreasonable.

John Bartram Hotel

BROAD STREET AT LOCUST
PHILADELPHIA, PENNSYLVANIA

Maître d'Hôtel: *Robert Timperio*
Chef: *Anthony Dardanelli*

IN A WAY, THE RESTAURANT AT THE JOHN Bartram Hotel is the most interesting in Philadelphia. For, in a city noted for the air of lethargy which pervades its restaurants, the John Bartram brings invention, ingenuity, and even excitement to the selection of its menu and the service of its food.

The John Bartram menu is unusually large and interesting; and Maître d'Hôtel Timperio and Chef Dardanelli have had the courage to bedeck it with such enticing dishes as Snails Sauté, Imported French Mackerel, Boula-Boula au Gratin, Bisque of Lobster *Nantaise,* Chicken *Cacciatore,* Rainbow Trout, Swordfish *Sauté Bretonne,* Broiled Pheasant, Hearts of Ceylon Palm Hollandaise, *Parfait au Rhum,* Chateaubriand *Bouquetière;* these in addition to all the usual steaks, chops, sea food, salads, soups, hors d'oeuvres, vegetables and desserts you'll find on any self-respecting menu.

The John Bartram has brought a delightful innovation to Philadelphia, and perhaps to restaurant eating, in their Gourmet Dinners, which must be ordered in advance (twelve to forty-eight hours) and served for from two to six people. Here is the menu for one such Gourmet Dinner:

Avocado Pear Stuffed with Crabmeat
and Caviar John Bartram

Hearts of Celery   Rose Radishes
Mixed Olives
Boula Boula
Diamond Back Terrapin Maryland, Amontillado
Filet of Beef à la Renaissance
Potatoes Champs Elysées
Belgian Carrots in Cream
Hearts of Palm Vinaigrette
Compote à l'Orangé

Demi-Tasse   Dinner Mints
$20.00 per person. Menu prepared for four or more persons.

The John Bartram has a good selection of wines, and recommends them wisely, but it suffers here as do all restaurants from rigid state control of wine and liquor, and the stupid and stultifying restrictions and difficulties that control puts on the getting of good wines.

Joseph's

279 DARTMOUTH STREET
BOSTON, MASSACHUSETTS

President: *Louis Corsini*
Maître d'Hôtel: *Spartaco (Nino) Scarpellini*
Chef: *Domenic Ruzzo*

OSEPH'S HAS A CHARACTER OF ITS OWN, AND a name of its own, but is, nonetheless, owned by and managed by Locke-Ober. That, of course, is good parentage and Joseph's does nothing whatsoever to besmirch the family name. It is one of Boston's better restaurants.

The Joseph's menu is a document to study and to cherish. It starts with the admonition, "Time is the essence of good food preparation. If we make you wait it is to serve you better."

Listed below are practically all the classical good dishes known to man, at least to man of the Western world. It is one of the most ambitiously complete menus in the United States today. Joseph's does have its specialties, though, and for those easily befuddled by a monumental menu, they single out Anchovies Joseph's; Baked Oysters Dartmouth; Baked Clams Casino; Clear Green Turtle Soup *au* Sherry; Baked Lobster Savannah; Filet Mignon of Beef Mirabeau; Breast of Duck, Sliced Orange, *Bigarade* Sauce; Breast of Chicken Richmond;

Sweetbreads Eugénie, *Crêpes Suzette,* Cherries Jubilee.

The wine list too is rather breath-takingly long, but commendable in the quality of both its labels and its vintages. Red Bordeaux and red Burgundies are particularly well represented, with a lesser, but good, selection of their white counterparts, and a respectable showing of champagnes, Rhones, Vouvray and Loire, Rhines, Moselles and Alsatians, Italian, sherry and port, and domestic wines.

Keeler's

STATE STREET
ALBANY, NEW YORK

Proprietor: *Simon Adler*
Manager: *Leon Pomerantz*
Chef: *Honoré Martin*

LBANY IS THE CAPITAL OF AMERICA'S greatest state (all right, Texas, calm down), America's *most populated*—and best-eating—state, so it would be nice and fitting to be able to say that it is a sort of capital of restaurants, too. Alas, it is not. In fact, it is not altogether unfair to say that there is only one really good restaurant in the entire city. That is Keeler's and a very good restaurant it is.

Keeler's is a venerable place, having served a succession of Governors and legislators for well over half a century—Theodore Roosevelt, Franklin Roosevelt, Thomas Dewey, Averell Harriman and others up to, and including, the present Nelson Rockefeller. It is a true American restaurant in that its menu, to veer dangerously toward punning, is a melting pot. That is, nestling together in the type on the menu, with Broiled Sea Bass, Cold Roast Leg of Lamb, Long Island Duckling, Sirloin Steak, and Calf's Liver and Bacon, are Vichyssoise, Consommé *Brunoise,* Alaska Crab Meat Newburg, Broiled Filet Mignon Henri IV with Béarnaise Sauce, *Escalopine* of Veal, Curried Chicken Maharajah with Chutney, Boiled Bermuda Potato, Kahlua Glacé, Siberian Punch, Gorgonzola Cheese, and other foreign-sounding foods and dishes.

Keeler's has an excellent wine cellar, with expertly selected French, German, and Italian wines. Also American, of course. In fact, this is the heart and headquarters of the New York State wine land, and it is strongly recommended that you try some of these fine wines.

It would be a distinct exaggeration to say that Keeler's is worth a special trip to Albany. But if you are in or near this somewhat Gay Nineties city it definitely is worth a visit and its reward of an excellent, unhurried, sympathetically served meal.

The Krebs

30 WEST GENESEE STREET
SKANEATELES, NEW YORK
(Open for dinner only)

Owners: *Mr. and Mrs. Frederic W. Perkins*

THE HUGE HOME-COOKED DINNERS OF OUR youth have just about vanished from the American scene, probably with benefit to the general health, or at least, the national waistline. But now and then it happens that a man feels a nostalgic longing to indulge again in one of those memorable feasts, to abandon for a few hours all concern for calories or capacity.

When that hunger strikes, there is only one thing to do. Avail yourself of the most convenient means of transportation and head straight for the Krebs, of Skaneateles, New York.

People enroute by car from one coast to the other have been known to make a 200-mile swing off their course to enjoy a dinner at this time-mellowed shrine of genuine American home cooking. Since the day when Fred R. Krebs opened the restaurant in 1899, very little has changed. The present owners, who inherited the business in 1936, are still serving the same enormous, garden-fresh table d'hôte dinner, except that they have added an intervening course or two.

You don't dine at Krebs: you eat. Yet there is nothing orgiastically festive about the place, in the Rabelaisian sense. The dining rooms are

[199]

neat and modestly homelike in their arrangements. And the atmosphere may remind you of dinner at your elderly Aunt May's on a Sunday afternoon, long ago.

Guests sit at long tables, elbow to elbow with strangers. But there is a spirit of friendliness, a companionship of the hungry, that catches hold before the soup and spreads with every course. The family feeling is emphasized by the fact that there is no menu at the Krebs and you take what is offered. There are six courses in all, served by several industrious young ladies, who carry trays from which you help yourself as your conscience permits. After the opening appetizer of shrimp cocktail, melon or fruit cup, you have a choice of three soups and an indiscriminate endowment of pickles and relishes.

Then each of the waitresses appears in turn. The first bears a vast platter, the contents of which are divided equally between fried chicken and sliced steak. The next girl brings mashed white potatoes and candied sweet potatoes. Shall we help ourselves to both? Why not? But be ready for the next girl, who is straining under a tray laden with gravy in a bowl, creamed mushrooms on toast, fresh vegetables in their season, home-baked brown bread and rolls, and cinnamon buns for the sticky-fingered set. An assortment of salads appears before you can whisper "Help!" and the final offering of desserts includes ice cream, pie, strawberry shortcake in June, local melon in late summer and heaps of chocolate brownies and angelfood cake in all seasons.

This, it need hardly be noted, is not exactly the kind of food that will appeal to the taste of the gourmet with continental leanings. It is, however, as American as strawberry festivals and back-yard barbecues. And it has the special old-time American quality of generosity—heaped up and running over. In this, it departs from the sort of food served at the tea room restaurant, which is also American, but hardly bountiful. An air of "refinement" may pervade Krebs, but nobody will cluck disapprovingly at the occasional glutton whose eyes bulge at the steady parade of good things and who tries desperately to gobble up everything in sight.

The unvarying charge for one of the Krebs' mammoth meals is

$5, regardless of how much you eat. Cocktails are available in the upstairs lounge and sitting rooms, but liquor is not served in the dining rooms. The cocktail lounge opens at four o'clock and dinner service begins at five o'clock every evening except Friday, when the restaurant is closed. On Sundays, dinner begins at noon.

Finally, it should be noted that the Krebs is one of the most widely discussed and highly recommended eating places in the land. The good word about it has been spread by devotees through all the states since the turn of the century. Serious eaters often make family pilgrimages to this rustic, beautiful part of northwestern New York, with a dinner at the Krebs the high point of the trip. The new Thruway has made the restaurant more accessible than ever. When guests at a wayside motel commune at twilight at the back door of their cabins, rarely does a discussion about food take place without someone exclaiming: "When it comes to real honest-to-goodness eating, give me the Krebs in Skaneateles!" As far as we know, no one who ever investigated this statement in person has ever offered an opinion to the contrary.

Locke-Ober

3 & 4 WINTER PLACE
BOSTON, MASSACHUSETTS

President: *Charles W. Little*
Maîtres d'Hôtel: *Fred Hammell, Adolf Cecchini*
Chef: *Gino Bertolaccini*

BY ANY MEASUREMENT, LOCKE-OBER'S IS ONE of the dozen or so best restaurants in the United States. And by the measurement of distinctiveness and atmosphere, it has no peer and few equals. Not many in the whole country can give you a comparable feeling of having stepped from this glittering day of chrome and hurry back into a softer day of glowing copper and measured time in dining and drinking—only a few such as Cavanaugh's in New York, Gage & Tollner's in Brooklyn, Galatoire's in New Orleans, and perhaps Ernie's in San Francisco.

Locke-Ober's stands at No. 3 & 4 Winter Place and is known to many of its constituents simply as "Winter Place." The building is narrow and not very large over-all, but the building itself is the only thing remotely puny about Locke-Ober's. The drinks are gargantuan, the food portions are outsize, the appetites and capacities are monumental, for this is primarily a place for men. In fact, women are not allowed in the first-floor dining room at all, except on two designated nights in the whole year. One of these is Christmas and the other, of course, is the night of the Yale-Harvard game, when it is played at Cambridge. As a whimsical sort of solace to the women, the management has, for some inexplicable reason, given them a bathtub in the ladies' room.

Locke-Ober's is more than eighty years old and has always shown a grim determination to keep the place looking as much as it was eighty years ago as is possible. The management has succeeded real well. The tabs for drinks are still punched out in a sixty-year-old version of a cash register that belongs more in a museum than a present-day restaurant. The L-shaped bar which runs along two walls of the downstairs dining room is the same L-shaped bar that the original owner had made of mahogany brought in from San Domingo and lavishly carved by French artisans. The one painting in the place is still the huge nude painting of Mlle. Yvonne which hangs over the bar. Her nudeness is interrupted only when Harvard loses to Yale when, in a passion of mourning, she girdles herself with a black sash. So determined are the owners to maintain things just as they were that they even keep a long row of huge steam dishes which today have no use whatsoever except as reminders of the past.

All this worship of antiquity and nostalgia is splendid but it would be for nought if the quality of the food and drink wasn't what it is, and what it is is simply superb. Perhaps the outstanding specialty of the house is Lobster Savannah, a huge Thermidor-type lobster with creamy sauce and tender morsels of lobster meat from close-by Maine. Part of the reason for its flavor is a generous use of sherry and fresh mushrooms and diced green pepper. Other specialties are Anchovies Winter Place, Filet Mignon Rossini, Eggs Fisherman Style, and Tuna Fish Colbert. Boston being a seagoing town, naturally sea food and shellfish are exceedingly popular.

All the customary drinks are here, and one that isn't so customary, which was invented in Locke-Ober's. This is the Ward 8 cocktail, named after a famous political ward of Boston. Primarily this is just a whiskey sour—a jigger of rye or bourbon, the juice of a lemon, ice and a little sugar. But somebody on the day of its invention in an inspirational moment dashed in an ounce of grenadine, shook it vigorously, poured it into an 8-ounce goblet, garnished it with a half slice of orange and gave birth to the Ward 8. The wine cellar at Locke-Ober's is not spectacular but it is, to say the least, adequate.

It is only natural that the long history of Locke-Ober's is studded with tradition and anecdotes, the anecdotes mostly the gay doings and gags of Harvard men. To show to what extremes the management will go to maintain its traditions, there is the story of Tack Hardwick. Hardwick was one of the football greats of Harvard. He was also one of the eating greats of Locke-Ober's. Each day, he would sit at the same table, sipping a cocktail and doing a crossword puzzle before ordering his lunch. This routine continued until just a few days before he died. When he did die, no one was seated at his table until after he had been buried. In the three days intervening, his old waiter quietly laid a plate face down on the table and beside it placed a crossword puzzle and a pencil.

Miller Brothers

119 WEST FAYETTE STREET
BALTIMORE, MARYLAND

Proprietors: *Fred M. and Ella K. Miller*
Headwaiter: *Theodore Cook*
Chef: *Sam Roggio*

ONE OF THE MOST SATISFYING TYPES OF restaurants, certainly the most unswerving in adhering to its traditions, is the sea-food restaurant of the Eastern seaboard. In its palmiest days, there were never many of this type, and today there are fewer, only a handful, in a handful of cities. Billy the Oysterman has faded from the New York scene, Hall's has lost its nice old building in Washington, Harvey's, also in Washington, has deteriorated considerably. Of the real old school there remain only the Union Oyster House in Boston, Sweet's and The Lobster in New York, Bookbinder's in Philadelphia—and Miller Brothers in Baltimore. Miller Brothers has as fine a birthright as a sea-food restaurant *can* have; it was born within smelling distance of Chesapeake Bay, and is still there.

Some of the best oysters in the world (notably Chincoteagues) come from the waters of Chesapeake Bay. So does some of the best crabmeat. So, in spring, does the earliest shad and roe to be served fresh along the Eastern seaboard. And so, of course, does terrapin, that superb Maryland delicacy, which seldom goes outside the borders of its native state, and which is to be found at its best at Miller Brothers.

All of these come to Miller Brothers dewy from the Chesapeake waters, and are prepared for you in a variety of ways, and with knowledge and skill won from well over a half century of lovingly handling these local delicacies. The place does well by steaks and chops and by game in fall (Chesapeake Bay, in addition to being richly endowed with sea food of rare goodness, abounds with wild fowl, as it is on one of the great flyways of the United States).

Miller Brothers clings fondly to its Gay Nineties decor which rather adds to the comfort and the pleasure. The bar is interesting. The selection of wines is good; and the imported and domestic beers on draught are perfect companions for sea food.

Mont d'Or Inn

SMITHTOWN, LONG ISLAND
NEW YORK

Proprietors: *Mario and Rita Morelli*
Headwaiter: *Jack Glathmann*
Chef: *Henry Payot*

THE INN, AS IT IS KNOWN AND JUSTLY admired in England, is not exactly nonexistent in the United States, but it is something of a rarity. One such rarity, and one of the most pleasant evidences that the inn actually *does* exist in this country, is the Mont d'Or, in Smithtown, Long Island, fifty miles east of New York City.

Twenty years ago, Mario Morelli left his job as a captain in the upstairs front room of 21 to open a small restaurant on New York's East 48th Street. It was called Mont d'Or and it's still a good little restaurant in a new location on East 46th. But Mario and his extremely attractive wife, Rita, are not there any more. They are in the charming white colonial home on Route 25A into Smithtown which is their new Mont d'Or restaurant and inn. This is the place they came to twelve years ago with the blissful intention of taking it easy, of sloughing off the pressures of running a restaurant in the heart of Manhattan.

Actually, they've been about as relaxed as the pilot of a jet plane. Not only did many of their old 48th Street friends frequently trek out to see them, but scores of dwellers in the lush seaside pastures of the Hamptons and other eastern Long Island communities discovered Mont d'Or and made it a habit, summer and winter, to stop on the drive out for luncheon on Thursday, Friday, or Saturday, and on the drive in for dinner on Sunday. So it has become famous, busy, and prosperous, and Mario and Rita have become unrelaxed, unretired and happily occupied.

Rita tends bar and a more enticing bartender is difficult to imagine. Mario divides his time between the floor (as maître d'hôtel), the kitchen, and the table-side chafing dish on which many of his specialties are prepared. Aiding them nobly is Jack, headwaiter, a handsome Smithtown lad, who has learned the restaurant business surprisingly well, and is an excellent painter in his non-serving hours.

One great specialty of Mont d'Or is Chicken *Echalote,* in which the chicken is sautéed in butter with shallots, flambéed with brandy, bathed with heavy cream, and doused with lemon juice. Another is a Mario production made in the dining room right next to your table, where you can watch the maestro at work. It is Filet Mignon *en Boite,* filet spread with mustard, cooked in a covered copper casserole, with shallots and brandy, a dash of Lea and Perrins and a spoonful of *fond de veau.* Then there are the soufflés. Most restaurants want you to bring the family if you're going to order a soufflé, but Mario has the rare attitude that if you want a soufflé, you shall have a soufflé, an individual one made in any flavor that happens to be your fancy at the moment.

The wine list is exceptionally good. If you were to try Mont d'Or, you would agree with the eastern Long Islanders who go out of their way to stop there for a meal, and agree with the authors of this book that it is indeed worth even a special trip from New York.

Park Schenley

3968 FORBES-ON-THE-PARK
PITTSBURGH, PENNSYLVANIA

Proprietor: *Frank G. Blandi*
Chef: *Dino Nardi*

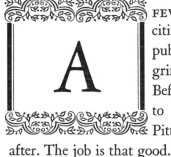 FEW YEARS AGO, A GROUP OF PITTSBURGH citizens well endowed with both money and public spirit, started a refurbishing job on their grimy, unkempt, unlovely city. Today, the Before and After photographs create disbelief to any viewer who did not actually know Pittsburgh before, and has not actually seen it after. The job is that good.

Public spirit, like many bad things and few good ones, can sometimes be contagious, and in Pittsburgh it has been to a surprising degree. The crusade, led intelligently and energetically by Mayor (now Governor) David Lawrence, has won a diverse following, not the least diverse of whom is Frank Blandi. Frank is a native Pittsburghian of Italian descent, who has been in the restaurant business for twenty-five years (he's only forty-five now) and who has culminated his successful career by establishing Pittsburgh's finest restaurant, the Park Schenley.

The Park Schenley is probably Pittsburgh's first bout with *haute cuisine,* and the fine wines which accompany it, and Pittsburgh is liking it fine. At a dinner to mark the Park Schenley's winning of the

[209]

Holiday Award for Dining Distinction, not only Pittsburgh society attended, but also the leading personages in the Pittsburgh newspaper, radio, and television worlds, and the leading Pittsburghian of them all, Mayor David Lawrence. He indicated that a refinement and improvement in food had a place in the city's over-all renaissance when he said, "The Park Schenley is more to Pittsburgh, or can be more, than just a great restaurant. It can serve as an inspiration to other restaurants and other restaurateurs to emulate the job it has done. Thus, it can raise the whole level of dining in Pittsburgh to a level any city, today, must attain if it wants to be ranked among the great cities of the world, as Pittsburgh definitely does."

The Park Schenley has a rolling beef wagon, copied from English fine restaurants (Simpson's, primarily), which serves beef as you like it, rare, medium (you shouldn't like it well done), and it is beautiful beef. It is also capable and anxious to do all the dishes, the traditional dishes, of *haute cuisine*: Rolled Filet of Beef, Cornish Hen with Wild Rice, *Coq au Vin, Boeuf Bourguignon,* and so forth. Frank Blandi also has the proper wines to go with these dishes, and while they might seem a bit strange in their environment now, they won't be so for long, because their environment is becoming more knowledgeable all the time.

The Patio

WESTHAMPTON BEACH, LONG ISLAND
NEW YORK

Manager: *Carlo Moratti*
Chef: *John Jones*

HIS IS THE SECOND OF THE SURPRISINGLY good "neighborhood" restaurants in the more westerly part of the Hamptons. The Patio is a hotel and as such is open every day, the year round. It is owned by a group of successful Westhampton businessmen, two of whom are also owners of the leading food store in town, which gives the restaurant something of an inside track on the supply of good foods. One of these owners is Milton Weixelbaum, who is an unusually skillful butcher, and who chooses for the Patio steaks of surpassing character. When one of these thick succulent sirloins is finished at your table-side, in a chafing dish, by Carlo himself, with his own maître d'hôtel sauce, it is a steak difficult to equal anywhere in this land. Carlo received his training on the Italian Line, at New York's famous and elegant Colony restaurant, and, before coming to the Patio, at the Waldorf-Astoria. As noted, the steaks (also the other meats) are outstanding. The Long Island duck and the abundant sea food from local waters are also good. And, if you appeal to Carlo's generous Italian nature, he'll prepare for you a dish of spaghetti with clam sauce, or of clams-stuffed ravioli that you simply cannot beat anywhere.

Stonehenge

ROUTE U.S. 7
RIDGEFIELD, CONNECTICUT

Proprietor: *Victor Gilbert*
Maître d'Hôtel: *Arthur Sims*
Chef: *Primo Mantegari*

 NE OF THE MOST PLEASANT TRIPS IN THE world today is to make an inn tour of England They're there, all over England, just as you've read about them in classic English novels and seen them in Old English plays and movies. So true to type are they, you wonder if they've been built like movie sets by the clever British Travel Organization. Then, upon inquiring, or reading Raymond Postgate's excellent *Guide to Eating in England,* you learn that the places have been there since seventeen hundred and something, that they have been visited by Johnson, and Sterne, and Walpole and Dickens, and God knows who else, and the furniture and pewter mugs go back to the beginning.

Many Americans, exposed to such inns, say, "Why don't we have this sort of thing back home?" And sometimes some brave soul actually does something about it. Victor Gilbert, while stationed in England during the war, had the familiar inn dream—and now has the inn itself, the Stonehenge in Ridgefield, Connecticut. It is an authentic old New England building, in lovely Connecticut countryside, with elderly spruce and maples surrounding it and a three-acre pond in back in which you can dip in summer and on which you can skate in winter. Stonehenge can put you up and fill you up, for it has both bedrooms and a kitchen of which it is inordinately proud.

People do stay there when touring New England, but they also drive over from the nearby countryside, and even from New York City, to dine.

Stonehenge is not a great restaurant, but it is a good restaurant, and its *ambiance* makes it seem considerably better than good. The menu has a slightly French accent, but in proper inn fashion, it also features good gusty steaks and chops, and such thoroughly American fare as strawberry shortcake. Proprietor Gilbert is particularly proud of two specialties, Creamed Chicken *Cannelloni* au Gratin, and old-fashioned Thick Planked Steak. The wine list is excellent.

Toll Gate Lodge

MANCHESTER, VERMONT
(Open for dinner only, June to October. Reservations advised.)

Owners: *Barbara and Mario Berry*
Maître d'Hôtel: *Frank Pugliese*

I F YOU SHOULD EVER TOUR NEW ENGLAND, you will inevitably reach a point where you are fed up with folksy Colonial taverns, hybrid tea-room/antique shops, and with roadside fare dominated by leathery fried clams, flaccid waffles, "chicken-in-the-basket," "giant shakes," "finger steaks" and other classics of American short-order cuisine. If you are lucky, you may then stumble on the Toll Gate Lodge, Vermont's sole claim to gastronomical achievement. Unquestionably, this will restore your faith, for a few days at least, in the possibility of finding civilized food and agreeable drink on the roads that lead away from New York.

At that, this is no easy place to stumble on. Actually, it is known to comparatively few people, being well off the important highways. Its clients are principally summer residents and weekend visitors from Boston and New York. The small, rambling house nestles, almost hidden, in the green and shadowy heart of a forest on the lower slopes of Peru Mountain, four miles from Manchester Center, just off Route 11. Nearby once stood an ancient toll gate, where travelers between Boston and Saratoga Springs halted to pay a state tax, wherefor the name.

Dining on its tree-shaded outdoor terrace, you sit at a table within a few feet of a mountain stream, which rushes past on a course parallel to the property, foaming over pebbles and scattered boulders and providing cool, singing music as a background for your table talk. The Lodge has two or three rooms for occasional guests and the more adventurous among them sometimes take early morning dips in the icy pool near a tiny footbridge.

It is the contrast between this wild woodland prospect and the smooth continental perfection of the food and service which constitutes the unique charm of this surprising little restaurant. When the weather is too wet or chilly for terrace dining, guests are served in the inside room, small and intimate. It has the indefinable but unmistakable look and aroma of a restaurant where the drinks are made correctly, the food is prepared with love and where you instinctively like the people at the next table.

When Mario Berry and his charming wife, Barbara, first came upon this lovely forest site, they could not rest until they were able to buy the old house and a considerable piece of land on either side of the brook. "This is where we will live when we retire," Mario told me, last summer. "It is exactly like one or two beautiful mountain places I knew in Switzerland and Austria. And there are no nicer neighbors anywhere than you will find right here in the Green Mountains."

A slender, polished and graceful veteran of long service in European hotels and restaurants, Mario is still in his forties and looks younger. He may remind you of the handsome tango dancer you once admired when you first visited the Riviera, or perhaps your favorite ski instructor at St. Moritz. But he is really a serious individual, with an excellent head for business. He cooks, does the marketing and keeps the accounts of this small but profitable enterprise, and everything he does, he does well.

Barbara, immaculately groomed and serenely pretty, makes the iciest, driest and purest martini to be found north of 21, and can be counted upon to do as well with most items of the barman's repertoire. In addition, she takes your order at the table, performs the duties of the sommelier, and occupies herself with a thousand details without ever losing her smile or appearing busy.

If the owners take a fancy to you and admit you to the inner circle of their friends, you will discover that they are not only talented in their craft but simple, delightful people who love nature with an almost naïve passion. Many of the wild creatures of the forest are their friends and guests, running or hopping in and out of the windows between mealtimes, with perfect trust and unlimited impudence. An albino skunk named Rosemary visits often and dines off a tray of selected tidbits. A striped chipmunk appears every morning to clean up stray crumbs under the tables and chatter companionably with Barbara and Mario while they are drinking their coffee. Squirrels, rabbits and other small animals are intimates of the establishment and Mario is fond of telling about a female black bear with two cubs who appear at odd intervals to sample leftovers at the back door.

The Lodge closes around the first of October and the owners migrate to Palm Beach, where they operate a restaurant which is a favorite of the white-orchid and maroon-cummerbund set. In the summer or fall, however, it is worth driving fifty miles to visit Toll Gate, if only for a single meal. The food is about what you are used to at your favorite small restaurant in New York, San Francisco, Paris or Rome, and so are the prices, which definitely are not low, but extremely fair.

Many familiar dishes of international reputation are on the menu, each cooked to perfection. Because Mario and Barbara know their clients and their America, they specialize in as fine a charcoal-broiled sirloin or filet mignon as you will find in the heart of Steak Row, New York City. Other recommended choices are the Cold Vichyssoise, the *Pâté Maison,* the Sautéed Brook Trout with *Sauce Amandine,* thin *crêpes* stuffed with King Crab, Baked Filet of Sole *Véronique,* Veal

Cutlet *Zingara, Coq au Vin à l'Estragon,* and broiled Whole Live Maine Lobster. I have dined there at least half a dozen times in recent summers and never fail to order the marvelous Potatoes Toll Gate, which are cut in shoestring shapes, moulded into a fat pancake and browned slowly in an iron skillet. They have an indescribably haunting flavor, due to no ingredient I could divine by tasting, or discover by asking.

Union Oyster House

41-43 UNION STREET
BOSTON, MASSACHUSETTS

Proprietor: *Laurence A. Greaves*
Chef: *Goldburn Goodridge*

T HE UNION OYSTER HOUSE CLAIMS TO BE THE original oyster house of Boston, and as it has been around some 130 years, there's no one left to dispute the claim. It's not only the original oyster house, but it's in its own original house, two buildings joined in holy wedlock, on Union Street, and plastered with signs reminding the world, or at least Boston, that *this* is "Ye Old Oyster House." (If for no other reason, the place deserves the patronage of people allergic to coyness, for leaving the terminal "e" off "Old.") Not only is the building the same, but the bar, over which many millions of oysters have been launched, is the original one of 1826.

Naturally, the Oyster House features oysters and clams in all the many ways these bivalves can be served. There are broiled oysters, fried oysters, oyster stew, combination stew of quahaugs and oysters, clam bouillon, clam chowder, fried clams, clam stew, oyster sandwich, and clam sandwich. But while all, or at least most, of these dishes are intriguing, the best way to eat oysters and clams is raw, opened individually at the bar, and seasoned only with a spot of lemon juice. The oysters recommended here are the Narragansetts, the clams the qua-

[218]

haugs, and the clam chowder, the Rhode Island. The steamed Ipswich clams, soft clams, are worth trying but lovers of sea food think they're pale indeed in comparison to their more muscular cousins.

Other classic sea foods, from the nearby paralyzingly cold waters off the New England Coast, are here, too—lobster in its manifold forms, crab, scallops, haddock, scrod. The management wistfully tries to remind the customers that it is also proud of its steaks, chops, chicken, and excellent roast beef, but nobody seems to pay much attention. The wine list is meager and undistinguished, but this is made up for, in a degree, by a fine list of beers and ale, including draught, and, in addition to the best American brands, beer from Denmark and Germany, ale from Canada and England, and stout from Ireland.

The Oyster House has a couple of hospitable customs the like of which we've never run into elsewhere. On Saturdays good old Boston Baked Beans are served to you, compliments of the management. And when the temperature goes over eighty-five degrees, a glass of iced tea is handed to you as you come in off the steaming Boston street. Very nice ideas.

Villa Paul

MONTAUK HIGHWAY, HAMPTON BAYS, LONG ISLAND
NEW YORK

Owner: *Paul Villa*
Chef: *Marie Villa*

VILLA PAUL IS OWNED BY PAUL VILLA (VILLA Paul spelled backward), who was formerly the owner of the Ambassador Inn, at East Quogue, and runs much the same kind of place in his new and charming inn. As told above, Paul and his wife retired for health reasons and returned to Italy. The comforting companionship of relatives and old friends, and the warm clean air that swept from the Mediterranean through their home town were healing enough to send them back hale, and to permit them to open a new restaurant and inn several miles down the Island from their old.

Villa Paul is located in a charming old white clapboard Long Island house, surrounded by a gleaming white picket fence, well back from bustling Montauk Highway, in a quiet grove of trees. It is such a favorite retreat of the home people of the Hamptons (the fashionable summer and year-round weekend set and the solid permanent residents) that it needn't depend on transients and always has a warm Italian air about it.

Paul is one of the most expert bartenders we've ever encountered (he's also very knowing about food and wine) and Marie is a superb cook. Villa Paul specializes in sea food of the vicinity, in Maine lobsters, and in all Italian specialties. If you're ever down that way, it's worth seeking out behind its white fence, restful in its grove of trees.

Villa Pierre

GLEN COVE, LONG ISLAND
NEW YORK

Owners: *Irene and Pietro Sacco*

A FAVORITE DREAM OF MANY FRENCH AND Italian restaurant people in New York is to own some day a little restaurant in the country. Not way out in the tall corn, but just far enough away from town so a man could raise a garden and a family, go fishing or hunting when he felt like it, and cook only as a form of self-indulgence.

One of the few who made this dream come true—or part of it, at least—is Pietro Sacco, a man still young, slender and handsome, who was born near Genoa and trained in the restaurants of France, where he learned to speak fluent French with a soft Ligurian accent. In subsequent years, Pietro became Pierre, maître d'hôtel of the Chateaubriand, one of New York's better French restaurants. Because he combined the seductive charm of his native land with an elegant worldly polish, Pierre made many friends and was one of the best liked headwaiters in the city. It was clear to most of his clients that inevitably a man of his talents would some day own his own restaurant. Pierre thought so too, but his particular dream took the form of an impressive country inn by the roadside, far from the clanging tensions of Manhattan.

He made his move a few years ago. His inn was christened Villa Pierre. It is a large remodeled country house, just off the Glen Cove Road in the opulent North Shore of Long Island. There, with the invaluable help of his pretty and energetic wife, he has built a loyal following from among the land-owning gentry of that lush section, so well described in Scott Fitzgerald's *The Great Gatsby*. His dream is a reality, except that today he has no time to give to gardening or fishing and is completely absorbed in the complicated and demanding project of dining and wining a couple of hundred fastidious guests almost every evening and some afternoons.

In the two hundred miles of Long Island countryside, there are only three or four top restaurants with a worldly background. Villa Pierre is now definitely one of them, and getting better all the time. It started as a place where people came for a fusillade of Scotch, bourbon or gin on the rocks, leading up to clams or oysters and a giant steak. Gradually the more discerning guests began to perceive that Pierre was capable of more noble gastronomical accomplishments. Appreciation of his classical French cuisine grew and the number of these subtle and elegant dishes on the menu increased with it. Today Pierre's repertoire is equal to many of New York's internationally famous establishments.

He has not forgotten his Italian origin and among the popular suggestions are: *Cannelloni Maison, Scampi Pierre, Consommé Raviolini, Spaghetti Bolognese* and *Fettuccini alla Crema*. This last is one of the numberless versions of the late Alfredo's Roman masterpiece. Pierre's homemade noodles are cooked *al dente* and then tossed in a copper pan over a flame in sizzling butter, heavy country cream and freshly grated Parmesan cheese. This simple but fantastically delicious treatment of *pasta* makes an excellent one-dish luncheon, with red wine, salad and fresh fruit.

Pierre is especially proud of his *Crêpes* Maryland, thin pancakes filled with crabmeat cooked in cream, white wine and shallots and served au gratin. He recommends the Maine Lobster, either grilled or Thermidor, the Long Island Duckling *Sauce Bigarade, Croûte Alsaci-*

enne, Poulet Flambé, Boneless Stuffed Chicken *Périgourdine,* and his home-baked chocolate or rum cake. Prime sirloin steak is still in top demand, and there is an impressive grilled chateaubriand with *sauce béarnaise,* served for two at around fourteen dollars. It will be seen that Pierre's is not exactly inexpensive, but the scale of prices still falls somewhat below New York's top dozen. The wine cellar is well garnished with superb vintages, including a Chambertin Clos de Bèze 1953, Chambolle-Musigny 1955, Château Cheval Blanc and Château Latour of 1953 and several of the legendary years of Lafite and Mouton-Rothschild.

The Warwick

LOCUST STREET AT 17TH
PHILADELPHIA, PENNSYLVANIA

Manager: *Paul J. McNamara*
Chef: *Henri P. Sidoli*

F REQUENTLY, IN SMALL CITIES, THE HOTEL is the only decent place in which to eat, but this is rarely true in the larger cities. Philadelphia is an exception. In Philadelphia, the two leading hotels, the Barclay and the Warwick, are definitely the best places in the whole city in which to eat. The Barclay is the more elegant of the two, and perhaps the more classically correct in a gastronomic way. But the Warwick, despite the fact that it leans toward the commercial, is more exciting and interesting in its food. These pleasant characteristics are due principally to the Warwick's knowing and alert manager, Paul McNamara, and dedicated chef, Henri Sidoli. Paul critically visits each of the dining rooms, every day, and sits, obviously enjoying a meal, in at least one of them. Henri also appears in each, every day, talks to the maître d'hôtel and perhaps a diner or two he knows, scans the food on the nearby tables, and aims a Geiger-sensitive look at the faces at table to determine whether or not they are pleased with the products of his beloved kitchen.

There are three dining rooms on the main floor of the Warwick; the Warwick Room, the Embassy Room, and the Coach Room. The

[225]

Embassy Room is formal; crystal chandeliers, that sort of thing; and has two levels, the street or entrance level, and a lower level, reached by a miniature grand stairway of some six steps, down which beautifully gowned women can make what they hopefully believe will be a dramatic and gasp-inducing entrance. The Warwick Room is gay and cheerful, at its best at luncheon time. At night, unfortunately, there is an orchestra, and dancing, but if you insist upon a table far away, the distraction from the primary business of eating may not be too great. At least it's a quiet orchestra. The Coach Room is all-male for lunch, but open to women after five o'clock, at which time it is particularly popular for cocktails. Up until about two years ago the Coach Room, at lunch, served only the Warwick's famous Shrimp Lamaze (shrimp salad with a special multi-ingredient, deliciously piquant sauce) and one or two hot steam-table dishes. Then an elaborate and attractive copper charcoal grill was built into the room, and an expanded menu offered, featuring such dishes as cooked-to-order giant hamburger, ham and eggs in skillet, eggs and Canadian bacon, Polish sausage and sauerkraut, omelettes with home-fried potatoes; good, hearty, masculine fare.

Chef Sidoli likes to spring surprises on his guests, so every day, in each of the three dining rooms, you're likely to find an unusual dish featured: today a Spanish dish, tomorrow a Chinese specialty, next day a recipe from the South Seas. The wine selection is far above the average for Philadelphia.

Waiter
and
Client

NE OF MANKIND'S TOUCHIEST RELATION-
ships, rivaling in delicacy the relationship be-
tween man and wife, mother and daughter,
employer and employee, emperor and subject,
teacher and pupil, is that between the diner
and the waiter who serves him. On certain
rare, almost nonexistent, occasions, it has over
the years developed into genuine friendship. Not too infrequently,
when diner and waiter see each other practically daily, there arises an
exceedingly close rapport, a sort of father-backward child, or nanny-
baby relationship with, of course, the diner always cast in the role
of the backward child or baby. More often, there's an aloof attitude of
meticulously courteous hostility, such as used to exist between the top
diplomats of two rival major nations. And sometimes it's just out-and-
out open warfare.

In this struggle the diner is the underdog. The waiter is way ahead
of him from the time he first walks into the restaurant, is seated at
the table, unfolds his napkin and places it on his lap, takes his first sip
of water and nibbles on his first chunk of bread. For the way the diner
does each of these things helps reveal to the waiter how he'll order,

how long he'll be at the table, how much his check will be, and how juicily he'll tip. This is not because waiters are master psychologists, but because they've learned that it's good for the income to find out as much as possible about the likes and idiosyncrasies of the diner, and nearly all of them have been around and observing for a long time. You practically never see a young waiter in a good restaurant; most of them have reached the age of flat feet, and started as busboys when they were thirteen years old.

According to Robert Sylvester, a long-time student of restaurants, nightclubs, bistros and their personnel, waiters have learned pretty precisely what to expect from a diner before he has been around long. If you've stopped somewhere along the route to the restaurant for a drink or two or three or four (and an old-line waiter can tell almost to the gram how much you've taken aboard), the waiter knows you're not going to be much of a connoisseur of food as far as that particular meal is concerned. If you're in a jolly tipsy mood, he knows you'll tend to pick at your food but explain in a friendly way that it's excellent but you're just not very hungry. If you're in a sulky tipsy mood, he knows you'll tend to pick at your food but explain in a grumpy way that it didn't taste right—no, you would not like something else.

If you sit down and gulp a couple of glasses of iced water, the waiter knows you'll have more or less the same cavalier attitude toward food as if you'd been drinking. If you eat more than two pieces of bread, you've started the waiter worrying about both the size of your check and the size of your tip.

If you're a member of a party of four or more, and if one person gives the order for the whole party, everyone has a better chance of getting just what he ordered than if the waiter is assaulted by a babble of orders.

If you snap your fingers, or go "siss," or bang your fork against your glass to attract your waiter's attention, you'll attract his attention all right, but you'll also incur his dislike. Nothing annoys him more, and why not? I was in Christ Cella's one day when an oaf banged his glass with his fork to attract the attention of the waiter. He succeeded.

He also succeeded in attracting the attention of Christ, a wonderful restaurateur and human being, who liked his waiters and respected their dignity. He stalked over to the diner, fixed him with an angry eye, and said, "Listen, if you ever do that again in my restaurant, I'll throw you right through that window, and I won't bother to open the window." The diner subsided into sheepish silence which, under the circumstances, was the wise thing for him to do because Christ was an enormously powerful man who not only was capable of throwing him through the window but through the solid brick wall if he felt like it. Not all restaurateurs would so fiercely protect the dignity of their waiters, but you can see nevertheless that banging a glass at a waiter can be a poor idea.

Waiters of different nationalities are varied in their dispositions and ways of treating customers.

There are very few purely American waiters around, as Americans don't go in much for waiting and, frankly, don't make very good waiters. They are friendly, even to the point of being pally, and expect friendliness from the customer even to the extent of his being pally in return. If the customer shows the slightest sign of being aloof, your American waiter is likely to sulk. And he takes an extremely dim view of criticism or complaints. But in his favor it must be said that he is usually bright, alert, and efficient, and if you show the proper spirit of togetherness, he will serve you well.

The French waiter is undoubtedly the most accomplished of all in the true Art of Waiting. Unlike the American, he wants to be aloof, is meticulous in his attitude toward the diner-waiter relationship. He lets you know, and not altogether subtly, that he knows more about food, and wine, and the art of eating, than you will ever know. He expects you to appreciate his knowledge and to call upon it in selecting your meal and the wine to go with it. In the unlikely event that he does put before you an inferior dish or a badly prepared one, or commits some gaucherie in serving you, he will accept your criticism respectfully and make amends. But you had better be right. He will be precise, correct, and courteous, and expects preciseness, correctness, and courtesy in return, which is a not altogether unreasonable attitude.

The Chinese waiter can only be described in the one word "inscrutable." There is rarely any conversation with him whatsoever, except the bare ordering of the meal. And even this is better done away with. Your wisest course in a Chinese restaurant, unless you are thoroughly conversant with Chinese food, is to let the waiter or the proprietor order for you. Perhaps, at some odd moment in history, a Chinese waiter has smiled, but this writer has never seen it.

In our opinion, the best of all waiters, and the one who contributes most to making a meal pleasant, is the Italian waiter. He likes you the minute you sit at his table and, as the meal progresses, he gets to like you more until at coffee time his affection for you fairly glows. If you are his regular customer, and frequent his restaurant and his station, his affection develops into fierce protection and possessiveness. He is likely to take all initiative out of your hands, to pamper and to coddle you, to shower you with attentions and courtesies, to anticipate and even create wishes for you, to make your cup run over. A man who has such a waiter in his favorite Italian restaurant is fortunate indeed.

As the Italian waiter is the best of all waiters, the Jewish waiter is the quaintest. He is, always and invariably, a Character. Perhaps he has been best described by that aficionado of Jewish restaurants, Hugh Foster, in a piece called "The Derma Road" he wrote several years ago for *Holiday*. Here is his description of the Jewish waiter:

> The Jewish waiter, unlike the stiff or obsequious Marcels and Jeans in the ritzy places, does not wait until he is spoken to, but fraternizes with his patrons. His name is usually Sam and he has been a "character" in metropolitan anecdote for generations. You will know him by his alpaca coat, his unservile air and his benevolent tyranny over customer and employer alike.
>
> Sam will tell you that you feel like "a nice piece pickled herring to start," and somehow you do. Then "a nice plate *mandel* soup"—*mandel* is a variety of crouton. In his lexicon everything is "nice" and the preposition "of" is unknown. Sam is not the kind of man who takes orders; he receives requests but prefers to make

suggestions. "You'll take a portion potted brisket beef with a side *derma* and *kasha,* gentleman." Sam never says "sir." Always "gentleman."

You say: "How is the stuffed breast of veal with—"

"Don't ask questions. *I'm* telling you, brisket beef."

And, apprehending him later, you point to somebody at the next table blissfully engrossed with *your* breast of veal with a "side *varenikes* and *farfel,*" tiny pieces of noodles served in soup or with meat, adapted from the Italian *farfarelli.*

With a nudge and a look, Sam will let you in on that the other fellow is a barbarian, and what he's wolfing down is good enough for *him.* If you visit the same restaurant twice, Sam will, by some trick known to this fabulous craft, know you by name. He will go to the kitchen door and call out loudly, "A nice piece smoked carp, special for Mr. Foster!" And if you can't surmount the last two *kreplach* on your plate, he will urge you on: "Eat up."

Unafraid of the proprietor, Sam has been known to knock off ten or fifteen per cent of your check because you passed up the dessert on the *prix fixe dinner.*

The chief barrier between waiter and diner, the major deterrent to friendship, is the villainous custom of tipping. It would be comforting to be able to feel that on some enlightened day not far away this custom which no one likes would be banished from the earth. But like taxes and death, two other fairly unpopular institutions, it is, alas, with us to stay. Restaurant owners, waiters, and customers have deplored it together, but no one has ever come up with a solution, and all accept its inevitability. The answer then seems only how best to live with it.

There are no hard and fast rules on tipping other than the quite obvious, Don't overtip, Don't undertip. The norm in a good New York restaurant is twenty per cent. (It's less in other cities; even in nearby Philadelphia fifteen per cent is a generous tip, and old-family Philadelphians stick meticulously to the archaic ten per cent rule. Warning to old-family Philadelphians: Don't try it in New York.)

Twenty per cent is an over-all figure, which means that there frequently is the nice problem of how to divide it between the various people who have ministered to you and hovered over you. First, there is the lordly and forbidding figure of the headwaiter or maître d'hôtel. If he actually does something for you, saves you a good table on the basis of your advance reservation, takes your order and makes helpful suggestions on food and wine, oversees serving and helps serve, for instance carves a bird, he is entitled to a tip of his own. If he merely greets you and turns you over to a captain or a waiter, he rates only a polite "good night" and "thank you." If you detect or suspect that the head-waiter deliberately holds out good tables for unsubtly hinted-at tips, you are in a dump, my friend, and you'd do well, hereafter, to avoid it.

In many restaurants these days there is a happy institution called the Tip Pool. Sometimes just the captains pool their tips, sometimes just the waiters, sometimes the captains and the waiters, and sometimes practically everybody gets into the act, the captains, the waiters, the busboys, the bartenders, the attendants in the men's room and the ladies' room, and the hatcheck girl. There is no notice in any restaurant that such a system is in effect, nor will any employee volunteer the information. But it is perfectly proper to ask your waiter if the place has a Tip Pool, and if he says "yes" the annoying business of tipping becomes much easier for you. You leave your twenty per cent in one chunk and it is meticulously divided so that everyone who has served you gets a portion he has agreed in advance is fair.

We have our own method for virtually abolishing the embarrassment and humiliation which so often accompany the sorry spectacle of figuring out the tip and fumbling with your change. In those places we know well and visit regularly we never pay a check and never leave a tip. Twenty per cent is added by the waiter or the owner to each check, and the total is put on the monthly statement. Thus we part with the waiter not with the fresh memory of a rather snide financial transaction with which neither of us is altogether happy, but with the pleasant and warming recollection of a good meal, well served and properly appreciated.

A bonus, beyond and above mere money, that can be given to a waiter, is common courtesy and respect for the job he does. Waiting is highly skillful work, and if you don't think so, just take a crack sometime at serving eight or ten people eight or ten different meals, all at once, all hot, and all on the basis of orders given in the midst of almost utter confusion. It is work which requires intelligence, concentration, and long, arduous training. The waiter frequently finds himself harassed out front by the customer, and backstage by the chef, who is usually one of the world's most consummate tyrants. He serves you primarily because he wants and needs that twenty per cent. But a couple of "please's," "thank you's" and a "good night" thrown in during the course of the meal will make him richer without making you the least bit poorer.

The South
& the Midwest

Antoine's

713-717 ST. LOUIS STREET
NEW ORLEANS, LOUISIANA

Proprietor: *Roy L. Alciatore*
Maître d'Hôtel: *Angelo Alciatore*
Chef: *John Daigle*

ANTOINE'S IS VERY LIKELY THE MOST FAMOUS restaurant in the United States, and very likely has hosted more famous people than any other restaurant in the United States. Of course, it has been at it longer than any others, but still the list is deeply impressive because practically no one of any note whatsoever comes to New Orleans without dining at Antoine's and practically everybody of any note whatsoever does come to New Orleans.

Mr. Roy Alciatore, the present owner, is a dedicated, experienced, and perhaps unsurpassed restaurateur.

Antoine's was opened in 1840, by a restaurant man from Marseilles, M. Antoine Alciatore. His son, Jules, followed him as proprietor and entrepreneur. Jules died in 1934, when Roy took over. Roy was the grandson of old M. Antoine, though the venerability of the reputation would have indicated that the restaurant was more firmly rooted in time than to be run by a mere grandson of the founder; and the youthfulness of Roy made it hard to believe that he was only the third in line in what had already become a world-famous institution.

The building which houses Antoine's is large, and truly New Orleans in style, including the iron grille balconies on the façade. It has the rich, mellow charm that all the fine old buildings of the French Quarter have attained over their long years. Inside, despite the overall size of the building, there is the illusion of intimacy, as the space is cut up into numerous dining rooms. You enter the main dining room which is the largest. Off that are other rooms, different in decor and in size. Many of these are used mostly by private parties and one is used almost exclusively by Roy Alciatore and his guests.

The ample wine cellar is on the same floor as the dining rooms, as one doesn't dig below street surface in New Orleans without incurring the displeasure and invasion of the Mississippi River.

Antoine's is almost always crowded, and it's wise to reserve well in advance; if you're only going to be in New Orleans for a day or two, write ahead for reservations. So determined are people to dine there, that they form long queues on the sidewalk of St. Louis Street, and wait patiently for tables. Everyone, including Roy Alciatore, deplores this. But he explains, "They'd be heartbroken if they had to go home from New Orleans and say they hadn't eaten at Antoine's, so we somehow take care of them all, and give them real Antoine food."

And real Antoine food is something to marvel over, to worship over, to revel over. Most famous of Antoine dishes is Oysters Rockefeller, invented for John D. himself by Jules Alciatore himself. There's deep mystery about the preparation of this dish, with dark intimations that the recipe, if written out at all, is buried in Fort Knox. Fundamentally, it's oysters, topped with finely chopped spinach and olive oil, broiled in a hot oven, and any really good chef can make a reasonable facsimile. But it's more fun to get it from the inventor, just as it would have been more fun to buy a light bulb from Thomas Edison than from the local hardware man. Other particular Antoine specialties are Orange *Brûlot,* coffee and liqueur served in a dexterously peeled orange which obligingly turns itself into a coffee cup; *Pommes Soufflées,* barely heavier than the air that fills them; Pompano *en Papillote,* pompano immersed in a wonderfully rich and creamy sauce imprisoned and cooked in a brown paper bag, and served when the bag is the color and texture of fine, brown, old parchment, slit at your table with a few deft strokes to release all the captive flavor, warmth, and goodness.

While these are the classic specialties of the house, there are a number of other delights which are actually more gastronomically sophisticated; *Filet de Boeuf Marchand de Vin; Bisque d'Ecrevisse Cardinal,* Bouillabaisse *à la Marseillaise,* Gumbo *Créole, Pigeonneaux Royaux au Sauce Paradis.* There is also the beautiful, plump, succulent Buster Crab (no relation to the swimmer and movie star of similar name), a native of New Orleans (the crustacean, not the movie star), *Filet de Boeuf en Casserole Robespierre,* and, cousin to Pompano *en Papillotte,* using the same delectable Gulf of Mexico fish, Pompano *Amandine.*

The wine cellar at Antoine's is superb, one of the best in the United States. This should not be surprising as owner Roy Alciatore, a Grand Officier of the Confrérie des Chevaliers du Tastevin, is one of the leading wine connoisseurs of the country. Membership in the Confrérie denotes an affinity and affection for Burgundy wines, and the cellar reflects Grand Officier Alciatore's tastes in its exquisite collection of Burgundy whites and reds. But it also generously plays host to the great wines of Bordeaux, of Champagne, of the Rhine and Moselle, of Italy, and to the sherries of Spain, the ports of Portugal, and the cognacs and marcs of France.

Over the years, many, many devotees of *haute cuisine* have visited New Orleans, have come from all over the country, for the sole intent of dining at Antoine's. It has always been worth it and still is.

Cape Cod Room

DRAKE HOTEL
LAKE SHORE DRIVE AND UPPER MICHIGAN AVENUE
CHICAGO, ILLINOIS

Director of Catering: *John R. Bogardus*
Manager: *Eddie Schweykowsky*
Chef: *John Kaufmann*

CHICAGO IS 1,278 MILES FROM THE SPOT where the Atlantic Ocean washes closest to it, which very likely accounts for Chicagoans' affection for the Cape Cod Room, the salty sea food restaurant in Michigan Avenue's Drake Hotel.

The Cape Cod Room for many years has brought to Chicago the wonderful things to eat the Atlantic Ocean offers and that is a godlike gift to an oceanless Midwest city, situated on a crustaceanless fresh-water lake, even though that lake is as big as a sea.

Lake Michigan does bring to Chicago tables a distinctively good fish, whitefish, and less worthy fish in lake perch and lake trout. But these are pale and pitiful cousins of the mighty fish of the Atlantic, the blues, and the sea bass, and the mackerel, and the swordfish, and even the mako shark. And there are, of course, no shellfish in the lake, no clams or oysters, no crabs, and, most tragic omission of all, no lobsters.

All of these are to be had in the Cape Cod Room, as fresh from the Atlantic's cold and salty waters as refrigerated express cars and airplanes can rush them, and that's about as fresh as you can get them anywhere unless you live right smack on the ocean and gather them in yourself or go down to the dock when the fishing boats come in and haggle with the skipper. Just to get you in the mood, the Cape Cod Room is decorated to convince you that the gentle zephyr you feel is not mere air-conditioning but a breeze that has kissed the Atlantic whitecaps and spray as it wafted in to you.

The Cape Cod Room not only *gets* the fruit of Eastern seas and bays, but it knows what to do with them after they float ashore in its kitchen. Sea food cannot, of course, be beaten in its raw or most simply cooked state; clams and oysters on the half-shell, lobster boiled or broiled, crabs boiled and picked, scallops dusted with flour and fried quickly in butter.

But good sea food also lends itself to an infinite variety of cookery, and on the Cape Cod menu you will find lobster in twelve different styles; broiled, steamed, baked in the half-shell as follows: Thermidor, Cardinal, *Parisienne* and Mornay, and served in a chafing dish *à la* Newburg, *a l'Indienne,* Tetrazzini, *Américaine, Bordelaise* and Mushroom Cardinal. But, one moment, I forgot to mention a specialty never encountered elsewhere; Imported French-Fried Lobster Dainties. You may call this the final tribute or the supreme insult to the sweet monster of the deep, according to your private notions about how he should be eaten. There are also a variety of culinary manipulations of fresh crabmeat, more or less along the lines described above. Scallops from Cape Cod or the ocean off New Bedford are another department all by themselves on the menu. The most tempting are the small bay specimens broiled *en brochette* with bacon and mushrooms. Pompano, imported French turbot, English Channel sole, and at least two dozen other fishes are always available, but the crowning treasure of the Cape Cod Room for this inveterate sea-food enthusiast is native lake trout or Lake Superior whitefish, broiled or sautéed with butter and lemon juice. The management is proud of its jumbo shrimps, its clams and

[243]

oysters, and makes a specialty of red snapper soup with sherry, as served in Philadelphia. Bouillabaisse *Marseillaise* is extremely popular on Fridays. There are shellfish stews of all kinds and frog's legs served every way but *au naturel*.

Along with sea food, the Cape Cod Room has imported from the East the New York idea of what a martini should be; dry enough so that dust forms on its surface, cold enough to numb the fingers which hold the glass, big enough to warm the heart of the most avaricious distiller of gin, and served with a sprightly twist of lemon peel rather than a glum and sodden olive. Other drinks are equally gargantuan in size, equally sophisticated in their making. The wine selection is excellent and there's good draught beer. The decor, as mentioned above, is all quite nautical—hawsers, lobster-pot markers, belaying pins, ships' wheels, compasses, fish-nets, all that sort of stuff—but it manages, somewhat miraculously, to skirt the precious. Prices are not bargain basement, but neither are they shattering. Altogether, the Cape Cod Room is worth going to, particularly for lunch, and even if you're a Cape Codder or Down Easter.

Charlie's Café Exceptionale

701 FOURTH AVENUE
MINNEAPOLIS, MINNESOTA

Owner: *Charles Saunders*
Headwaiter: *John Skeg*
Manager: *Harold Ahlman*
Chef: *Alfred Mahlke*

THE GREATEST RESTAURANT GUIDE IN THE world is France's Guide Michelin, and the greatest accolade given by the Guide Michelin is three stars (***) and it is given to very few restaurants (last count was fourteen) in all of France. In the Guide, and in the knowledge of gourmets who have been following it through these many years, three stars means "worth a special journey."

In the United States, we have not as yet reached that precise designation of restaurants. Probably, with our overwhelming distances, we never will.

But if that gastronomic happy day ever should arrive, there's an excellent chance that a midwest—Minneapolis—restaurant would be awarded a three-star rating. It would by no means qualify as a three-star restaurant in the Guide, nor could it sanely be compared with the restaurants which hold this coveted designation, but in its way, and within reason it is "worth a special journey." The restaurant is Charlie's Café Exceptionale. And it is an exceptional (English spelling) restaurant. It is exceptional in a purely, strictly, American way.

For instance, Charlie's is one of the last strongholds of that superb American invention and dish, the planked steak. Our fathers and their fathers before them wallowed in this great slab of beef, garnished with all the vegetables in the garden, and served on an inch-thick plank of wood. Few of us now even know it, for very few restaurants will take the time to prepare and present it properly.

Before you are served your entrée at Charlie's, you will have set down before you a somewhat gargantuan tray of hors d'oeuvres—fresh shrimp with special cocktail sauce, chopped chicken liver with a generous embellishment of onion, pickled herring, spiced beets, corn relish, spiced pickled string beans (a lovely thing), cottage cheese if you want it, celery, olives and radishes if you can take them.

These are all in lavish portions and on a circular tray, a sort of Lazy Charlie. It's a fitting introduction to, and preparation for, the planked steak. The steak is the dish to have if you have never before been to Charlie's, and if it looks as though it will be some time before you get back. But it does not exhaust the resources or skills of the place. The menu is rich and sophisticated, with superb beef, and chops, chicken, Cornish hen, and game in season, Midwest frog's legs, sea food flown in from both oceans, and rarefied specialties such as Chicken Kiev (a Russian concoction in which boned chicken is stuffed with butter and served golden brown and oozing) and a highly-seasoned steak made to a South American recipe. You can have your good old American pie, of course, but you can also get an expertly made soufflé or *crêpes Suzette* done dazzlingly at your table.

Charlie also features some special drinks which he and his deputies will be glad to tell you about . . . and an exquisitely cold and dry martini, which in this civilized era seems to be a universal accomplishment in the United States. Adequate wines are to be had but this really is more bourbon and beer country. The prices are ample but not overwhelming.

[246]

Commander's Palace

WASHINGTON AVENUE AT COLISEUM STREET
NEW ORLEANS, LOUISIANA

Owner: *Frank Moran*
Maître d'Hôtel: *Otto Orser*
Chef: *J. M. Evans*

WHEN, OUTSIDE NEW ORLEANS, THE CITY IS mentioned in conjunction with food, as more often than not it is, the first two names to come to tongue are Antoine's and Galatoire's. They are the restaurants known everywhere. To people a bit more knowing about the town, Brennan's and Pontchartrain are not far behind the two paragons. But to people who live in New Orleans, it's not a twosome or a foursome, but a fivesome, and the fifth restaurant in the very select group is Commander's Palace.

Commander's Palace is not at all a fancy place but its old-fashioned decor is pleasing and somehow conveys a promise of good things to come; and the promise is no hoax. The cuisine is Creole, French, and Italian, but the hard core of it is American, in the best American tradition. As do the other good New Orleans restaurants, Commander's Palace features food from the nearby Louisiana waters, cooked with a definite Creole accent—Crab Meat Imperial, Turtle Stew, Trout Alexander. And of course there is gumbo, gumbo in its soup form, and gumbo in its non-soup form, served as a separate dish or as a side dish with your main course. Commander's Palace is also justly proud of its broil-blackened steaks and chops.

Commander's Palace makes those two fine and original New Orleans drinks, the Sazerac cocktail (Pernod, bourbon, Peychaud bitters) and the Ramos gin fizz (gin, lemon, white of an egg, soda), with both affection and skill. It takes art and time to make these two superb drinks, and it is worth getting a ringside seat at the bar to watch the maestro in his act. The wine list is simpler than the elegant production at Antoine's, but is adequate in variety, and the wines are carefully selected.

Le Cordon Bleu

DANIA
FLORIDA

Owner: *Thérèse Lauder*
Maître d'Hôtel: *Paul Arpajou*
Chef: *Marcel Ballestra*

THE IDEA OF ENCOUNTERING, ON GARISH U.S. Highway Number One, in a small and sleazy Florida crossroads, a restaurant comparable to the better restaurants in the Burgundy or Bordeaux sections of France, is obviously absurd; unless, of course, you're aware of the fact that in Florida, as in Southern California, the absurd is frequently the norm.

Anyway, there it is—Le Cordon Bleu, in Dania, Florida. In appearance, Le Cordon Bleu is the antithesis of most of Florida's fancier eating places; where they are pretentious, it is plain; where they are ugly in an ostentatious way, it is ugly in a folksy way. On the outside, that is; inside, it is friendly and attractive.

The name is come by honestly. The owner, Mrs. Thérèse Lauder, is a diplomée of the Cordon Bleu, the world's most famous school of *haute cuisine*. She is also a Commandeur of the Confrérie des Chevaliers du Tastevin, an accolade which goes only to men and women who are proven connoisseurs of the best in food and in wine. It is unusual for a woman to get it. The maître d'hôtel is Paul Arpajou, formerly of the Pavillon in New York, and the staff is entirely French.

The kitchen crew, too, is French; the *chef de cuisine,* Marcel Ballestra, a Niçoise. The fact that he is a Niçoise is not insignificant, because he brings from his native Nice a gustiness and zest in cooking for which that once-Italian city is naturally famous.

Proprietress Lauder would prefer to have a bit of advance notice if she is to give you a really memorable dinner, and promises, with that notice, to provide practically any de luxe dishes you may desire. But being a sane person, and realizing that even people who are dedicated to "being in Key West by nightfall" may have discerning appetites, she has a menu of daily specialties. On this, you will find such Cordon Bleu inspirations as *Escargots Bourguignon* (half doz. $1.25), *Pâté Maison,* Duck *Bigarade* ($4 for the dinner), *Café Diable* ($1.50), Chicken *Sauté Cordon Bleu* ($3 for the dinner), *Crêpes Suzette* ($1.25); and such local representatives as red snapper, pompano, and sirloin steak.

Food and wine are not given away at Le Cordon Bleu, but the prices are definitely reasonable for the quality. It would be worth trying to arrange, on your trip to or from a Florida destination, or on your stay there, a meal at Le Cordon Bleu. Call in advance.

Galatoire's

209 BOURBON STREET
NEW ORLEANS, LOUISIANA

President: *René Galatoire*

T HE BEST KNOWN RESTAURANT IN NEW Orleans, as far as the country outside New Orleans, and, for that matter, the world at large is concerned, is Antoine's. But probably the favorite of the crusty old families of New Orleans is Galatoire's. Roy Alciatore, who owns Antoine's, is an old and good friend of mine, so I am not going to get into any compromising argument about better or best. There is honor enough for both, for Galatoire's, like Antoine's, is a great restaurant, one of the greatest in the entire United States.

It is at 209 Bourbon Street in New Orleans, in a block below Canal Street, a block lined with the seamiest of the Bourbon Street night clubs, a slum-looking neighborhood in the cruel light of day and not too much better in the softer glow of night-time. But it itself is immaculate, white-painted on the outside, three-storied, and so narrow it looks almost one-dimensional. The inside is plain and of a distinctly earlier day, and it somehow says to you, as you enter, that you will eat there as in another day, a day that was richer, quieter, more bountiful, and calmer in the preparation and service of food.

[251]

Very little has changed at Galatoire's in the last half century. The floor is white tile, cracked, and somewhat uneven. Strips of worn red carpet run down the aisles. The walls on both sides are lined with old mirrors with wavering lines in the glass and little brown spots in the silver. On the mirror frames are brass coat hooks. From the very high ceiling hang dozens of two-bladed electric fans, and under each is a circle of glaring, unshaded electric lamps. The fans serve only in the interests of nostalgia, for now that the place has been air-conditioned they no longer are needed or used. In the back of the restaurant is a towering mirror with an ornate gold frame; across it are shelves of liqueurs. The whole effect is rather like a restaurant in the French provinces.

As I recall, my last dinner at Galatoire's was this:

First, two Sazeracs, that Pernod-flavored bourbon drink which originated at the old Sazerac Bar in New Orleans. Then, local Gulf Shrimp *Rémoulade,* with the spicy red *rémoulade* sauce which is so different in each New Orleans restaurant. Then Crawfish Bisque, a dark red soup with piquant stuffed crawfish heads dropped in the bisque just before serving. I ordered several extra heads on a side plate, an old New Orleans custom. With these courses goes garlic bread, hot French bread which has been specially baked for Galatoire's and adorned with a butter-garlic dressing and a touch of paprika. It might be said that Galatoire's, unlike many fine restaurants, goes in rather heavily for onions, garlic, bay leaf, cayenne and other muscular seasonings and condiments. The bisque was followed by chateaubriand, accompanied by Potatoes *Soufflé,* as good, I might say, as I have eaten anywhere in the world. I eschewed dessert, unless you want to call Brie cheese and a fresh apple dessert, and, as I had had an excellent Richebourg with my chateaubriand and Brie, I stayed Burgundian and had, with my coffee, a Marc de Bourgogne, and another with my cigar.

Galatoire's has had a long history of good food. In the last half of the nineteenth century the house was occupied by Victor's Restaurant, a name some people remember with pleasure even today, for Victor Bero was one of the best chefs in a town that had plenty of good ones. But by the turn of the century he had retired and Victor's was closed. Then in 1905 Gene Galatoire took it over.

There are, of course, many specialties at Galatoire's. The most popular Galatoire dish of them all is Trout Marguery, which is trout in a hollandaise sauce.

Then there is the delicately flavored pompano, which New Orleanians, and indeed most Southerners, consider the best of all fish. Galatoire's Pompano *en Papillotte* is baked in a thick sauce of shrimp, crabmeat and subtle seasonings. Of course, this shocks many, including myself, who feel that the proper way to serve pompano is broiled with a bit of maître d'hôtel sauce.

There are other, less rich, dishes: Shrimp Creole, with tomatoes and green peppers, and served over rice. And Red Fish Court Bouillon, a kind of glorified fish stew with tomatoes, flavored with thyme, garlic, onions and bay leaf.

Less distinctly Creole in flavor are the chicken dishes: *Bonne Femme,* or *Turenne* (with a red wine sauce containing mushrooms and artichoke hearts). And, to end the proper dinner at Galatoire's, *Crêpes Maison:* pancakes filled with jelly and served in a sauce of orange Curaçao with almonds and tiny curls of orange peel.

One of Galatoire's real delicacies is the crawfish which are served in the bisque, and also by themselves. These delectable small crustaceans look like stunted Maine lobsters and come from the fresh waters around New Orleans. Unfortunately they are available for only a few months each year—February until May—at least in theory. Actually they are often far too small early in the season and it's March before they reach the pot.

Galatoire's is perhaps the world's greatest citadel of traditional Creole cooking which is basically, though not purely, French. There are many other elements: the Spanish (in its use of pepper and spices); the African (the word gumbo comes from a Congo dialect and means okra); the Italian (in the liberal use of olive oil); the American Indian (the indispensable *filé,* which is ground sassafras leaves, was a favorite seasoning of the Choctaws).

[253]

If you visit New Orleans you can try calling Galatoire's for a reservation. The chances are you will be rebuffed, as they don't like to hold tables. If you go at conventional mealtimes you will probably have to take your place in a queue that pours out of the doors and up the street. This definitely doesn't appeal to me, so I go at unconventional hours and eat in a leisurely and uncrowded way, and I advise you to do the same.

Gaucho Steak House

AMERICANA HOTEL
9701 COLLINS AVENUE, BAL HARBOUR
MIAMI BEACH, FLORIDA

Maître d'Hôtel: *Frank Pavlo*
Chef: *Hugo Hunccke*

OR THE LAST TEN YEARS OR SO IT HAS BEEN the annual custom, in Miami Beach, to open a hotel bigger, lusher, plushier, more gadgety and more gimmicky than the previous year's bigger, lusher, plushier, more gadgety and more gimmicky hotel. A few years ago it was the Americana; and one of its more satisfactory gimmicks was a restaurant called Gaucho Steak House, after the South American cowboy of the same name.

The Gaucho is more intimate, cozier, and simpler than most restaurants in big hotels, especially the big "this year's" hotels. As its name suggests, it specializes in beef, the very best beef that can be had. It is rolled up to your table on a wagon, and sliced off in an impressive chunk of roast beef, or it is brought to you by a highly efficient waiter in one of steak's many forms, charcoal broiled prime sirloin, charcoal broiled ladies' prime sirloin, charcoal broiled filet mignon, chateaubriand, mignonettes of beef tenderloin *en brochette,* charcoal broiled ground tenderloin. For beef-dissenters, there are lamb chops, Virginia ham steak, fresh Florida pompano, Maine lobster, and broiled whole mountain trout.

There is an excellent pastry wagon, on which the prize exhibit is a rich, thick, brown-to-black chocolate pie. The Gaucho will serve you wine, graciously even, but it does not make a Big Thing of it.

Gourmet Room

TERRACE HILTON HOTEL
15 WEST SIXTH STREET
CINCINNATI, OHIO

Maître d'Hôtel: *Henri J. Guglielmi*
Chef: *Vito Locaputo*

HE GOURMET ROOM, SPARKLING ATOP THE twentieth floor of the Terrace Hilton Hotel (*née* Terrace Plaza) is the third of Cincinnati's triumvirate of fine French restaurants, the first recorded in this book, and the first in point of time, for it was established in 1948, before either of the other two existed. One of these three, the Maisonette, is owned by a young American businessman, Lee Comisar; another, Pigall's, is under the knowing ministration of, of all things, a genuine Frenchman, a great chef, Maurice Gorodesky; and the third, the Gourmet Room, is presided over by an Italian, Henri J. Guglielmi.

The Gourmet Room is attractive physically. The walls are all glass, and give a fine view in three directions, of the downtown area of the city, of the Ohio River, marching majestically along to its wedding with the Mississippi, and of some of the seven hills on which Cincinnati, like Rome, was built. But the idea of coming to a fine restaurant is not to look, but to eat, and this the Terrace Room enables, and encourages, you to do. The view is a bonus.

The Gourmet Room is intimate, as its name indicates . . . a *room,* not a banquet hall as are so many hotel restaurants. Among the Gourmet Room's specialties are Curry Soup, *Coquilles* of Lobster and Crabmeat, Guinea Hen with Wild Rice, Sauce Grand Marnier, *Crêpes Suzette,* and Soufflé Grand Marnier.

These are, for the most part, classic French dishes, done in the classic French way. But if you get Henri in one of his freer moments he might himself preside over one of his cooked-at-the-table specialties, such as *Escalopes de Veau* Henri.

The wine list at the Gourmet Room is very good indeed. The prices are not exactly painless, but neither are they lethal. As the room seats only fifty-six people, you can see that it's wise, almost essential, to reserve well ahead of time.

London Chop House

155 WEST CONGRESS STREET
DETROIT, MICHIGAN

Owners: *Lester and Sam Gruber, Albert J. Woolf*
Maître d'Hôtel: *Alfred*
Chef: *Philip Velez*

L ONDON CHOP HOUSE IS DETROIT'S MOST famous restaurant, a fame achieved in almost equal parts by excellent food, excellent wine, and excellent publicity. The owners, Lester and Sam Gruber, and brother-in-law Al Woolf are shrewd businessmen and promoters, so shrewd that they know slick stunts alone won't make a restaurant flourish. The waiters wear plaid or paisley jackets. An itinerant artist will dash off a caricature of you if you don't fend him off. If you make an advance reservation, matches with your name printed on the cover will await you at your table. You will be showered with bulletins, birthday and anniversary greetings, messages of good cheer. But even though you might consider most of these stunts expendable, you'd be well advised to go to the Chop House for the food itself. The owners are very serious when it comes to the food and wine they serve. They have collected some 2,000 books on food, wine and tobacco, thousands of menus, and constantly travel in this country and abroad seeking recipes and ideas. They claim their list of vintage French wines is surpassed in this country only by the Waldorf and 21.

[259]

The Chop House, naturally, in deference to its name, features superb chops and steaks. But as it is in the Great Lakes area, it also proudly specializes in Great Lakes fish. Dwellers along the East Coast, basking in the bounty of Atlantic sea food, are inclined to be cavalier toward the lesser fish of the Lakes. That's a mistake. The whitefish from Lake Superior, the perch from Lake Ontario and the baby frog's legs from the shores of Michigan have a delicacy and a gentle flavor all their own and are prepared lovingly and skillfully at the London Chop House. Particularly recommended is the Boneless Perch Dobler, named for M. Dobler, the original Chop House chef who invented the dish.

Warning: After 9:30 P.M. a space is cleared, an orchestra appears, and benighted souls actually leave their tables to dance. The Chop House is a favorite of Detroit's motor and other tycoons; important, if seeing tycoons in the flesh spurs your appetite.

The Maisonette

505 WALNUT STREET
CINCINNATI, OHIO

Proprietors: *Lee and Michael Comisar*
Maître d'Hôtel: *Drago Mitrovich*
Chef: *Pierre Adrian*

O NE OF THE ODDEST FACTS ABOUT FOOD IN the United States is that Cincinnati has more good French restaurants than any other city in the country except New York. Of course, New York has dozens, while Cincinnati has only three, but those three still put it ahead of San Francisco, New Orleans, Chicago, Los Angeles, and Boston, our only other great eating centers. Please remember, we said *French* restaurants; serving real, traditional French food. The three in Cincinnati are the Gourmet Room atop the Terrace Hilton Hotel; the Maisonette; and Pigall's. The Gourmet Room started it all; the Maisonette was, in a way, inspired by the success of the Gourmet Room; and Pigall's was, in its way, an offshoot of the Maisonette.

Lee Comisar, despite his rather misleading last name, is a clean-cut young American, and his career an inspiring example of the efficacy of Free Enterprise. Lee's family, his mother, Mrs. Knight, and his uncle, Ben Comisar, have been in the restaurant business in Ohio, Dayton and Cincinnati, for some years. The restaurants they ran were good wholesome American places, serving good, hearty American food.

Then Lee, and his father, Nat, good American Free Enterprisers, with good American backgrounds, decided that if the Gourmet Room could succeed, and valiantly, in Cincinnati, so could another and even more authentic French restaurant. They set out to prove their point by calling on the Club Vatel, a club named after the famous chef who impaled himself on his sword because the turbot, which was the *pièce de résistance* of a dinner for Louis XIV, did not arrive on time. The club is a headquarters for the French chefs of the United States. The chef they recommended was Maurice Gorodesky.

It would be nice to say that the discerning palates of Cincinnatians immediately recognized the superior quality of a great French chef's works, and made the Maisonette an overnight success. They didn't even have the opportunity, for the Comisars knew that the good burghers of Cincinnati simply do not respond to rapid change, especially if it is inspired by foreign lands (any place outside Cincinnati); so he proffered the new food, the *Soufflé Grand Marnier,* the *Escargots Bourguignonne,* and the *Coq au Vin,* gently and in easy stages. In fact, the process was so gentle that it was a full two years before the Maisonette emerged as a true French restaurant, one of the best in the entire country. And by that time it was a real success; it still is, and a quite astounding success, not only with the worldly people of Cincinnati, the many New Yorkers who visit Cincinnati regularly for business or artistic reasons, the advertising executives, the bankers, the musicians, the actors and the opera stars. All the traditional French dishes, immaculately cooked, are here; authentic onion soup and bouillabaise, snails, chicken in champagne sauce, soufflés and *crêpes.* The fish, from English Channel sole to Colorado rainbow trout, is exceptionally good. So are the roast beef and the steak.

Realizing that serving superb French food without the proper wines to accompany it would be a commendable job only half done, Comisar stocked an excellent, sagely chosen wine cellar. And it's pleasant, at the bar, to encounter unimpeachable versions of old friends from New Orleans, the Sazerac, absinthe frappé, and Ramos gin fizz, made by Bill Richmond who had his own bar in New Orleans for a number of years.

This story of the Maisonette ends on a sad note. Maurice Gorodesky, the chef, and Lee Comisar had a squabble and Maurice left. But actually, this sad event has its own happy ending; for the Maisonette remains a really fine restaurant, and Maurice opened his own place which is also a fine restaurant, enriching Cincinnati and delighting lovers of fine food who come there, those same advertising executives, bankers, musicians, actors and opera stars, who now have not two fine French restaurants to enjoy, but three.

Las Novedades

EAST BROADWAY AND 15TH STREET
TAMPA, FLORIDA

Owners: *Manuel Garcia, Sr. and Jr.; Lorenzo de Palacio*
Maître d'Hôtel: *Louis Perez*
Chef: *Arnaldo Gonzalez*

LAS NOVEDADES, IN YBOR CITY, THE COLORful Spanish section of Tampa, has grown since 1890, when it started, from a tiny coffee shop to what is probably the most authentic Spanish restaurant in the United States.

As a device to get you quickly into the proper exotic mood, the owners have made the main dining room a patio transplanted from Seville, complete with balconies, Moorish arches, mission bell, fountain, and a real, honest-to-God, fruit-bearing orange tree. This may give you something of a start at first, but the first cocktail should put you on the road to recovery.

You can get all the conventional American drinks, and, for that matter, all the conventional American dishes at Las Novedades; but this is a restaurant of Spanish specialties, and you'll enjoy it more if you indulge in its specialties from start to finish. Put behind you that devil's urge for a martini, and have instead a Las Novedades creation, a Tamborine, a Piruli, a Goya, or a Las Novedades Special. The ingredients are all listed on the menu, so you won't be going too deeply into uncharted firewaters.

Helpfully, Las Novedades lists complete Spanish dinners, which simplifies ordering but is, in a manner, a coward's way out. It's more exciting to order Spanish Hors d'Oeuvres or Spanish Bean Soup, and then try one of Las Novedades' special dishes, Chicken *à la Acosta, Arroz con Pollo* (chicken on golden-colored rice), *Bistec de Filete Cacerola,* Pompano *Relleno* (baked, boned, and skinless, stuffed with sea food and cream sauce), *Paella* (yellow rice and a rich assortment of sea food from the nearby Gulf), *Langosta á la Mantequilla.* There are others, but these should give you an idea. After whatever you choose for your entrée, by all means try some of the restaurant's Spanish pastry, for Las Novedades started in life as a coffee and pastry hole-in-the-wall, and was named for *las novedades* (novelties) of pastry served there.

It is fitting to drink Spanish wines with these dishes, of which there is a good selection in both white and red; and to finish it all off with Cuban coffee and Spanish brandy. Oh—and a cigar imported from Havana.

The Old House
Restaurant

432 SOUTH FIFTH STREET
LOUISVILLE, KENTUCKY

Proprietor: *Erma Biesel Dick*
Headwaiter: *Seymour Ellis*

I'S UNFAIRLY CYNICAL TO FORM A PREJU-
dice against a place because it's called Old
House, and is in the South, and is in a senti-
mentally Colonial-type manse. We did, however, even before we ever had been there. But
we have been forced to exorcise our prejudice.
Louisville is probably the most sophisticated
and enlightened of all Southern cities and it's proper that it would have
a fine international restaurant, even though hidden behind a Ye Olde
South façade. The Old House gets Dover sole from the cold waters of
the English Channel, lobster from the equally cold waters off the
Maine coast, shad roe from Maryland's Chesapeake Bay, and shrimp
from the Gulf of Mexico. It goes to provincial France for *escargots* and
marrons. And its Angus beef comes from Kansas City and Chicago.
Appropriately, it serves Old Kentucky ham but in keeping with its international aspect, it also serves Romanoff Beluga caviar. One of the
dishes of which it is most proud is Pheasant Minnesota, cooked with

such tempting allies as double cream, sherry, truffles, and mushrooms. Also proudly offered is the special salad made with Kentucky Bibb, preserved stuffed orange, riced Philadelphia cream cheese, and their own special dressing. The wine list is not sensational but it is adequate. There are a couple of items on it that could be criticized as being more for show than for enjoyment. There's a Château d'Yquem 1909 at $50 a bottle. This is a great wine, of course, but it's syrupy sweet and should be drunk only by the thimbleful with an ultra-rich dessert. There is also a Graves 1893 at $35 a bottle. This is simply too old for a wine to be, and while it is still good, it must have lost much of its life. There is also a special list of whiskies at $5, $7.50 and on up to $15 a drink. We'd recommend instead the more modern and less fancy Jack Daniels, Old Fitzgerald, or Johnny Walker Black Label.

Pigall's

462 EAST FIFTH STREET
CINCINNATI, OHIO

Owner-Chef: *Maurice Gorodesky*

AURICE GORODESKY WAS BROUGHT TO CIN-cinnati when the Comisars, a successful family of restaurant owners, decided to give Cincinnati a true, faultlessly French restaurant. They succeeded; and Maurice, as chef, became known and respected about town. Then his wife, Nanette, opened her own small restaurant, and while Maurice tried to remain aloof, and continue to give his all to the Maisonette, he inevitably found himself in with his wife's new venture and a partner in Pigall's. Together, they preside over the kitchen, and together they have created a restaurant which, while hardly out of its infancy, is already something of an institution in Cincinnati.

In the world of *haute cuisine,* Maurice is something of a prodigy. At the age of eighteen, he not only was in the sacrosanct kitchen of the Paris Ritz, but for his work there was awarded, by a jury of gourmets, the First Prize of the City of Paris. A few years later he had bestowed upon him the *Prix d'Honneur* of the Paris Chamber of Commerce which had selected him as the best young chef in France. Today, he is a member of a surprising number of chefs', gourmets', and wine-bibbers' societies in Europe and the United States, though still in his early forties. When he was offered a job in Cincinnati, some of his compatriots asked, "Why go?" His answer was, "Let's take French cooking and French wines wherever we have the opportunity."

So France has invaded Cincinnati and Cincinnati loves it. Pigall's menu starts with the admonition *"Soyez Patient, La Bonne Cuisine Demande du Temps."* (Be patient, good cuisine demands time.) This is a reassuring and hopeful sign to lovers of good food. The menu itself tends to make these hopes glow, for the character of a restaurant can frequently be read from the menu alone. Here are some of the poetic names of dishes from Pigall's menu: *Pâté du Chef aux Truffes, Coquille* of Fresh Sea Food *au Champagne, Moules Rémoulade, Soupe à l'Oignon* Pigall's, *Coq au Vin Maison au Vieux Bourgogne du Chevalier, Pommes Dauphine, Petits Pois au Beurre, Gâteau du Chef, Escargots de Bourgogne,* Imported English Sole *au Chablis,* Pompano *Sauté* "Paris-Paris," Steak *au Poivre du Chef,* Chateaubriand, *Poire Belle Hélène, Crêpes* Pigall's, *Parfait Glacé* Nanette, and *Café Filtre* "Sidewalk Café."

Pigall's wine cellar is small, but chosen with meticulous understanding of the best wines and the best vintages of recent years. The champagnes, with such delectables as Dom Pérignon 1943, Krug, Brut Réserve, and Pommery Rose Royal; and the Burgundies, with Bâtard-Montrachet 1953, Moulin-à-Vent 1943, and La Tache 1943; are superlative.

Plaza Spanish Restaurant

1426 FIRST STREET
SARASOTA, FLORIDA

Proprietors: *B. Alvarez, C. G. Fernandez, John C. Hagerman*
Chef: *Earl Heine*

**A**LL ALONG THE WEST COAST OF FLORIDA there are heritages of its Spanish days, principally, remnants of bad Spanish architecture and oases of good Spanish food. The Plaza Restaurant, in Sarasota, is one of these oases.

There are many Spanish specialties on the Plaza menu, but those of which the owners are proudest are their Stuffed Shrimp, their Chicken and Yellow Rice, and the inescapable Florida favorite, Pompano *Papillo* (pompano cooked in a brown paper bag). With these, the Plaza can serve you imported Spanish wines: Brillante (Spanish sauternes), Cepa de Oro (Spanish Chablis), Marqués de Riscal (Spanish claret). The wine of Spain, incidentally, is very good.

The Plaza also has a complete American menu with such decidedly un-Spanish items as roast beef, sirloin steak, grilled sea trout (from the Gulf right off Sarasota), ham steak, pork chops, lamb chops, and old-fashioned strawberry shortcake. There's also a fetching little item called "Fried Fingers of Snook," whoever Snook may be.

[270]

The Plaza wine list is a bit on the slim side, but if your favorite wine is not there, you might try to console yourself with a fine imported beer, a Heineken's, or a Löwenbrau, or a Dortmunder.

The Plaza is attractively housed and has an excellent bar and cocktail lounge.

Pontchartrain Hotel

2031 ST. CHARLES AVENUE
NEW ORLEANS, LOUISIANA

President and Managing Director: *E. Lysle Aschaffenburg*
Maître d'Hôtel, Caribbean Room: *Douglas Leman*
Chef, Caribbean Room: *Daniel Evans*

NE OF THE VERY BEST PLACES TO EAT IN New Orleans is the Pontchartrain Hotel at 2031 St. Charles Avenue, on the way from New Orleans to Lake Pontchartrain. But because of its location outside the city and out of range of the raucous but pleasant sound of Bourbon Street, it is generally not known to tourists.

The Pontchartrain is without doubt the first hotel of the area, though not as well known as the loftier Roosevelt and the old-time St. Charles. The proprietor, Lysle Aschaffenburg, has an inborn New Orleans feeling for food and knowledge of food, and he has enhanced this feeling and knowledge by frequent trips to Europe, largely for the purpose of studying food and wine, and frequent visits to the eating centers of the United States: New York, Chicago, San Francisco and Los Angeles.

The most interesting place to eat at the hotel is in the Caribbean Room, which is an appropriate name for a New Orleans restaurant, as it does have an affinity with the Caribbean area. Yet the menu is not of the shrimp and rice, and beans and rice, and exotic rum drink

genre of the Caribbean, but properly New Orleans in character, with its accent on French and Creole food.

The specialties of the house are Lump Crabmeat Remick, Breast of Chicken Hawaiian (what's this doing in a Caribbean Room!), Trout *Véronique, Pot au Crème,* and a dessert they're very proud of, Ice Cream Pie. The Crabmeat Remick is an appetizer in casserole form. The Breast of Chicken Hawaiian is breast of chicken on toast with a grilled pineapple ring and béarnaise sauce. Trout *Véronique* is fresh lake trout with a delicate white wine sauce, hollandaise and grapes. The *Pot au Crème* is *pot au crème* and the Ice Cream Pie is pie with ice cream, over which the Pontchartrain chef works some magic he seems reluctant to reveal.

The Pontchartrain has the traditional Shrimp *Rémoulade* and Crabmeat *Rémoulade,* Louisiana Gumbo *Créole* soup, and Gulf sea food in season.

The last time in New Orleans I came as an officer of a gourmet society which included the leading gourmets of New Orleans. We had the official semi-annual dinner of the society, then were entertained with special dinners, at the leading restaurants in the city. I was told repeatedly by these connoisseurs that the best food in New Orleans today was being served at the Pontchartrain. This may very well be true, and you most definitely should try it; but still visit, in addition, Antoine's, and Galatoire's, and Brennan's.

Proprietor Aschaffenburg, an officer in the Chevaliers du Tastevin, has chosen the wines affectionately and expertly.

The Pump Room

AMBASSADOR EAST HOTEL
1300 NORTH STATE PARKWAY
CHICAGO, ILLINOIS

Manager: *Philip L. Boddy*
Maître d'Hôtel: *Henri Jabeneau*
Chef: *Albert Bonelli*

ONE OF THE BEST KNOWN, BEST LIKED, AND most waggish innkeepers and restaurateurs our times have known is the late Ernest Byfield. He first became known when he opened the College Inn in the Hotel Sherman in Chicago's Loop, where such nostalgic names as Coon-Sanders and Ben Bernie held forth for the raccoon-coat set. He then took over the two Ambassador hotels, Ambassador East and Ambassador West and, for some reason unknown to living man, decided to transplant Bath, England, to Chicago, Illinois. The underground passage between the two hotels was called the Sarah Siddons Walk. The restaurant in Ambassador West was named—or perhaps we should get in the Old English mood, and say y-clept—"the Buttery." But the crowning achievement and child of Ernie's fertile and lively brain was the Pump Room. This was supposed to be an adaptation of the famous restaurant in Bath, run by the eighteenth-century dandy, Beau Nash, and destroyed by the twentieth-century madman, Adolf Hitler. It is, to say the least, an embellished adaptation. It's hard to believe that the original Pump Room had waiters bearing flaming food on swords, Nubian coffee boys with three-foot high ostrich plume head-dresses, and martinis served in stemmed soup dishes.

As we said before, Ernie Byfield was a waggish fellow, and a great deal of his tongue-in-cheek outlook toward the world went into the founding and establishment of The Pump Room. But don't get the idea that it is a joke; it is, indeed, one of the great restaurants of the whole world. The great people of the world who pass through Chicago are to be seen there, even if their stay is as ephemeral as the wait be-tween the Twentieth Century from New York in the morning and the Chief or Super Chief to the Coast in the afternoon. While Ernie was alive, names in the news felt it practically compulsory to drop in on him and partake of his wit, his charm, his vittles and his booze.

Stock Yard Inn

4178 SOUTH HALSTED STREET
CHICAGO, ILLINOIS

Manager: *Robert M. Foss*
Maître d'Hôtel: *John Holman*
Chef: *Harry Oakley*

THERE ARE TWO SURPRISINGLY GOOD RESTAUrants within the famous Chicago stockyards. One is a club, where the present-day executives of the meat companies sit and enjoy their products under the stern and watchful eyes of their predecessors and ancestors whose portraits hang on the wall above them. The other is a restaurant open to the public, the Stock Yard Inn, which is the best place to eat if you visit the stockyards, one of the great tourist sights of Chicago.

It would be nice to be able to say that here, in the greatest stockyards in the world, you'd be able to get the world's best beef, but regrettably, that's not so. You can get better beef in dozens of places in New York, in several places in California, and even in a few restaurants in the center of Chicago. But the beef at Stock Yard Inn, nevertheless, is awfully good. And there's an excitement about the propinquity of the lovely beasts, headed for good restaurants throughout the country, that gives an extra succulence to your meal. Naturally the Inn specializes in beef in its manifold forms, including Marinated Beef Slices, with

[276]

onion, salt and pepper, lemon juice, sour cream, and lettuce, which is particularly worth trying at lunch time. The management is to be congratulated on the wines, particularly the properly gusty Burgundies, it has chosen to go with its fine beef. And there is good draught beer to appeal to those many discerning people who feel that the best drink of all with a thick steak or an oozing red slab of roast beef is beer.

Weidmann's

208-210 22ND AVENUE
MERIDIAN, MISSISSIPPI

Proprietor: *Mrs. Dorothy Weidmann*
Manager: *Thomas E. McWilliams*
Chef: *Henry Foy*

ERIDIAN, MISSISSIPPI, IS NOT ONLY AN UN-likely place to find a good metropolitan restaurant, it's even an unlikely place to find oneself in. But if you're traveling on the main southern route from Los Angeles to New York, you can't avoid it, no matter how hard you try. If you should arrive there around evening, you might just as well stay overnight, for pushing on into the sparsely hoteled regions of Mississippi would be at best a poor gamble. Besides, there is an even more compelling reason for staying in Meridian, and it's called Weidmann's.

A few years ago, my wife and I were eastbound for New York and happened to drive into Meridian at nightfall. We had heard about Weidmann's, or perhaps had read about it somewhere. So we headed there as soon as we had bathed and changed. Walking through the door of Weidmann's was walking out of Mississippi into New York City. There was the immediate realization that this was really a big-time restaurant. As in Sardi's, and Reuben's, and Dinty Moore's, and Jack Dempsey's, there were autographed photographs of celebrities on the walls, portraits of actors and actresses and boxers and other athletes who had eaten there. The proprietor and the waiters were big-time; there was that air which makes you feel at once that you are in a good restaurant.

Meridian is not on, but within the area of the Gulf and all its wonderful sea food, especially Gulf shrimp. The menu features such succulent shrimp dishes as Gulf Shrimp *Rémoulade,* Gulf Shrimp Buena Vista, Iced Shrimp Peeled, Stacked Shrimp *Ravigote,* "Garlic Broiled Shrimp" (the quotes are theirs), Stuffed Jumbo Shrimp, Baked Shrimp au Gratin, Creole Shrimp and Rice, and Fried Fantail Shrimp. These Gulf shrimp are considered by the shrimp-enchanted to be the very best, the richest, the meatiest, the most delectable shrimp in all the world. Despite the bonanza of shrimp, I ordered marinated herring instead. The atmosphere suggested it. My homesickness for New York sharpened my appetite for the dish. It turned out to be marinated herring at its wonderful best, that great combination of the essentially opposite flavors of sour cream, vinegar, bay leaves, onions, and the herring itself. The four temples of marinated herring are, in my estimation, Lindy's, Reuben's, 21, and the Oak Room of the Hotel Plaza, all in New York. Weidmann's can be added to that select foursome.

Weidmann's sea-food menu is a complete menu in itself, containing some thirty different dishes, among which, in addition to the shrimp specialties mentioned above, are Crab Lump Cocktail, Crab Belvedere, Trout *Amandine,* Maine Lobster, Danish Baby Lobster Tails, Broiled Spanish Mackerel, Broiled Salmon Steak, Pan Fried Rocky Mountain Rainbow Trout, Broiled Oysters *en Brochette,* and, "For the Seafood Lovers . . . Special Seafood Platter." The works, probably.

Weidmann's has a considerable reputation for good red meat, for steaks, and chops, and liver. The way to eat good red meat, is, of course, red and plain. Steak *au Poivre,* steak covered with peppercorns, a touch of cognac and a few other intruding ingredients, as served at Le Pavillon in New York, and the Calavados in Paris, is permissible. But generally speaking, good meat buried in sauce is to be seriously deplored. However, Weidmann's has a Stuffed Steak of which they're inordinately proud, and which is worth trying, as long as you don't let it become a habit. It is a choice piece of filet mignon, split and broiled slightly, then stuffed with a mixture of Roquefort cheese, chopped mushrooms, chopped garlic and parsley, lemon juice, a dash of Lea and Perrin's sauce, sherry wine. Stuff this into the split steak, pin it together, and give it the required amount of additional fire. It's so good and so unusual that for the time being, at least, you forget the enormity of desecrating a fine piece of beef.

For dessert at Weidmann's, it's almost compulsory to have Black Bottom Pie. This is a pie which sends most Southerners into ecstasies, but rarely finds its way above the Mason-Dixon Line. Roughly, it rests on a bottom crust made of ginger snaps; has a filling of scalded milk, egg yolks, sugar, cornstarch, bitter chocolate, vanilla, gelatin, egg whites, whiskey and custard, and is topped with whipped cream and shavings of bitter chocolate. If that sounds tempting to you, you'll find it at its best at Weidmann's.

I have not been back to Weidmann's since, but have had regular reports on it, from qualified people, and am happy to be able to recommend it as before. Henry Weidmann died in November of 1956. His wife Dorothy is now the active owner; his son-in-law, Thomas Mc-Williams, is manager; Mrs. Billie Mahoney is his assistant, and Chef Foy directs the kitchen. I am sure they will keep things at Weidmann's on the same high plane that I remember. As long as they continue to do so, you will always have an excellent excuse for stopping off at the town called Meridian, Mississippi.

The Future of American Restaurants

NOT TOO LONG AGO THE NEW YORK TIMES ran an excellent piece on the theme that elegance of cuisine is on the wane in the United States. The *Times* considered this sufficiently newsworthy to start it on the front page. The points Craig Claiborne, the writer, made in this piece were that the influx of master chefs ended with stricter immigration laws, that efficiency experts dedicated to cutting expenses had taken control of the kitchen away from the chefs, that training facilities for cooks and waiters are virtually nonexistent, and that the great chefs were dying and retiring and the new younger ones simply not coming up, indeed not even entering the profession. It was pointed out that the average age of the great French chefs in the United States was now sixty-three and that the only new young great French chef in the whole United States is Pierre Franey, formerly of the Pavillon.

These things are all true and it is proper to deplore them. But the picture isn't altogether that dismal. The fact remains that there are superb restaurants in the United States, not a few of them, but many; and that new ones are opening, and will continue to open, and that the quality of many of them is surprisingly high. The reason why this trend will continue and even accelerate is a quite simple one; the restaurant business can be greatly rewarding both in satisfaction and in a financial way. Owning a restaurant, a good one, is a first-rate way to get rich rather quickly and to live off the fat of the land while you're doing it. You can get rich running an exquisitely elegant, astronomically priced, shamefully snobbish, restaurant like Le Pavillon, as evidenced by M. Soulé. You can get rich by running a habitat for celebrities, and make your whole family rich with you, as has been proven by the Berns and and Kriendler clans of 21. You can get rich by setting up a smoothly operating organization to open restaurants with a gimmick, as indicated by the success of the Restaurant Associates Corporation which runs the Hawaiian Room in New York's Hotel Lexington (Hawaiian food and entertainment gimmick), the Forum of the Twelve Caesars (old-Roman gimmick), the Four Seasons (grandeur gimmick) and other lucrative places. You can get rich by quietly and economically opening a small, predominantly family-run place, as evidenced by Tony Gugnoni of New York's San Marino. You can get rich by opening a better mousetrap or food-trap, as indicated by Mario and Rita Morelli and their Mont d'Or Inn in remote Smithtown, Long Island. There are wealthy restaurateurs all over the United States. In every city, in a number of small towns and in suburban and even rural areas. And it's a very pleasant business even though it is hard work. A good restaurateur is a standout citizen in his community, gets to know and become real friends with personages and big shots, gets the best service in the world from accomplished chefs and waiters, commands the last word in food, wines and liquors, cigars and other pleasantries of life. He never has to pick up a tab or resort to his Diners' Club account whether he eats alone, or with the whole family, or entertains a group. Any such business is bound to attract people of intelligence and taste, and to cause them to learn the preparation and serving of good food. Maybe French chefs are growing old and tired and their number diminishing. But it isn't altogether essential that a chef be of French birth and instruction. In our estimation, Italians are every bit as good chefs as the French, and a good Chinese chef can maybe show both a thing or two. We've encountered superb colored chefs, Yugoslav chefs, Japanese chefs, Russian chefs, male chefs and female chefs, teen-age chefs and even boys-from-Brooklyn chefs. Things are awfully good for restaurants and restaurateurs now, and they can hardly help but get better as time goes on. A hundred years ago Americans ate about one meal in two hundred away from home. Today we are eating about one meal out of four away from home. And there is no indication whatsoever that this percentage will do anything but increase. All the proof you need of that is to go out and try to hire a maid.

With rewards such as good and well-run restaurants offer, it is inevitable that intelligent young people will be attracted to seeking them. They will learn about the business end of a restaurant by taking business courses, about running a restaurant by apprenticing themselves to good ones, and about cooking from studying under good chefs. They can learn a great deal about cooking simply by practicing doggedly at home; but they can learn more by spending time in a good restaurant kitchen, by going to one of the few good cooking schools which exist in this country (their names can be obtained from the Vatel Club, 349 West 48th Street, New York City) or by going to the Cordon Bleu in Paris. Studying abroad has become quite the thing for young Americans, and studying at Cordon Bleu or the famous hotel school in Vienna would entitle a student to all the privileges he would receive in any other recognized institute of learning.

There are already indications that the restaurant career is about to become, for young people in this country, the fashionable thing it has become for young people in England. Young people there in colleges and recently graduated from colleges are studying cooking like mad and a number of them have already gone in the restaurant business. Perhaps the outstanding example there is Perry Smith, the bearded owner and maestro of the "Hole in the Wall" in Bath. Smith, a graduate of London University, and an amateur of good cookery, honed the edges of his amateurism by study in Paris and became a professional by opening the Hole in the Wall. This happens to be one of the very best restaurants not only in England but anywhere. The last time one of us was there, after a superb meal, he complimented Smith, who very graciously replied, "I'm so glad you found it good. It so happens I didn't cook tonight; I've been training one of our waitresses who has a great flair for cooking and she did every bit of the dinner you had." So you see it is possible to learn fine cooking in the proper surroundings and under the proper tutelage.

The signs in this country all seem to us to be good. More and more people, men particularly, are learning to cook and regularly cooking, and young people no longer look to the kitchen as a den of drudgery. Fine food from all over the world has found its way into shops in every respectable-sized city and even into those citadels of food mediocrity, the supermarket. Despite the tendency of gourmets to sneer at frozen foods, frozen products have become infinitely better since Clarence Birdseye invented the process and many exciting foods and even whole meals are now being made available in frozen form. American wines, too, have improved immeasurably since the blighting hand of Prohibition was lifted from our vineyards. The United States today is, in our opinion, growing the best wine of any countries except France and Germany. There is a growing opinion that America is growing better rosé even than France; and champagne second only to the master product from France.

Probably the brightest ray in the whole spectrum of eating is the motel. This once tawdry part of the American scene has become quite a thing of beauty and elegance. And in the competition for the touring customer, the forward-looking motel owner has learned there is no lure comparable to a fine restaurant. It is our prediction that in the next few years some of the best restaurants in the United States will be found in, or as adjuncts to, motels.

The Southwest & the West

Alexis' Tangier

NOB HILL
1200 CALIFORNIA STREET
SAN FRANCISCO, CALIFORNIA

Proprietor: *Alexis Merab*
Maître d'Hôtel: *André Jouanjus*
Chef: *Vladimir Skvortsoff*

HE FOOD AT ALEXIS' TANGIER IS AS GOOD AS there is in San Francisco, as good as there is on the West Coast. (Lucius Beebe rates it even higher—at the top, in fact.) Please note that the stress is on the *food*. That is superb, whether it's Alexis' famous Chicken Kiev, or some one of his noteworthy dishes of Middle East origin. But all is not paradisiacal in this gourmet paradise. Alexis' seems to have gotten the quaint notion that overcharging is a form of elegance and superiority, and that people are terribly, terribly impressed by terrible, terrible prices. Knowing people simply are not. This fiscality is evident mostly in the wine list where the better clarets are priced at an absurd $25 and onwards and upwards. Another disenchanting note, to some serious diners, who like to concentrate on what they're eating and drinking, is a tendency toward excessive pallyness on the part of Alexis.

Having purged ourselves of these few carping comments, let us say again that the food at Tangier is exquisite. The menu is long, full, fascinating, and enticing, with the dishes associated with superior international cuisine, and a number of exotic things as well. Some of the more off-beat items on it are *Yalanji Dolma* (stuffed grape leaves); *Blini* (pancakes with black caviar, sour cream); Chicken Baghdad (with mangoes, ginger, wine, curry); Boneless Squab Istanbul; Lobster Tails Baghdad (with mangoes, ginger, wine, curry); Shish Kebab of Lamb *à la* Kazbek; *Loukhum,* Turkish delight; Mangoes-Lichis *à la* Alexis; and *Café Turc.*

The wine list at Alexis' Tangier is outstanding (if you can keep your eyes off that right-hand column), the decor interesting and conducive to relaxing, pleasurable wining and dining.

Amelio's

1630 POWELL STREET
SAN FRANCISCO, CALIFORNIA

Owner: *Mrs. Amelio Pacini*
Maître d'Hôtel: *Dave Viani*
Chef: *Ernest Lavino*

HENEVER SAN FRANCISCANS START TALKING about their fine restaurants and how much finer they are than other fine restaurants anywhere (and that's a pet subject of conversation in San Francisco) the name of Amelio's inevitably comes up. It's one of the old-timers of San Francisco and one of the most respected. It's also extremely jealous of its reputation and takes pains to see that no one, including the customers, does anything to tarnish it. (There's even a conspicuous notice which sternly admonishes, "Patrons entering these premises unescorted must remain unescorted while in this place of business." Out, masher, out, adventuress!)

Amelio's is Italian and proud of it, and the menu is studded with Italian dishes—Antipasto, *Prosciutto è Melone,* Minestrone, Veal *Parmigiana, Rollatine,* Chicken *Cacciatore, Zabaglione,* and, of course, spaghetti, *tagliarini* and *fettucini* in all their varying and enchanting forms and dresses. When pressed, the owners will confess that their own favorite dishes are Asparagus *della Casa,* Boneless Squab and Chicken *Vecchia-Usanza.* The wine list is adequate, with proper favoritism shown to the excellent wines of California.

Arthur's

3701 MCKINNEY AVENUE
DALLAS, TEXAS

Owner: *Arthur Bates*
Maître d'Hôtel: *James Harrison*
Chef: *John Siegrist*

ALLAS DOES NOT HAVE THE FOOD ITS SIZE, wealth, and growing sophistication merit, but it does have some fine restaurants, and Arthur's is one of them. Arthur's doesn't fool around with trying to be French, or Italian, or Spanish or anything else but good old Arthur's, Texas, U.S.A. The only French items on the menu are Vichyssoise and Roquefort cheese dressing.

Arthur's specializes in steaks, chops, and Maine lobsters, and, according to Texans, that's proper food for a Texan, and therefore for any other good red-blooded American. And so it is. As befitting all things Texan, the menu is large and crowded with good things, with a pleasing, taste-titillating, thoroughly American sound to many of the dishes.

Listen to the names—Fresh Gulf Shrimp, Texas Grapefruit, Cream of Tomato Soup, Maine Lobster, Long Island Scallops, Lake Superior Whitefish, Wall-Eyed Pike, Old-Fashioned Ham Steak with Red-Eye Gravy and Hominy, Charcoal Broiled New York Sirloin Steak, Idaho Baked Potato, California Fruit Salad, Old-Fashioned Strawberry Shortcake, Philadelphia Cream Cheese. These random choices from the menu are pleasant and nostalgic reminders of the rich variety and goodness of American food. And it is to Arthur's credit that he brings into his place the good things of *all* the United States, and that he serves them so well.

And surely no decent, fair-minded person will object to a few touches of Texan expansiveness such as Curried *Jumbo* Shrimp, *Jumbo* Silver King Squab, and *Colossal* Ripe or *Jumbo* Green Olives.

The Blue Fox

659 MERCHANT STREET
SAN FRANCISCO, CALIFORNIA

Owners: *Mario Mondin and Piero Fassio*
Chef: *Tony Penado*

HE BLUE FOX IS KNOWN AS THE 21 OF SAN Francisco, which is a rather nice way to be known in restaurant circles. It attracts an interesting crowd of intellectuals, as does 21, and it does well by them, as does 21. The Blue Fox also, in a macabre way, boasts that it is opposite the city morgue if that sort of proximity has a titillating effect on you.

While the menu here is international, there is a definite leaning toward Italian dishes—*scampi, vitello tonnato,* stuffed *lasagne, tortellini,* and so forth.

The wine list properly features the better California wines, but is also abundant in wines from Burgundy, Bordeaux, the Rhine and Moselle valleys, and Italy. This is one of our country's better restaurants and should not be missed when you visit San Francisco.

Chasen's

9039 BEVERLY BOULEVARD
LOS ANGELES, CALIFORNIA

Proprietor: *Dave Chasen*
Maître d'Hôtel: *Louis Bianco*
Chef: *David Nisi*

I F YOU'RE GRAYING AT THE TEMPLES AND balding at the forehead, you'll probably remember one of the great entertainers of history, Joe Cook. Joe had one of the funniest vaudeville acts of all time, "The Four Hawaiians," and also played in some highly successful revues in New York and on the road. He was one of the first performers, along with the zany Ted Healy, to have stooges in his act. Joe's chief stooge was an actor and comedian called Dave Chasen. Dave had been playing in vaudeville and on the legitimate stage for some years before Joe encountered him and put him in the act. One bit made Dave famous. It is impossible to describe, as all he did was to wave his hand slowly across his face while smiling puckishly at the audience.

When Joe was playing in New York, and his stint was finished at night, he would drive to his rather fantastic home in Lake Hopatcong, New Jersey. There the show went on, far into the night or, more accurately, into the morning. Dave would go out with him. So, frequently, would Ed McNamara, known in New York stage and intellectual circles as "the Singing Cop"; Harold Ross, editor of *The New Yorker*; Franklin P. Adams, the FPA of columnar fame; and others. They would drink at Joe's waggishly decorated bar, eat in his baronial dining room, and be merry. They were served by Joe's then butler, properly clad in knee breeches and silk stockings, Mr. Walter Sweeney of the hilarious vaudeville act "Mr. Duffy and Mr. Sweeney." Mr. Sweeney was no longer welcome on the monopoly stages of Mr. B. F. Keith because his partner, Mr. Duffy, had told off a Memphis audience who was responding to the act's subtle waggery with unusual iciness, by walking to the apron and saying, "I will now sing 'The Holy City' while Mr. Sweeney passes amongst you and beats the bejesus out of you with a baseball bat."

At these gatherings, Ed McNamara and Dave Chasen were the chefs, and extremely effective ones.

Time marches on.

Joe's health started to fail him. Dave's work started to fail with Joe's health. Harold Ross felt that Dave could better his fortunes and benefit mankind by putting his culinary talents to public use. The result was Dave Chasen's Restaurant in Beverly Hills.

Dave's is new as National Institutions go, born 1935, and known then as Southern Pit Barbecue, spareribs 35¢, chile 25¢, all drinks 35¢. Even in this simple state, Dave drew celebrities, Jimmy Stewart, W. C. Fields, Henry Fonda, Spencer Tracy, Nunnally Johnson, and others of the then Hollywood big shots and wags. But spareribs and chile, as a steady diet, can strain the stoutest bonds of friendship, and the faithful after six months or so of throat-searing, began to implore Dave to broaden his food horizons. Maybe he, too, was beginning to tire of his limited fare, or maybe his inherent respect for the duties of friendship asserted itself, but in any event, Dave decided to blossom out, and in a really heroic manner. He started with steaks flown from New York, trout from Colorado, pompano from Florida, shrimp from New Orleans, salmon from Canada, and oysters from Baltimore. Periodically, Dave adds to these winged delicacies, one of his latest additions being turbot from France.

But with all these fancy pants, lifted-pinky goodies, the most popular, and maybe the best item on the Chasen menu is a number by the elegant name of Hobo Steak. This is a recipe Dave learned in his pre-restaurant days from Ed McNamara, that great favorite of Chasen's good friends Joe Cook and Harold Ross, and from him, in Joe's kitchen at Lake Hopatcong, Dave learned the secret of this wonderful salt-encrusted steak. The recipe for it will be found in the recipe section.

Chasen's is worth going to in order to see celebrities in their native habitat, or to bask in the warmth of Dave's hospitality, but most of all it's worth going to for as good food as there is in all the United States.

Ernie's

MONTGOMERY STREET
SAN FRANCISCO, CALIFORNIA

Owners: *Victor and Roland Gotti, Mario DeFenzi*
Maître d'Hôtel: *Carlo*
Chef: *Raymond Capitan*

RNIE'S CLAIMS TO BE THE OLDEST RESTAU-
rant in San Francisco, but so do several others.
It might also, with some reason, claim to be the
best. But as both claims must necessarily be
contentious let's settle, in this report, for the
facts that it is very old, very attractive, and very
good indeed.

Ernie's is in an old part of the city, and in a building which has its
memories, but there's nothing creaky about it, nor anything frayed or
threadbare about its decor. It was refurbished and redecorated a few
years ago in authentic, well-done Victorian style, and its brocaded wall-
paper, heavy crystal, Turkish carpets, open fireplace, oil paintings and
bric-a-brac, redolent of the champagne days of the bonanzas, make a
soothing and superb setting for superb food.

The owners, maître d'hôtel, and chef are Italian or of Italian descent,
and many of the specialties of the house are also of Italian heritage.
But all Italian restaurateurs of long experience understand French cooking as well as Italian, and the two schools meet amiably, in an irresistible harmony of flavor and aroma, in the kitchens of all really

great Italian restaurants. And Ernie's is really great. In deference to the nationality of the owners and chef, you'd probably do well to start your meal at Ernie's with an Italian specialty.

If you ask Victor or Mario, they'll probably suggest *Tortellini alla Romana,* a *pasta* that's brought to the very brink of being *too* rich, but blessedly doesn't go over.

Entrées of an exalted nature are *Tournedos* Rossini, Chateaubriand Richelieu, Cornish Hen *à l'Orange,* Breast of Capon with a rich *périgourdine* sauce of *foie gras* and truffles. Somewhat on the simpler side are Frog's Legs *Provençal,* and San Francisco's own beloved abalone.

Even salad gets something of the maestro touch at Ernie's, as it receives separate billing on the menu, is of good greens without intruding radishes or other unworthy entries, and is mixed deftly at your table. For dessert, you could do worse to close, as you opened, on an Italian note, and have wonderfully good, wonderfully light, heroically beaten *Zabaglione,* an Ernie specialty. And at the very end, *caffé espresso,* naturally.

Ernie's wine list is excellent, replete with the proper Burgundies, Bordeaux, champagnes, and Italian Chiantis, Orvietos, Barolos, and Soaves. But Ernie's properly stocks superb California wines and it's a rather nice and polite gesture to look at this section of the wine list when you visit there. Incidentally, it's open only for dinner.

Fleur de Lys

777 SUTTER STREET
SAN FRANCISCO, CALIFORNIA

Owners: *Robert and Chérie Charles*
Assistant Manager: *Maurice Amzallag*

IF THE FLEUR DE LYS WERE LESS GOOD, IT would be a brash upstart, for it is already mentioned in the same breath with the venerable greats among San Francisco restaurants, with Jack's, and the Palace, and Ernie's, and Amelio's. But it happens to be very good indeed, and happens also to belong in that same breath.

The proprietors of the Fleur de Lys are not long out of France and the restaurant they ran there in a château above Nice. They came to the United States on a visit, went to Dallas, to New Orleans, to Los Angeles, to San Francisco—and that was the end of the visit.

They first opened a tiny restaurant in the small California town of San Anselmo. While the townsfolk were a bit startled to find suddenly an authentic corner of France in their midst, they responded hospitably, first, and enthusiastically, second. Soon, more than townsfolk were responding and the tiny corner of France became sadly inadequate. The decision to move was made, and the lavish Fleur de Lys is the result.

It is as truly French as any restaurant in the United States, richly French, elegantly French. The linen, china, silver are superb, the decor rich but soothing. These are all nice things to have in a restaurant, but

actually, all that really counts is what comes out of the kitchen and the wine cellar; and what comes out of the Fleur de Lys kitchen and wine cellar is a series of minor miracles.

While M. Charles is perfectly capable of being his own chef (as are the owners of all really fine restaurants) he does have an accomplished artist in the kitchen, from France naturally. The French dishes you would expect, from *Soupe à l'Oignon* to *Soufflé aux Liqueurs,* are on the menu. But if you want to bring the light of gladness to the eyes of both M. and Mme. Charles, you will order *Délices d'Escargots, Suprême de Volaille, Tournedos au Poivre,* or *Grenadin de Veau.*

The Fleur de Lys wine cellar is not vast, but it's very sagely chosen. There are the usual fine Burgundies and Bordeaux, the Alsatians and the Beaujolais, and the champagnes. But there are also some excellent, and in this country rather rare, wines from the Loire Valley—Anjou, Vouvray, Sancerre, and Grand Saumur. And there is an enticing list of California wines, as there should be.

The bar is extremely attractive; and—a delightful feature of it to those who have stayed at the Hotel Raphael in Paris—it was formerly presided over by Maurice, the handsome, courteous, and deft entrepreneur who used to conduct the enchanting little bar at the Raphael. Maurice has now moved from behind the bar to the more exalted position of maître. But he still sees to it that his old friends are taken care of at the bar, and that they are reminded of pleasant days at the Raphael.

Jack's Restaurant

615 SACRAMENTO STREET
SAN FRANCISCO, CALIFORNIA

Owners: *Michel, Paul and Emile Redinger*
Maître d'Hôtel: *Paul*
Chefs: *Otto Hurter and August Zipper*

T HIS VENERABLE ESTABLISHMENT IS ONE OF the few surviving and still-flourishing restaurants that originally established San Francisco's reputation as the only center of civilized eating west of the Mississippi. Now Los Angeles is putting up a stiff challenge for the honors, but Jack's, at least, hasn't slipped from its ancient excellence. It is still doing business at the old stand, and business is good. The premises are mellowed and stained by time, with a certain serene and established look which to the dedicated gastronome is more beautiful than the most fashionable orchid-and-chrome decor.

Jack's is filled, especially at luncheon, with well-groomed gentlemen who have offices in the financial district downtown. Each has his favorite waiter and table and seems to enjoy life with the leisurely appreciation of his French or English counterpart. It is customary here to take a couple of hours for the midday meal, which means a prelude of tingling icy martinis, three or four slowly prepared and well-served courses, and a bottle of wine.

French cooking is supposed to be the house specialty, but the menu is dominated by strong California influences. West Coast crab legs, for instance, are offered in several delectable styles—with cocktail sauce, *à la* Newburg, sautéed with *sauce béarnaise,* or the way which I can recommend most highly, boiled in the shell, cracked for easy eating, and served cold with plenty of thick, creamy mayonnaise. Jack's has the old-fashioned touch with other familiar favorites like local sand dabs fried in butter, Rex sole *meunière,* Alaska cod with boiled new potatoes, grilled rump steak and a luscious club steak with beef marrow sauce.

The owners, the Redingers, are particularly proud of certain dishes with which Jack's has been identified since the late years of the last century—Chicken *Sauté à la* Jack's, with mushrooms and artichokes; Frog's Legs *Sauté à Sec* or *à la Poulette,* Filet of Sole *à la* Marguery and that special delight of blue-eyed blondes—Sweetbreads *Sauté* with Mushrooms, or Broiled on Toast.

La Rue

8631 SUNSET BOULEVARD
BEVERLY HILLS, CALIFORNIA

Owners: *Bruno Petoletti and Orlando Figini*
Maître d'Hôtel: *Bill Prause*
Chef: *Orlando*

SEVERAL YEARS AGO, A FRENCH FRIEND OF mine opened a restaurant in New York and on opening night said proudly to me, "This is the only French restaurant in New York that doesn't have a single Italian in the kitchen."

This might have been commendable chauvinism, if chauvinism ever is commendable, but it was bad restauranteuring, for within a year the place folded. MORAL: Don't start a French restaurant without an Italian in the kitchen.

One of the finest French restaurants in the United States has followed this precept so meticulously that it is also one of the most successful restaurants in the country. It not only has Italians in the kitchen, but Italians in the dining room, at the bar, and in ownership. It also will, if properly approached, gleefully bootleg a small Italian menu to you in place of the more ostentatious, regular French menu.

The name of the restaurant is La Rue, on Sunset Boulevard, in Beverly Hills, California. The owners are Bruno Petoletti and Orlando Figini, two restaurateurs of long experience in Italy, France, England, New York and points west. Bruno, a tall, lean, jovial type, presides in

[305]

the dining room, and his equal partner, Orlando, reigns in the kitchen. La Rue has not attained the national prominence that Romanoff's and Dave Chasen's have, but it is a pet, perhaps *the* pet, of Beverly Hills connoisseurs and knowing visitors to Beverly Hills. It is quieter than its more illustrious competitors but caters to just as many celebrities.

You enter La Rue through the bar, an attractive one, and you might choose to eat at one of the six tables in the bar. But you would be more likely to go up the three steps into the elegant, but restful, main dining room. You sense, when you enter it, that you are going to eat well.

The last time I ate (well) in La Rue, I first stopped at the bar and had two absolutely perfect martinis. (NOTE: don't let yourself be cowed by the propaganda that the martini destroys all sense of taste for food and wine that are to follow. Made properly dry, it titilates the palate and improves the taste, or at least the enjoyment, of good, not too rich food, and good, not sweet wines.)

While at the bar, I consulted with Bruno about the meal. This was a two-menu consultation, the traditional French menu, and the more-or-less surreptitious Italian menu. From this consultation evolved the meal I had in the main dining room, which I happen to prefer to the bar. It started with *lasagne* as the first course, a feather-light *pasta,* stuffed delicately with minced chicken, bathed gently in double-strength chicken broth, and snowed lightly with true Parmesan cheese, imported from Parma.

The main course was authentically French—Capon *à la Fine Champagne La Rue.* Into the preparation of the capon had gone heavy cream, sweet butter, fresh mushrooms, celery, onions, bay leaves, brandy, Worcestershire, salt and pepper. Luckily, dandelion salad was in season, so I had that; then another specialty of the house, *Poire Farcie Maison,* or stuffed pear, or pear treated rather magically with candied marrons, vanilla ice cream, egg yolks, sugar, Marsala wine, whipped cream, anisette, brandy, vanilla, shredded sweet chocolate. Had enough? Well, so had I, almost. Except for a beautiful black and strong espresso coffee; and the wines; and the liqueur; and the cigar.

With the *lasagne,* I had a genial Soave, perhaps the most pleasant of all Italian white wines. With the capon, that greatest of all white wines, Montrachet (1952), seemed practically compulsory. And with the coffee and a Larranaga cigar, I had my favorite brandy, a Marc de Bourgogne, although most people, I think, would have preferred a good cognac, and rightly so.

By the time all this was consumed and appreciated, La Rue had thinned out a bit, and Bruno had time to relax and chat. We talked about his days on the Italian Line and in New York, about his friends Gene of Leone's, Tony Gugnoni of San Marino, Pietro Sacco of Villa Pierre, in Glen Cove, Long Island, Mario and Rita of Mont d'Or in Smithtown, also Long Island, Alex Hounie and Roger Parizot of Chateaubriand, Guiseppe Cipriani of Harry's Bar in Venice, and Nino of Nino's in Rome.

Bruno had a cognac and I had another marc and another espresso. I left well fed, content, and clear enough of faculty to realize that La Rue is one of the fine and gracious restaurants of the United States today. If you find yourself in the Los Angeles area, visit it.

Mario's

4300 LEMMON AVENUE
DALLAS, TEXAS

Proprietor: *Mrs. Christine Vaccaro*
Maître d'Hôtel and Chef: *Dominick Russo*

DALLAS IS ONE OF THE MOST SOPHISTICATED and exciting towns in the whole United States, proud of its economic vitality, commendable for its cultural achievements. As such, it should have many outstanding restaurants. But let's face it, it does not.

Famous Neiman-Marcus has a good place in its Zodiac Room, but this attractive and excellent dining room is open only for lunch except on Thursday, Dallas' shopping evening. Arthur's is a good place, Old Warsaw is superb; and ranking up with it is Mario's.

Mario's, being in the heart of Texas cattle-land, features steak in its manifold forms; sirloin, chateaubriand, filet mignon, ground. And the steak is New York cut, not the pancake-flat, too-fresh beef you usually get in Texas. It also has the traditional chops, sweetbreads, ham, rock Cornish hen, and chicken. But Mario's is especially proud of its authentic Italian dishes, and they're here in all their tantalizing aroma of garlic, olive oil, tomato paste, and freshly ground Parmesan cheese. You can, for instance, start Italian and finish Italian; *Lasagne,* Shrimp Mario with garlic and lemon, Chicken Tetrazzini, *Scaloppine* with

[3 0 8]

mozzarella and *prosciutto, Zabaglione,* and *caffé espresso.* Each of these has many Italian alternates . . . and there are always spaghetti and noodles in their infinite and infinitely pleasing variety.

There is no wine list at Mario's, but you can get good Italian wine, some imported, some Californian. It is not open for lunch, only for dinner.

The Old Warsaw

3914 CEDAR SPRINGS
DALLAS, TEXAS

Proprietor: *Stanislaw A. Slawik*
Maître d'Hôtel: *Ignatius Urbanek*
Chef: *George Patry*

BEFORE THE SECOND WORLD WAR, THERE was a young student of law and economics at the University of Cracow in Poland named Stanislaw Slawik. At the same time, there was a beautiful young actress on the Polish stage in Warsaw named Janina Wilcz. The actress went to Paris and attended the Sorbonne while appearing on the Parisian stage. The young law and economics student, after the war broke out and Poland fell, found himself in London, in the Polish Government-in-Exile. In 1941, he was sent by that Government-in-Exile to the Polish Embassy in Washington and later to the Polish Consulate in New York.

Along the line and the years, the law and economics student and the beautiful young actress met and were married, and settled in New York. The Polish Consulate, as are all consulates, was a rather gay place, accustomed to fine eating and drinking, to caviar and champagne, to parties and receptions, to entertaining and being entertained. It was supposed to reflect the doings at court in the old Poland, and indeed it did. But there came the day when Poland fell to the Communists, and the United States fell out with the Communists, and the days of old Poland and the old court doings were no longer in favor.

Stanislaw Slawik and his wife were, to put it bluntly, out of work. To two such dashing and resourceful people this was not altogether a disaster. They dug in their pockets and bought a somewhat battered jalopy, decided to head west from New York, and since it was winter and rather bitter, to head west by way of the South. They got as far as Dallas, Texas, where the jalopy broke down. Broke down is something of an understatement. It expired. Forced to stay in Dallas for a period, and having friends there, they got around enough to realize this was the place they were seeking, the place in which they wanted to settle down and live.

In their various activities, they had learned how to entertain, how to appreciate and prepare fine food, and how to know the good wines of the world. It was a fairly natural step, therefore, for them to go into the restaurant business, especially as good friends urged them to do exactly this. They found a sort of funny little Mexican restaurant, and with the financial help of good and generous friends took it over. When they did, it ceased to be a funny little Mexican restaurant and became, appropriately, an unfunny Polish restaurant. And while the accent is Polish, the food and the wine are quite definitely French, as is the official name, *La Vieille Varsovie*.

At that time, while Dallas was not altogether a raw-boned, yippee Texas town, and while it was most definitely emerging into a center of wealth and culture, it was not wholly prepared for the full treatment in French food and wine. Stanislaw had to pioneer in introducing his wine cellar to Dallas. Incidentally, wine cellars in Texas have to be street-floor affairs, because if you dig a cellar it is likely to be filled with water or oil before you can occupy it. So the cellar at the Old Warsaw is actually a most attractive private dining room. But when it was opened, it was only a laughing matter. The wise ones of Dallas predicted that this poor, misguided chap from overseas would be out of business in six months. That was ten years ago.

Stanislaw Slawik also introduced *escargots* to Dallas, which was the greatest act of courage since the defense of the Alamo. At first he had to give them away as a nameless hors d'oeuvre, detaching them from their shells and serving them on a piece of bread, and never mentioning the horrid word snails. Today he is serving more than a hundred dozen a week.

He also serves game imported from Europe, grouse, wild duck, pheasant and partridge, and sea food imported from Long Island and New England. The importation is done by plane, now by jet, at three hours from New York. He is an acknowledged expert on wine, a Chevalier of the Confrérie du Tastevin, and his wine cellar reflects his knowledge and his taste.

Texas law, fatuously, forbids the serving of hard liquor publicly. Clubs can serve it but restaurants cannot. The Old Warsaw respectably and legally gets around this prohibition by having a separate room which is a club and which you can join even as a visitor to Texas. The initiation fee is painless, and the drinks, including a beautifully cold and dry martini, are expertly made by a former Polish judge.

Perino's

4101 WILSHIRE BOULEVARD
LOS ANGELES, CALIFORNIA

Proprietor: *Alexander B. Perino*
Chef: *Attilio Balzano*

IF YOU WERE TO COME OUT WITH THE FLAT statement that food in Los Angeles is better than food in San Francisco, you would not only be hunted down and despatched by an angry posse of San Franciscans, but would be looked upon generally as the kind of idiot who would say that food in Baton Rouge is better than food in New Orleans. Not wishing either fate, we'll simply suggest that the theory can be entertained, if not embraced, that the Los Angeles area may very well have better restaurants than San Francisco. Submitted as evidence are these names: Chasen's, Romanoff's, La Rue, Scandia, Bel Air Hotel . . . and Perino's.

Any city which contains a restaurant of the stature of Perino's can claim to have reached maturity in the world of gastronomy. Its most enthusiastic regular patrons insist that it is *the* best restaurant in the United States. That's commendable as loyalty, but dubious as fact. But it is high praise indeed to be able to say that such acclaim, while probably overblown, is not ludicrous.

Perino's is very much on the elegant side, in appearance, in appointments and in service. As you would expect from its combination of virtues it is also very much on the expensive side.

[313]

One Perino aficionado (one of those, incidentally, who insist it is the best restaurant in the United States), when asked in what Perino's specialized, replied with praiseworthy objectivity, "They specialize in specialties." But such an enthusiast is inclined to go a bit ecstatic when he lovingly describes to you the tenderloin of beef stuffed richly with *pâté de foie gras*; the filet of saddle of baby lamb, really infant, cooked to a babyish pink, and served with potatoes *Boulangère* and *sauce béarnaise;* the pheasant cooked slowly in a bath of chartreuse; and the *pastina all'uova,* which is chicken broth *doublé* into which *pasta* the size of tapioca is mixed, and an egg yolk the size of an egg yolk is whipped.

Perino himself is a handsome man, with a flashing Italian smile and a puckish sense of humor. He is a North Italian village boy who has come a long way, just about to the top of the list as far as restaurants west of the Mississippi are concerned, and a person respected and liked by the great of the Southern California area, movie and "Old California" types alike.

Old hands at Perino's say the maestro somehow manages to see, and approve, *every* dish which comes from his kitchen; if you watch you will notice him softly telling a waiter to use a different spoon for serving, or changing the decor of a silver platter of Filet of Rex Sole Doria.

Perino is a restaurateur of the old school; that is, he is charming at the welcoming door, and gracious in the dining room as a host and maître; yet he considers his real work to lie in the kitchen. He hovers over his stock pots and his stoves, and, each day, he visits his suppliers not only of meats, but even of such apparently mundane things as vegetables and salad greens. It wouldn't seem that there could be much difference in such foods, especially when the market is meticulously chosen in the first place. But there is; and it takes great knowledge and experience to perceive that difference by the feel and look of a head of lettuce, or the crumbling of a pinch of fat, or the marbling of a piece of beef.

[3 1 4]

Perino's chef is Attilio Balzano, who has been with him since the place opened in 1932.

Perino hates to close the restaurant and as a consequence the place stays open seven days a week.

As the dry martini seems to have become America's national drink, it perhaps is appropriate to comment here that Tony Cadero, Perino's head bartender, makes as good a one as you'll find across the land. He uses French vermouth, naturally, and an English pot still gin, and serves the drink in an exquisitely thin blue-stemmed glass custom-made for Perino's.

"The ice is the most important thing in a martini," says Tony. "Ice picks up odors. Ice from the average home refrigerator is strong enough to kill a superior vermouth. My ice comes from a firm which delivers it freshly made each day, and directly to the bar; it never sees the kitchen. Even so, I taste a bit every day to make sure."

As Perino's clientele is cosmopolitan, so is its menu. He draws freely on the French, Italian, Swiss and, in the area of broiled meats, even on the English tradition.

There are only two things which he cannot do. The first is to use frozen food. His kitchen literally never uses frozen items. If a food cannot be had fresh, Mr. Perino believes it should not be had at all. Nor can he tolerate the extravagant use of garlic. Naturally, there is garlic in the kitchen, but it is used sparingly and reluctantly.

Scandia

9040 SUNSET BOULEVARD
HOLLYWOOD, CALIFORNIA

Proprietor: *Kenneth Hansen*
Maître d'Hôtel: *Fred Christiansen*
Chef: *George Peterzen*

WE'VE ALL BECOME RECONCILED TO THE FACT that *anything* can be found in the Hollywood area, including one of the finest Scandinavian restaurants anywhere, including Scandinavia. This particular Hollywood production is the Scandia, located, appropriately, on the fabulous stretch of Sunset Boulevard called the Strip.

The Scandia serves truly Swedish food (which is among the best in the world), not an Americanized version of it. But Swedish food is not so exotic that one has to acquire a taste for it, on the contrary, it's almost always love at first meeting. It is almost compulsory that the first meeting should be with *Smörrebröd*. You can choose *Leverpostej* (Danish liver *pâté*), Icelandic herring with sour cream, Danish open-faced sandwiches, smoked salmon on French bread with scrambled egg, or any of a few dozen other appetizers. But you'd find it more interesting if you could persuade Ken Hansen, the owner, or one of the waiters, to make up a selection for you, and a quite wondrous selection it will turn out to be.

Just as the *Smörrebröd* is almost compulsory, so are the drinks

[3 1 6]

which accompany it; aquavit and beer—not aquavit *or* beer, but aquavit *and* beer.

In the regular section of the menu, you will, of course, find some good old American favorites; Eggs Benedict, whole live lobster, ham and eggs, fresh cracked crab, grilled hamburger, sirloin steak, roast beef.

But there are also some stalwart Scandinavian dishes such as *Frickadeller* (Danish meat balls with spiced red cabbage), Filet of Veal Oscar (garnished with asparagus, crab legs, *sauce béarnaise*), Swedish *Biff Lindstrom.*

If you're still game and conscious, there are some wonderful Scandinavian desserts to send you blissfully out into the balmy air of southern California; *Aeblekage Med Floedeskum* (Danish apple cake—anybody knows *that*), *pannekager* (Danish pancakes with strawberry jam), cheese cake with lingonberries.

Just to remind you that you're in Hollywood, you'll find a pair of binoculars on your table. For what? Well, the day's menu is written on a blackboard hanging on the wall, and the binoculars are for those with weak eyes or weak resistance to gadgetry, to view it. That Hollywood environment can do things even to the imperturbable Scandies.

Trader Vic's

20 COSMO PLACE
SAN FRANCISCO, CALIFORNIA

Proprietor: *Victor Bergeron*
Maître d'Hôtel: *Alex Kaluzhny*

NTIL ABOUT TWENTY-FIVE YEARS AGO, THERE was no such thing as an "island" restaurant in the United States. There were plenty of Chinese, and in New York and San Francisco, one or two Japanese, restaurants, but no place that served the exotic dishes of the islands of the South Pacific. Even most of the Chinese restaurants were spurious, striving for oriental mystery with hideous combinations of lacquer, bamboo and beads, and covering a total ignorance of true Chinese cooking with strictly American inventions such as chow mein and chop suey.

The invasion of the United States by Polynesia and the other South Sea islands started, appropriately, in Hollywood, when a traveler in the islands, one Don the Beachcomber, opened a garish barn of a place which in its interior expressed all the exquisite taste and authenticity of a set for a poor B movie. There were pine trees with burlap bark, coconuts everywhere, South Sea artifacts, wind machines emulating typhoons, and fake tropical rain pouring down the outside of fake windows. But, strangely enough, the food was not only truly exotic, but good. And the ingeniously contrived, subtly potent rum

[3 1 8]

drinks made the falsest of settings seem enticingly real. Hollywood loved it, and turned out in swarms. All the stars were regular patrons, and each had his own pair of chopsticks, labeled and displayed prominently in a glass case in the middle of the dining room: Clark Gable, Norma Shearer, Lewis Stone, Gloria Swanson, Rod La Roque, Vilma Banky, and all the other reigning stars of the day. Anna May Wong and Sessue Hayakawa alone were missing—probably not impressed. After a while, Hollywood turned to some other fad, and Don turned to greener pastures, Chicago, then Honolulu where he is now.

But in the meantime, several hundred miles to the north in Oakland, a new island restaurant was opened which was not only to grow, and thrive, and expand, but to start a vogue for island food across the country: Trader Vic's. Vic's did not start as a full-blown South Sea island restaurant, but as a small chop, steak and whiskey place. But Vic drew on his background and knowledge of the far reaches of the Pacific, its mores and its foods, and soon converted to the present style of Trader Vic's. The place was a rather dull and arduous drive from San Francisco over the Bay Bridge and through Oakland, but San Franciscans and knowledgeable visitors to San Francisco felt the trip fully worth while, and as Trader Vic's flourished its fame spread. It probably was inevitable that Vic himself would cross the Bay Bridge, and establish in San Francisco, which is what he did; and while there are now several restaurants run or inspired by Trader Vic's, the San Francisco place is the real, the true, and the headquarters of the great man himself.

Trader Vic's lure is three-fold; exotic atmosphere, superb tropical food, and enticing island drinks, mostly with a rum base. Look out for those drinks; they taste so good, and they look so innocent, but their effect can be as subtle as a blackjack or a set of brass knuckles. There are over ninety different ones on the drink list, bearing such names as Zombie, Missionary's Downfall, Gun Club Punch, Doctor Funk of Tahiti, Navy Grog, Tonga, Tahitian Tiara, Kava Bowl. There is also the Scorpion, mysteriously made of a half a dozen different rums, and feigning innocence by bearing a white gardenia. Vic has assembled most of the rums known to man, including Antigua, Demerara, Barbados, Trinidad, Virgin Islands, Puerto Rican, Jamaica, New England, and St. Croix. More conventional liquors and drinks are available of course, bourbon and gin, and Scotch, but who cares?

But you are strongly advised not to get so immersed in the rum drinks that the goodness and flavors of the food elude you. For Trader Vic's is a truly fine restaurant. It is well to start eating with your pre-meal drinks, to nibble away at the fried shrimp or the spareribs, done in a special sauce and charcoal broiled. Or you might want instead, or in addition, Crab *Crêpes* Bengal, or Egg Roll, or Malayan Tidbits (*Rumaki,* Cheese Balls, Curry Puffs); or Bongo Bongo Soup, which is another way of saying Cream of Oyster, or *Kon Tiki Toheroa,* which is another way of saying New Zealand Clam Purée.

While Vic does not do the actual cooking, he has an inventive way with food, and many of the dishes on the menu are his own brain-children, or improvisations made from dishes he encountered out in the islands. Among his own personal favorites are Tahitian Lobster, lobster boiled with herbs and onions, a splash of a hot island sauce a bit like A-1, paprika, green pepper, shallots, parsley, curry and an abundance of fresh butter; Monterey Shrimp, which are shrimp fried in oil, then steamed in a bath of butter, garlic, that same A-1-like sauce, French vermouth, salt and freshly ground pepper; and Chicken-in-Coconut, which is a highly complicated concoction involving diced chicken adorned with and immersed in curry; green peppers, peeled tomatoes, sliced pineapple, onion, minced garlic, ginger root, and several other ingredients.

Trader Vic's menu is large and varied. You can get island food, American food, and Chinese food. You can also get ham and eggs, but even these show an island influence, because they're cooked with pineapple and bananas. When you go to Trader Vic's, phone as far ahead as possible for reservations as a large number of other people will have the same idea for dinner. Read, study, and enjoy the menu, but before you finally order have a friendly, helpful chat with the waiter or captain, and heed his advice.

The Zodiac Room

NEIMAN-MARCUS
DALLAS, TEXAS

Director: *Helen L. Corbitt*

S TANLEY MARCUS HAS A VERY SIMPLE PHI-losophy of storekeeping; fill the place with the best of everything from all over the world and wait calmly for the customers to swarm in.

The Zodiac Room in his Neiman-Marcus store in Dallas is not the best restaurant in the world. It probably isn't even the best in Dallas, but it is almost certainly the best restaurant to be found in a department store, anywhere, and as such doesn't depart too much from the Stanley Marcus philosophy.

The Zodiac Room is open during store hours only, which means it is open for lunch and tea six days a week and for dinner on Thursday evening, which is shopping night in Dallas. As would be expected of a department store restaurant, its clientele at lunch is made up to a great extent of women, but the neighborhood businessmen are also to be seen in considerable numbers and the menu most definitely does not ignore them. There are veal chops and breast of turkey and broiled baby lamb chops and steak and ham and king crab, among other things, and there's a whole page full of salads and sandwiches on the menu. There is even a salad beckoning particularly to the masculine trade called "My Man's Salad," made of thick tomato slices, hearts of

[321]

romaine and julienne ham and chicken, Roquefort cheese and clear French dressing. Most of the salads, proper to their Texas setting, are heroic in size and deleterious to wasp waists. The Thursday-night dinner has its own menu and is not just a luncheon served in the evening. It features such dinner specialties as Roasted Sirloin with Stroganoff Sauce, Veal Cutlet filled with *mozzarella* and *prosciutto,* Broiled Baby Lobster Tails, Roasted Leg of Spring Lamb, etc.

No public restaurant is allowed to serve spirits in Texas, but the Zodiac Room has been ingenious in the drinks they can serve within the law. The favorite cocktail is a champagne cocktail made with Veuve Clicquot, Champagne Krug and Almadén Rosé champagne. Other wines are available as are imported Heineken's and Tuborg beer, Bass ale and Guinness stout. Black Velvet is quite a favorite here, too, made in the traditional way of half champagne and half Guinness stout.

The Zodiac Room is under the direction of Miss Helen Corbitt, who is one of the famous personages in the field of foods in the United States. Before coming to Neiman-Marcus she was manager of the Houston Country Club, director of foods at Joske's of Houston, and executive manager of the Food Department at the Driskill Hotel in Austin. She writes a bi-weekly food column for the Houston *Post* and is also the author of a cookbook which is shamelessly displayed throughout Neiman-Marcus.

The Zodiac Room is extremely attractive, the service is excellent and going there one has the added incentive of being able to travel up to it (it's on the fifth floor) and down from it by the escalator that runs through the center of the store and from which you get an enticing and unobstructed view of the superior merchandise from all over the world which has been gathered in this Texan oasis of good taste.

A Few

Remarks

on

Cookbooks

T HE WORLD OF EATING AND DRINKING, OF food and wine, is really two worlds, one a world of fact, one a world of mythology. We have treated some of the myths in the chapter on wines and in other sections of this book, and we would now like to mention another more-or-less accepted myth, the myth that popular cookbooks are worthless.

It so happens that they are not, and that on the contrary, they are not only useful, but for the most part extremely good.

One of the most maligned of these books, perhaps because it is the most popular of them all, is the Boston Cooking School cookbook, which is usually mis-called "the Fannie Farmer Cookbook." The correct name is *The Boston Cooking School Cook Book* by Fannie Farmer. Fannie Farmer is no longer with us, but the men and women who put the book together and who have periodically revised it and brought it up to date are both familiar and effective with their pots and pans and measuring implements, and their effort is decidedly to be recommended, especially to the neophyte at cooking.

The Boston Cooking School Cook Book is not the only unfairly demeaned cookbook. There is, for instance, Mrs. Irma S. Rombauer's *The Joy of Cooking,* which has sold upwards of two million copies, and which has not only delighted those millions with its sprightly writing, but has helped them through the kitchen mazes.

If paying for cookbooks is against your thrifty nature, you can get a number of effective ones simply for the asking. There are the commercial cookbooks put out by the big food companies such as General Mills, General Foods, H. J. Heinz and Company, the Borden Company, and the others whose coupons are to be found in every issue of every women's magazine. One great contribution these companies have made to cooking literature is to standardize measurements. Before the advent of their aseptic and grimly businesslike kitchens, measurement directions were blithe and airy . . . "a pinch of salt," "a dash of pepper," "season to taste," "a teaspoonful," "a cupful," and so forth. As pinches, and spoons, and cups varied in size, finished dishes also varied. The food companies, by determining that a spoonful meant a level filling of a standard measuring spoon, and a cupful meant eight fluid ounces, and a pinch or dash meant less than one-eighth of a teaspoon, and a tablespoon meant three teaspoons, brought more order and certainty into the kitchen.

The paperback publishers have also contributed nobly to aiding the aspiring cook. Their contribution is not so much in the reprinting of hard-covered cookbooks, as in the origination of books of their own. The most famous and best-selling of these is *The Pocket Cookbook* by Elizabeth Woody, who as head of one of the commercial kitchens probably contributed more than anyone else to the standardization of measurements. There is also *The Meat Cookbook* in a paperback edition, and others which you will find at your neighborhood drugstore.

Probably the greatest cookbook in the world today, put together by the greatest chef of modern times, is *A Guide to Modern Cookery* by the incomparable Escoffier. Escoffier died in 1935, but his awesome reputation lives on. He was one of the most inventive chefs of all time and was reported to have created at least one new dish a day. He served in some of the greatest eating establishments in France, then as chef to Kaiser Wilhelm of Germany on the Kaiser's yacht. He was lured to London by his friend César Ritz, who managed the Savoy Hotel, which was at that time the finest hotel in London and one of the finest in the whole world. After a few years, Escoffier retired from the Savoy and returned to France, but emerged from retirement to come to New York to consult with Charles Pierre, another old friend, who was engrossed in plans for the new Hotel Pierre, construction of which was starting at 61st Street and Fifth Avenue. Escoffier never really served as chef at the Pierre but did act as consultant on the food problems of the hotel, and was instrumental in getting his pupil Scotto to open as chef. His book is in the classic tradition of French cooking and is not for the bride who is twittering through the preparation of her first meals in her new home. But it is a book that every conscientious cook should have eventually for reference and inspiration. It is available in English as well as in French, and any respectable bookstore will be able to get it for you.

Of course there is practically no limit to the number or varieties of cookbooks, and you could very well go both broke and mad if you attempted to keep up with their output. The New York Public Library, for instance, has the appalling total of some 2,500 different titles under the heading of books on food; and *Publishers' Weekly* estimates that a couple of hundred new ones are published each year. There are regional cookbooks, specialty cookbooks, occasion cookbooks, and national cookbooks.

In the regional field there are, to name a very few, *The New Orleans Cookbook, The Virginia Cookbook, Two Hundred Years of Charleston Cooking, The Thomas Jefferson Cookbook.*

In specialties, there are, again to name just a few, *The Omelette Cookbook, The Wine Cookbook, Soups, Salads and Desserts, The Modern Meat Cookbook, The Derrydale Cookbook of Fish and Game* (two volumes, elaborately boxed, and very fancy indeed).

In occasion cookbooks there are such items as *June Platt's Party*

Cookbook, The Picnic Cook Book, Cooking for Christmas, Cooking Afloat, The Perfect Hostess Cookbook, and the *Just for Two Cookbook.*

In national cookbooks, you will find, amongst others, *The English Table, La Cuisine d'Aujourdhui, The South American Gentleman's Companion, L'Arte nella Cucina* (Italian) and *The Italian Cookbook.*

Not a cookbook, but perhaps the most inspirational volume ever written about food, is the great classic, *The Physiology of Taste, or Meditations on Transcendental Gastronomy,* by Jean Anthelme Brillat-Savarin. It was written at the time of Washington and Jefferson and Franklin, and deals to quite an extent with Brillat-Savarin's trip to America at that time and his discovery of, among other delicacies, American wild turkey; yet it is still in print today and still a frequently referred-to book on thousands of American bookshelves. There are even books *about* cookbooks, one of the best of which is *Old Cookery Books* by the famous English essayist, William Hazlitt.

So much for cookbooks and the myths that surround them. One other myth with considerable circulation is that a great chef will adamantly refuse to give you any of his prize recipes; or if he does give it to you, he will slyly leave out an important ingredient, or change a vital measurement so that your result will be inferior to his. Your result probably *will* be inferior to his, but it will not be because he has resorted to chicanery. Some chefs simply cannot define or put on paper the precise way they cook a given dish; much of it is, with them, in the realm of instinct and they find it impossible to encompass it in mere words. It is a little like the situation in which Fats Waller, the famous jazzman, found himself when a befuddled lady asked him, "Mr. Waller, won't you please tell me what jazz is?" and Fats gave her the classic answer, "Lady, if you have to ask, you'll never know."

Some chefs feel that way about cooking, so it is almost impossible for them to put a recipe into words, oral or written. But most great chefs are invariably happy and proud to *try* to tell you how they make their most cherished dishes.

Our research for this book took us into many kitchens and we came

to know many chefs. We asked them to entrust us with a few of their favorite recipes. A selection of these recipes follows.

We might say that it is customary, in compiling recipes, to test each one by preparing the dish in advance, carefully following the directions and correcting any errors that are found. The writers of this compendium avoided this tedious procedure. Apart from the difficulties involved, we felt that the recipes were as accurate as were needed under the circumstances. Moreover, we are convinced that cooking is not an exact science but an art—with all the freedom of creation that word implies.

The recipes we have garnered are yours to follow, precisely, if you wish. But it surely will be more fun to change, substitute and add a touch here and there that is distinctively your own. These are not the usual home recipes, but professional cuisine at its most sophisticated. As such, they present a challenge to any real cook, male or female, who loves to adventure in the boundless world of gourmandise.

We hope you will think it worth your while to tackle a few of these fine dishes, complicated or exotic though they may seem. If you do, all we can say is—*"Bonne chance et bon appétit!"*

Recipes
from the
Great
Restaurants

Hors d'Oeuvres

BLUE SPRUCE INN

Shrimp-in-Dill

3 POUNDS FRESH UNSHELLED SHRIMP
2 QUARTS BOILING WATER
1 TABLESPOON SALT
1 CLOVE GARLIC, PEELED, CRUSHED
1 BAY LEAF
3 PEPPERCORNS
1 TEASPOON VINEGAR

Wash shrimp. Put in kettle with the other ingredients. Simmer covered 10 minutes or until tender. Allow to stand in liquid 20 minutes. Shell, strain, saving liquid. Serve surrounded with the following sauce:

[333]

Thicken 2 cups of shrimp liquid with 4 tablespoons flour, stir till smooth. Reduce to half 1 cup dry white wine, add 6 scallions, minced. Add the cream sauce, bring to boil, stirring. Strain and add 8 tablespoons finely chopped dill, season with salt and dry sherry and serve hot.

JOHN BARTRAM HOTEL

French Pâté de Foie Gras

6 OUNCES GOOSE LIVER	SALT AND PEPPER
1 SMALL TRUFFLE	2 PATS BUTTER
¼ CARROT	4 DROPS TABASCO SAUCE
1 PIECE CELERY	1 BAY LEAF
½ SHALLOT	1 EGG YOLK
2 TABLESPOONS WHITE WINE	1 TABLESPOON HEAVY CREAM

Boil the goose liver in goose broth for 15 minutes; remove from pot and dry. Grind goose liver very fine; sauté shallot in butter; add white wine and truffle, carrots, celery, 4 drops of Tabasco sauce, 1 bay leaf, pinch of salt and pepper. Allow to simmer together for 25 minutes. Remove from fire and add heavy cream, yolk of egg and stir. Serve in terrine on ice. *For 1 person.*

LOCKE-OBER

Canapé Martha

¼ POUND FRESH LOBSTER MEAT
1 TABLESPOON BUTTER

1 TEASPOON PAPRIKA

1 OUNCE SHERRY WINE

½ CUP BASIC CREAM SAUCE

1 TABLESPOON GRATED PARMESAN CHEESE

Melt butter in saucepan, add lobster and paprika and cook until lobster is heated through, add sherry wine and cook slowly about 5 minutes. Add cream sauce and stir until mixture is well blended. Place a piece of toast in a heatproof dish and spoon lobster mixture over it. Dust the mixture with grated cheese and place in 450-degree oven until top is well browned. *One portion.*

Cream Sauce

1 TABLESPOON FLOUR

1 TABLESPOON BUTTER

1 CUP SCALDED LIGHT CREAM

Melt butter in a small saucepan, add flour and stir until well blended. Slowly add hot cream and stir briskly until mixture is well blended. Cook very slowly for 5 to 10 minutes stirring intermittently. Strain sauce and use when needed. *Yields 1 cup.*

THE BLUE FOX

Scampi

Cut scampi into five-point stars, then soak in milk for 15 minutes. Take from milk, and drain.

Mix in flour very lightly, and fry in deep fat till they reach golden brown.

Meanwhile, make a sauce—heat ¼ pound butter, and mix with one pint dry white wine. Stir and let wine reduce.

After scampi have been browned, put them in the sauce, add parsley, and let scampi remain in sauce until sauce has penetrated the scampi. Serve with French bread and lemon. *Fifteen individual scampi.*

STOCK YARD INN

Marinated Beef Slices

I POUND SIRLOIN STEAK, COOKED   I OUNCE LEMON JUICE
I ONION, SLICED   I CUP SOUR CREAM
SALT AND PEPPER   LETTUCE

Slice cooked sirloin into julienne strips. Add sliced onion and salt and pepper, to taste. Sprinkle lemon juice over meat mixture and blend in sour cream. Mix well and serve on lettuce leaf.

CHATEAUBRIAND

Escargots Bourguignonne

To make the butter for about 5 dozen *escargots*:

GARLIC, $1\frac{1}{2}$ TO 2 OUNCES
SHALLOTS, I OUNCE
FRESH PARSLEY, I OUNCE
FRESH BUTTER, IO OUNCES

Chop garlic very fine with parsley and shallots. When well chopped, mix well and remove all moisture by squeezing through a linen. Add I ounce of absinthe (Pernod, Ricard or Pec). Salt and pepper to taste. Add the butter and mix well. Let cool.

[336]

Place some of this butter, *first,* deep in the *escargot* shell, then the *escargot* itself that you will have well drained from the can. Place more of the butter till shell is filled. Arrange on its special *escargots* dish, taking care that opening of the shell is on top. Place in hot oven till butter is sizzling. Remove and sprinkle with dry white wine. Serve very hot.

CHASEN'S

Shrimps Maison

Take eight fresh raw jumbo shrimp, shell and split. Sauté in butter. Add touch of garlic and sprinkle with ½ ounce dry white wine. Add cream and glaze under salamander. Serve in china casserole dish. *Serves 2.*

LE CAFÉ CHAMBORD

Coquille

INGREDIENTS: ½ cup each of the following: cooked shrimp, cooked crabmeat, cooked lobster and uncooked scallops. A few mushrooms, shallots, 3 tablespoons white wine, cream sauce, mustard, chives, parsley, salt, pepper and herbs.

Heat buttered pan. Add mushrooms. Fry until they are a golden brown for about 1 minute. Add chopped shallots and white wine. Add all sea-food items, cover pan. Cook for about 2 minutes.

Add cream sauce and cook for 5 minutes. Remove from fire and add ½ teaspoonful of golden mustard with chives and parsley. Also *fines herbes.*

Place in shell or buttered dish and cover with grated cheese. Broil until brown.

[337]

COVENTRY FORGE INN

Pâté Maison

Simmer ½ pound onions and ½ cup chicken fat and ½ cup rich chicken stock until onions are soft and golden in color. Pour onions and cooking liquor over 2 pounds chicken livers and season with a little Parisian spice. Cover kettle and simmer until livers are tender. Drain liver and put through sieve or food blender and add to them 1 cup each heavy cream and sherry in which is dissolved 2 tablespoons cornstarch. Add 3 lightly beaten eggs. Correct seasoning and add finely diced truffles if desired.

Pour *pâté* into well-buttered loaf tins, allow to set, then butter tops to prevent drying. Keep in refrigerator. For a firmer *pâté,* place tins in a water bath and bake in a cool oven until firm. Butter tops. This *pâté* improves if allowed to cure for 4 or 5 days in refrigerator.

MONT d'OR INN

Vitello Tonnato

Place 2-pound leg of veal in a pot, cover with water, 1 glass wine vinegar, 1 onion, 10 cloves and boil for 35 minutes. Let cool in same broth.

Sauce:

1 CAN IMPORTED TUNA FISH
10 FILETS ANCHOVIES
3 TABLESPOONS CAPERS IN VINEGAR

Put everything through a fine sieve. Add mayonnaise to obtain a light, creamy sauce. If too thick add a little cold water and lemon juice. Slice veal very thin, cover with sauce. Serve cold.

PIGALL'S

Escargots Bourguignonne à Ma Façon

12 SNAILS AND 12 LARGE SHELLS
1 CUP SOFT, FRESH BUTTER
2 TABLESPOONS FRESH, FINELY CHOPPED PARSLEY
1 TABLESPOON FRESH, FINELY CHOPPED CHERVIL
1 TINY PINCH TARRAGON
5 CLOVES GARLIC, FINELY CHOPPED AND POUNDED
1½ SHALLOTS, FINELY CHOPPED
1½ TABLESPOONS SALT AND FRESHLY GROUND PEPPER MIXED IN PRO-
    PORTION OF 2½ TO 1 RESPECTIVELY
½ PONY VERY GOOD MARC DE BOURGOGNE
    (IF COGNAC IS SUBSTITUTED, REDUCE AMOUNT BY HALF)
1 TABLESPOON RED BURGUNDY WINE
½ TABLESPOON FRESH LEMON JUICE

Melt butter and add all seasonings. Stir thoroughly with wooden spoon.
When the delicate aroma of the blend becomes noticeable, check one
last time for flavor and add a drop or two of walnut oil for smoothness.
Stuff snails into shells and fill to the brim with sauce. Arrange on snail
plate or *escargotière* and warm in a 325-degree oven for 8 to 10 minutes.

CHARLIE'S CAFÉ EXCEPTIONALE

Chicken Liver Pâté

1 POUND FRESH CHICKEN LIVERS	1 TEASPOON SALT
1 CLOVE GARLIC, DICED	¼ TEASPOON FRESH GROUND
1½ TABLESPOON SLICED ONIONS	BLACK PEPPER
¼ CUP CHICKEN FAT	½ CUP CHICKEN BROTH

Sauté onions and garlic in chicken fat to turn a golden color, then add all the remaining ingredients except the broth.

Sauté the livers until they are cooked through but not brown. Put all through fine food chopper and whip to a smooth paste. If too thick, add chicken broth.

Serve cold with diced onions, and chopped hard-boiled egg and rye melba.

PARK SCHENLEY

Clam Shell Stuffed with Crabmeat

Place 1 pound of fresh crabmeat into a mixing bowl. Dice 4 slices of pullman white bread (remove crust). Add 1 tablespoon of Coleman's dry mustard, a pinch of salt, 2 dashes of Lea and Perrin's sauce and 1 cup of coffee cream. Mix gently and stuff in clam shells. Sprinkle with bread crumbs and dampen with melted butter. Bake 5 to 8 minutes at 350 degrees to golden brown. *Three dozen individual servings.*

THE PUMP ROOM

Canapé Ambassador

I HARD-BOILED EGG	½ GREEN PEPPER
6 FILETS OF ANCHOVIES	I PEELED TOMATO
3 OUNCES OF TUNA FISH	

Chop above ingredients very fine and mix in salad bowl. Take four pieces of toast, place same in *crêpes Suzette* pan. Fry toast in 8 pats of sweet butter, place ingredients on top of toast, cover with 1 tablespoon of Russian dressing, garnish with Lea and Perrin's sauce and serve immediately. *Serves 4.*

GOURMET ROOM

Stuffed Clams

Take a dozen clams, open them, clean well in cold water. Chop them finely and mix with their own juice.

In a saucepan put 3 tablespoons of butter, 1 teaspoon each of shallots and green peppers, chopped very thin, let cook for 2 minutes. Add the chopped clams, cook for 5 minutes, add 3 tablespoons of Chablis wine and a half cup of heavy cream, mix well. When starting to boil, take off the heat, refill the clam shells with this stuffing and serve very hot. Put a pinch of chopped parsley on each filled shell.

COMMANDER'S PALACE

Crab Meat Imperial

1 GREEN PEPPER, FINELY DICED
2 PIMIENTOS, FINELY DICED
1 TABLESPOON ENGLISH MUSTARD
1 TEASPOON SALT
½ TEASPOON WHITE PEPPER
2 WHOLE EGGS
1 CUP MAYONNAISE
3 POUNDS LUMP CRABMEAT

Mix pepper and pimientos, add mustard, salt, white pepper, eggs, and mayonnaise, and mix well. Add crabmeat and mix with fingers so the lumps are not broken. Divide mixture into eight crab shells or casseroles, heaping it in lightly. Top with a little coating of mayonnaise and sprinkle with a little paprika. Bake at 350 degrees for 15 minutes. Serve hot or cold. *Serves 8.*

THE WARWICK

Grilled Tidbit

Mash a canful of sardines and season well with onion, salt and pepper and a *little* lemon juice.

Spread mixture on bacon strips. Roll jelly-roll fashion and broil until crisp. Serve with a cool drink.

GALATOIRE'S

Shrimp Rémoulade Sauce

⅔ CUP OF OLIVE OIL
5 TABLESPOONS CREOLE MUSTARD
1 BUNCH GREEN ONIONS
2 TABLESPOONS PAPRIKA
SALT AND PEPPER
⅓ CUP VINEGAR
1 STALK CELERY
2 CLOVES GARLIC
1 SPRIG PARSLEY

Grind all vegetables very fine, then add the mustard, paprika, salt and pepper. Mix all of these ingredients thoroughly. To this mixture add the vinegar gradually; then add the olive oil.

After the shrimp are boiled and peeled, soak them in this sauce for 3 hours. Shrimp should be served on shredded lettuce with tomatoes as a garnish. *Makes 1 quart.*

THE WARWICK

Lamaze Sauce

For shrimp, lobster, crabmeat, cold fish salads and cold eggs

I PINT OF MAYONNAISE
I PINT OF CHILI SAUCE
½ CUP INDIA RELISH
I CHOPPED HARD-BOILED EGG
I TEASPOON CHOPPED CHIVES
I TABLESPOON PREPARED MUSTARD
SALT
BLACK PEPPER
A-I SAUCE

Pre-chill mayonnaise, chili sauce, relish, chopped egg.
Use well-chilled bowl for mixing.
Mix well in following order:

MAYONNAISE	PREPARED MUSTARD
INDIA RELISH	CHOPPED CHIVES
CHILI SAUCE	HARD-BOILED EGG

Add salt and pepper to taste. Dash of A-I sauce over dressing when serving. *Serves 8.*

NOTE: Lamaze sauce must be kept in refrigerator at all times until served.

THE FORUM OF THE TWELVE CAESARS

Golden Eggs of Crassus

14 EGGS
½ BOX BREAD CRUMBS
2 EGGPLANTS, SLICED IN 1-INCH PIECES
1 POUND LOBSTER MEAT, CHOPPED VERY FINE
12 OUNCES TOMATO PURÉE
2 OUNCES PAPRIKA
3 OUNCES SHERRY
2 OUNCES BUTTER
  SALT
  FLOUR

Boil 12 of the eggs for 3 minutes. Cool and peel. Roll the eggs in flour. Beat remaining 2 eggs. Roll the floured eggs in the beaten eggs and then in bread crumbs. Fry lightly in deep fryer for about 1 minute.

Sauté lobster in butter. Add sherry and tomato purée. Season with salt and paprika and cook slowly for 5 minutes.

Fry eggplant slices until cooked, about 2 to 3 minutes. Cover eggplant with lobster sauce and place eggs upright in the center. Serve at once. *Serves 6.*

THE FOUR SEASONS

Carrot Vichyssoise

5 POTATOES, SLICED
7 LARGE CARROTS, SLICED
2 LARGE LEEKS, SLICED
1½ QUARTS CHICKEN STOCK
1 HAM SHANK

1 TEASPOON SUGAR
1 TABLESPOON
  PINCH PEPPER
1 QUART HEAVY CREAM

Cook vegetables and ham shank in stock until potatoes and carrots are done. Put through blender, season with sugar, salt and pepper. Add cream. Serve very cold with julienne of raw carrots. *Serves 6.*

LA CRÉMAILLÈRE À LA CAMPAGNE

Filets of Pompano Horizon

Take 4 filets of pompano, about 8 ounces each, half a cup of chopped shallots, half a cup of chopped parsley, salt and white pepper to taste, 1 pint of dry French vermouth, 2 cups of bouillon, 8 heads of good-sized mushrooms, one stalk of celery.

Place the filets in a buttered shallow saucepan, cover with the shallots, the parsley, salt and pepper. Add the celery, the vermouth and bouillon. Set it on the fire to boil. Cover with waxed paper. Put into 350-degree oven so it will keep bubbling for 10 minutes.

Now, drain the juice into a deep saucepan and let cook until you have about 2 cups of liquid left. Then add 2 cups of hollandaise sauce, stirring gently on top of the stove, but do not boil. Put the heads of mushrooms, that you have cooked separately with the juice of a lemon and a half a cup of water and a little salt, on top of each filet. Pour the sauce over this and put under the broiler until well browned. Before serving, decorate your platter, dish or saucepan with either crayfish or shrimps. *Serves 4.*

AMBASSADOR INN

Mussels Marinara (Genovese)

Black shell mussels. Clean thoroughly. Steam with olive oil, garlic and parsley. Cooking time about 10 minutes.

THE PATIO

Cucumber and Caviar Rounds

Peel the cucumbers, cut in 1½-inch rounds. Scoop out the center seeds, leaving the sides and bottom much like a basket. Soak in a weak vinegar and salt solution for several hours in the refrigerator. Drain and dry them off. Make a paste consisting of cream cheese and sour cream, add a bit of chopped chives. Fill the cucumber hollows and top each with ¼ teaspoon of caviar.

COPAIN

Periwinkles Provençale

Boil live conch for four hours, remove from shell. Put through grinder. Then finely grind one small, peeled clove of garlic and ½ Spanish onion per conch, lightly sauté. Then mix all ingredients well, sauté them lightly to prevent spoilage. Add juice of ½ lemon, salt and pepper. Bottle. Serve cold with piece of lemon. This will last for a long period under refrigeration.

NOTE: The conch juice can be reduced and used as a soup stock.

Entrées

BLUE SPRUCE INN

Long Island Duckling Bigarade

Roast a 6½-lb. dressed weight Long Island duck for 2 hours in a 450-degree oven.

Strain duckling's roasting stock, completely remove its grease and reduce it over a slow fire until it is very thick.

In order to bring the sauce to its normal consistency, add the juice of 3 oranges and half a lemon per pint of sauce and simmer for 10 minutes. Finish with 2 ounces of Curaçao and small pieces of orange and lemon rind cut finely julienne fashion and scalded previously for 5 minutes.

Cut up duckling into 4 portions, place into individual cassolettes (low open fireproof casseroles) several thin slices of peeled oranges on top, pour good portions of sauce over it, reheat in hot oven and serve in casserole.

JOHN BARTRAM HOTEL

Breast of Guinea Hen, Cumberland

1 2½-POUND GUINEA HEN (BREAST ONLY)	SHALLOTS
2 TABLESPOONS SOUR CREAM	BUTTER
SALT AND PEPPER	VIRGINIA HAM
2 TABLESPOONS FRENCH BRANDY	MUSHROOMS
2 TABLESPOONS WHITE WINE	WHITE GRAPES

Sauté the breast of guinea hen in butter, brown on both sides. Add chopped shallots and allow to simmer for 10 minutes. Add white wine, French brandy, brown sauce, white grapes, sour cream; allow to simmer for 25 minutes. Place a slice of Virginia ham and mushroom caps on top, and allow to simmer for 5 minutes. Serve under bell (glass).

LOCKE-OBER

Coq au Vin (under glass) Bourguignon

2 3-POUND CHICKENS, SPLIT IN FOURS	1 BAY LEAF
½ POUND FRESH MUSHROOMS, SLICED	2 STALKS CELERY, DICED
½ POUND WHITE ONIONS DICED FINELY	1 CARROT, DICED
2 SPRIGS THYME	2 CUPS RED BURGUNDY WINE
1 CLOVE GARLIC, CUT IN HALF	2 TABLESPOONS FLOUR

Put cut chicken in crock. Add garlic, thyme, bay leaf, celery, carrot, and onion with 1 clove. Cover with the red wine and marinate 24 hours at least. Remove chicken and pat dry with clean towel. Sauté chicken in butter until well browned on one side. Turn chicken and add mushrooms. Continue to cook until mushrooms are tender. In another pan, melt 2 tablespoons of butter. Add flour and stir until well blended. Add remaining liquid in crock and simmer until mixture reaches a desired thickness (15 minutes). Strain this sauce over chicken and mushrooms and simmer very slowly (10 minutes) or until chicken is cooked. Place chicken on shirred egg dish and cover with sauce and mushrooms. Sprinkle with chopped parsley. Then place glass bell over and serve.

THE BLUE FOX

Pheasant en plumage (for four)

2 YOUNG, 3½-POUND PHEASANT CHICKENS	I MEDIUM ONION (DICED)
4 BAY LEAVES	3 CUPS RICH CHICKEN BROTH
¼ POUND BUTTER, MELTED	2 DICED CELERY STALKS
2 STEMS ROSEMARY	I PINT BURGUNDY WINE
	SALT AND PEPPER

Singe and clean the pheasants. Rub inside and out with salt and pepper. Brush with melted butter, and place in roasting pan with bay leaves, rosemary, onions, and celery. Bake in hot oven (450 degrees) until birds become golden brown. Reduce heat to 350 degrees. Add chicken stock and wine and cook approximately 45 minutes longer, basting occasionally with butter. When birds are done, remove from roasting pan to serving platter. Blend 3 tablespoons flour in pan drippings to thicken sauce. Serve with wild rice and candied yams.

(The Blue Fox serves this creation on a silver platter, covered with plumage.)

STOCK YARD INN

Stock Yard Inn's Way of Broiling a Steak

Season the steak with freshly ground black pepper and salt, and dip in oil.

Put the steak on broiler (full heat) for 2 minutes on each side. Be sure that all pores are closed. Then turn down fire and broil to the person's taste.

STONEHENGE

Plantain Pancake Flambé à la 'Henge

Split and bake 2 bananas. Dot with butter. Fold same into 2 thin pancakes (*crêpes*). Garnish with strips of bacon and a small segment of fig banana.

Flambé over spirit lamp or Sterno with banana liqueur.

Creamed Chicken Cannelloni au Gratin

1 WHOLE CHICKEN	SALT AND PEPPER
6 MUSHROOMS	1 SMALL GLASS SHERRY WINE
BUTTER	CREAM SAUCE

Boil chicken, mince. Mince and fry mushrooms in butter. Add chicken, salt and pepper to taste. Add sherry. Mix together in regularly prepared cream sauce.

[350]

Hollandaise

3 EGG YOLKS

2 TABLESPOONS CREAM SAUCE

½ POUND BUTTER (MELTED)

SALT

FRESH LEMON JUICE

Beat egg yolks over a hot fire until half cooked. Add melted butter and a pinch of salt, together with cream sauce to prevent curdling. Add fresh lemon juice to taste.

Pancakes

1 EGG

½ CUP FLOUR

1 GLASS MILK

Beat to a smooth batter and fry. Pour very small quantity in the pan and let it run until very thin.

Place creamed chicken in pancake and roll. Cover with hollandaise, sprinkle lightly with Parmesan cheese and place under broiler for a few minutes, until brown.

CHASEN'S

Hobo Steak

2 SIRLOIN STEAKS, CUT 2 INCHES THICK

1 TEASPOON FRESHLY GROUND BLACK PEPPER

4 CUPS SALT

1 CUP WATER (ABOUT)

½ POUND BUTTER

8-12 BREAD SLICES, THINLY CUT

Season steaks with black pepper. Place side by side in large skillet or deep broiler pan with fat edges toward perimeter of pan. Slip 2 lengths of cotton string under each steak (crosswise of steak and dividing steak roughly into thirds lengthwise); tie up steaks.

Combine salt and water to make soft mush; spread half the mush about 1½ inches thick over tops of steaks.

Place skillet or pan on broiler rack with top of steaks about 3 inches below unit or tip of flame. Broil 15-20 minutes, or until layer of salt begins to separate from meat. With broad spatula or pancake turner, lift off salt; turn steaks.

Using remaining salt mush, cover uncooked surface of meat. Continue broiling 15-20 minutes, or until salt begins to separate or rise from meat.

During last few minutes of broiling period, toast bread; keep it warm.

In another skillet or heavy frying pan, melt butter, allowing it to sizzle but not brown. At end of broiling period, remove salt from steaks; cut steaks in ¼-inch slices. Add slices to butter in pan; sauté ½ minute or less on each side. Place on toast; serve immediately. *Serves 4 to 6.*

LE CAFÉ CHAMBORD

Baron d'Agneau Bouquetière: Saddle of Lamb for two

INGREDIENTS: Saddle of lamb, about 3 pounds. One cup each of cooked baby carrots, French style string beans, fresh peas, lima beans, cauliflower, Parisian potatoes, broiled tomatoes, mushrooms; salt, pepper, 1 bay leaf, thyme, garlic, 1 onion, 2 stalks celery, and 1 cup of beef or lamb stock.

Place saddle of lamb in a roasting pan, garnish with a few slices of onions, and celery. Add one bay leaf, and a pinch of thyme. Season lamb with salt and pepper.

Roast for 45 minutes at 325-350 degrees. Remove from oven. Dispose of all grease in roasting pan. To the remaining stock in the roasting pan add 2 more cups of beef or lamb stock. Cook for 15 minutes. Add

1 piece of crushed garlic to this gravy and cook for another 5 minutes. Strain.

Place the meat in a large skillet. Garnish with the following vegetables which have been heated in butter: baby carrots, French string beans, fresh peas, lima beans, cauliflower, Parisian potatoes, broiled tomatoes and mushrooms. Serve.

COVENTRY FORGE INN

Baked Shad with Roe Filling

Take the roe from a 3-pound shad and poach in lightly salted water for several minutes. Drain and work through a coarse sieve. Add a *panade* made with 2 slices of bread and 2 to 3 ounces butter to the roe along with 5 to 6 finely chopped shallots, 3 tablespoons chopped parsley. (A little chopped tarragon and chevril may be added.) Season to taste. Place half of shad in well-greased baking dish, spread with roe filling, cover with other filet and bake in a hot oven, basting with white wine. When done (not overdone) remove and garnish with lemon slices dipped half in parsley and half in paprika.

GALATOIRE'S

Chicken Turenne

3 SPRING CHICKENS ABOUT 2 POUNDS EACH
12 BOTTOMS OR HEARTS OF ARTICHOKES PARBOILED AND SLICED
8 OUNCES OF MUSHROOMS SLICED
12 OUNCES OF BROTH
½ PINT OF SHERRY WINE
1 TABLESPOON FLOUR TO THICKEN BROTH

[353]

Disjoint the chicken and season with salt and pepper; fry same in butter until brown. Let chicken simmer in pot with the broth, sherry and garnishes for about 45 minutes. Serve same on hot platter. *Serves 6.*

MONT D'OR INN

Chicken Sauté

Sauté quartered, boneless chicken in butter and shallots to golden brown. Flambé with brandy, then blend in cream, salt, pepper, a dash of cayenne, and several drops of lemon juice. Cover and let simmer for about 10 minutes. Serve with Noodles Mont d'Or.

Filet Mignon en Boite

Place well-trimmed filet mignon in small casserole with butter, small amount of French mustard, a dash of Lea and Perrins sauce and shallots. Cover and let cook for about 5 minutes, then drain fat, add pinch of rosemary, salt and pepper, a good pony of brandy, cover again for a few minutes, and then serve.

PARK SCHENLEY

Shrimp Barsac, en Cocotte

Place 1 dozen fresh, raw, clean shrimp (large) in a skillet and sauté with butter. When golden brown add a pinch of chopped fine garlic, a pinch of parsley and 2 ounces of Barsac wine and cook for 1 minute. Place contents in a casserole, sprinkle with fresh white bread crumbs and pepper, and dampen with melted butter. Place in slow broiler until golden brown and serve.

PIGALL'S

Le Coq au Vin en Casserole du Chevalier du Tastevin

2 CHICKENS ABOUT 2 POUNDS EACH, CUT IN PIECES
7 OUNCES SALT PORK CUT IN LARGE JULIENNE STYLE
12 FRESH MUSHROOM CAPS
1 TABLESPOON FINELY CHOPPED SHALLOTS
½ BAY LEAF
1 PINCH POUNDED GARLIC
1 PINCH THYME
16 TINY NEW POTATOES
12 TINY WHOLE ONIONS
1 TABLESPOON FINELY CHOPPED PARSLEY
1 SMALL SPRIG PARSLEY
½ BOTTLE GOOD POMMARD OR CHAMBERTIN WINE
1 PONY GLASS VERY GOOD COGNAC
1½ PINT THICK VEAL GRAVY
½ PINT CLEAR VEAL OR CHICKEN BROTH
3 OUNCES BEEF FAT
SALT, PEPPER

Heat beef fat in a copper *sauteuse* or Dutch oven. Season chicken, dip in flour and sauté, turning carefully until golden brown. Remove from pan. In same fat, sauté onions, mushrooms and salt pork. When onions are light brown, return chicken to pan, add shallots and garlic, simmer for 5 minutes. Then add cognac, set it aflame. After a few seconds add wine, veal gravy and clear broth. When the first bubbles appear, add bay leaf, thyme, salt, pepper, parsley sprig. Boil slowly

[355]

about 20 minutes, then add potatoes (already ¾ boiled in salted water.) Simmer slowly for 10 minutes. Check seasoning. Skim off fat, if necessary. Turn into casserole. Top with croutons cut in shape of heart and sautéed in butter. Sprinkle with chopped parsley. Serve very hot.

CHARLIE'S CAFÉ EXCEPTIONALE

Pheasant Suprême

2 YOUNG PHEASANTS
1 HALF CUP BUTTER
1 HALF CUP FLOUR
1 8-OUNCE CAN SLICED MUSHROOMS
  (USE LIQUID WITH MILK)
1 QUART MILK (SCALDED)
  SALT AND PEPPER TO TASTE
3 OUNCES SHERRY WINE

Disjoint pheasants. Season with salt and white pepper. Sauté in butter, using heavy cast-iron skillet. When pheasant is golden brown, put in 325-degree oven for 30 minutes or until pheasant is tender.

Remove pheasant from pan and sauté the mushrooms in the same butter that the pheasant was fried in, add flour and stir until smooth, but do not brown. Add the hot milk and mushroom liquid and keep stirring until sauce is smooth. Return pheasant to the sauce and add the sherry wine and simmer for 10 minutes more.

Serve in a chafing dish with wild rice.

THE PUMP ROOM

Chicken Hash

Preparation requires the use of two skillets.

I CUP CHICKEN	SALT
¼ CUP DICED CELERY	PAPRIKA
½ CUP SUPREME SAUCE	3 OUNCES MADEIRA WINE
I EGG YOLK	I OUNCE ESCOFFIER SAUCE
I TABLESPOON CREAM	½ CUP CHICKEN BROTH

SKILLET NO. 1: Place some chicken broth in skillet, add diced celery and chicken and simmer well.

SKILLET NO. 2: Pour in Supreme sauce and heat. Add cream to thin. Add to this Escoffier sauce, salt and pepper. Allow to simmer well and then add Madeira wine.

Now, return your attention to Skillet No. 1 and strain off liquid and blend contents into those of Skillet No. 2.

Take yolk of egg and whip, adding a dash of cream and mix all well and allow to cook until done.

Serve in pastry shell using paprika and a sprig of parsley as decor. *Two servings.*

THE WARWICK

Chicken and Virginia Ham Shortcake

Simmer 6 slices of Virginia ham in a pan with 5 lumps of butter for 5 minutes. Remove the ham and put the meat of a cooked small chicken, minced, into the ham gravy, simmering it 10 minutes. Season with salt, pepper and a dash of nutmeg. Add ½ glass of white wine; simmer for 5 minutes.

Add ½ pint thick cream and yolk of 3 eggs, stirring smoothly and constantly to blend without curdling.

Place ham slices on toasted corn bread, top with chicken mixture and gravy, sprinkle with Parmesan cheese, brown under the broiling flame and serve piping hot.

For your corn bread, mix 3 cups of corn meal and 1 cup bread flour with three eggs and ½ cup bacon fat. Add salt and sugar to taste. Two tablespoons baking powder, 1 pint of milk; bake 25 minutes in a slow oven. *Serves 6 people.*

Suprême of Sole au Chablis

6 MEDIUM FILETS OF SOLE	1 TEASPOON CHOPPED SHALLOTS
1 GLASS CHABLIS	½ POUND BUTTER
3 EGG YOLKS	1 CUP AND 4 OUNCES CREAM
6 TABLESPOONS WHIPPED CREAM	½ LEMON

Cook shallots in butter until soft, but do not brown. Add wine, poach fish in wine and shallots and season. Add enough water to wine to nearly cover fish. Cover pan and cook for about 6 minutes. When poached, remove the fish. Add the cream to the cooking juice, and let reduce to approximately half. Allow to cool until almost lukewarm and then add egg yolks, melted butter gradually, whipping until thick. This operation should be done on the side of the oven where it is not too hot so as to prevent curdling. When thick add a pinch of cayenne pepper, juice of ½ lemon and the whipped cream.

Arrange the filets in a row on platter. Cover fish with sauce and glaze for about 10 seconds or until light brown, and serve at once.

COMMANDER'S PALACE

Trout Alexander

I 3-POUND SPECKLED TROUT	½ PINT CREAM
4 OUNCES BUTTER	4 GREEN ONIONS
¼ POUND BOILED SHRIMP	I GILL FISH BROTH
½ FLORIDA LOBSTER	2 OUNCES SHERRY WINE
2 TABLESPOONS FLOUR	4 SPRIGS PARSLEY
6 OUNCES MUSHROOMS	3 BAY LEAVES
I CLOVE GARLIC	SALT AND PEPPER TO TASTE
½ PINT MILK	

Poach trout in milk and a little water with salt and bay leaf. Sauté mushrooms in butter until nearly brown. Add shrimp and lobster, let sauté 5 minutes. Add garlic and green onions, cook until done. Blend in flour, add cream, milk and fish broth, cook slowly for 10 minutes. Add sherry wine and parsley. Serve piping hot, with the trout. *Serves* 4.

Turtle Stew

6 POUNDS SOFT-SHELL TURTLE	I½ CUP PURÉE TOMATO
I POUND ONIONS	I SMALL SPICE BAG
I MEDIUM-SIZE GARLIC	I CUP BRANDY
I STALK CELERY	I GILL WHITE WINE
I½ CUP PLAIN FLOUR	I GILL SHERRY WINE
2 CUPS OIL AND SHORTENING	½ POUND BACON DICED AND FRIED
½ BUNCH CHOPPED PARSLEY	

Braise turtle meat in oven until about half cooked. Add celery, onions, garlic and cook. Make gravy with shortening and flour until hazel brown. Add water and tomato purée to your turtle meat above.

Put in spice bag, sherry and white wine. Simmer until thoroughly cooked. Shred the soft shell of turtle and boil until tender, add to the above stew. Add bacon, mushrooms, brandy. Serve with dry toast or rice. *Serves* 8.

CHATEAUBRIAND

Coq au Vin

I 3½-POUND CHICKEN *or*
2 2-POUND CHICKENS CUT IN 8 PIECES
12 SMALL WHITE PEELED ONIONS
I OR 2 MINCED GARLIC CLOVES
2 OR 3 MINCED SHALLOTS *or*
    2 OR 3 MINCED SMALL WHITE ONIONS
½ CUP DICED PORK OR BACON
I TEASPOON SALT AND PEPPER, TO TASTE
12 SMALL MUSHROOMS
2 TABLESPOONS FLOUR
2 CUPS RED BURGUNDY WINE

Parboil pork and cook it in 2 tablespoons of butter till brown, in a large skillet or saucepan. Remove and set aside pork scraps. Season the chicken with salt and pepper to taste.

Brown the chicken in fat in which pork was browned, add the onions and the mushrooms, cover and cook over low heat till onions are lightly browned, turning occasionally.

Pour half of the fat in the pan into another saucepan. Blend in the flour, add the minced shallots or onions and the minced garlic. Cook over low heat stirring constantly till thickened. Remove from heat and gradually add the wine while stirring. Return to heat, add reserved pork, bring to a boil, stirring, and add the whole thing to the chicken.

Cover and simmer till chicken is tender, about half an hour. To serve, arrange the chicken, vegetables and pork in a deep dish or casserole. Skim fat from gravy and season to taste. Pour over chicken. *Four servings.*

THE FOUR SEASONS

Sautéed Calf's Liver with Avocado

12 THIN SLICES CALF'S LIVER
18 THIN WHOLE SLICES AVOCADO
½ CUP VEAL STOCK
3 OUNCES WHITE WINE
1 TEASPOON CHOPPED PARSLEY
1 TABLESPOON CHOPPED CHIVES
5 OUNCES BUTTER
  JUICE OF 2 LEMONS

Sauté together very quickly the sliced liver and sliced avocado. Arrange on hot plates 2 slices liver and 3 slices avocado per plate. Serve with Bercy sauce which is made by adding the wine to the veal stock and bringing to a boil. Brown butter in pan, add lemon juice, herbs and stock. Pour over calf's liver and avocado. Serve at once. *Serves 6.*

THE FORUM OF THE TWELVE CAESARS

Filet Mignon, Caesar Augustus

6 12-OUNCE FILETS
6 1-OUNCE CHIPS OF *pâté de foie gras*

Press 2-inch cookie cutter into top of each filet until about halfway through. Remove cookie cutter and with a sharp knife cut piece indented by cutter. Place chip of *pâté* in hole of each filet. Place the cut-out piece of filet on top of *pâté*. Broil filets as desired. *Serves 6.*

LA CRÉMAILLÈRE À LA CAMPAGNE

Peas à la Normande

Take 2 pounds of fresh fine peas; 1 head of Boston lettuce (shredded); 1 chopped onion; 2 ounces of diced salt pork. Cook lettuce, salt pork, onions together with 1 cup of bouillon for 10 minutes. Add the peas, salt and pepper, 1 *bouquet garni*. Let cook slowly until peas are tender. Add 1 teaspoon of sugar, and 1 cup of heavy cream mixed with 1 yolk of egg. Stir gently until thickened.

Bouquet garni: Sprig of thyme leaf; 1 bay leaf, some parsley branches; tied together with some string.

Blanquette de Veau à l'Ancienne

3 POUNDS BREAST OF VEAL, CUT INTO LARGE CUBES
I POUND FRESH BUTTON MUSHROOMS
I *bouquet garni*
10 SMALL WHITE ONIONS
2 CRUSHED GARLIC CLOVES
2 EGG YOLKS
I CUP HEAVY CREAM
SALT AND WHITE PEPPER TO TASTE

Put the veal cubes into a skillet or deep saucepan, cover with cold water and bring to a boil. Let boil for 2 minutes. Put under the cold water faucet, wash the meat thoroughly. Drain, put the meat back into the skillet with half a cup of melted butter. Let cook on medium fire for 5 minutes. Add the onions and garlic, let cook briskly for 1 minute. Add 1 cup of flour, mix with the meat. Add to cover the meat some white bouillon, the *bouquet garni,* salt and pepper. Bring to a boil. Put into 400-degree oven. Let cook for about 1 hour. Sauté the mushrooms in butter for 1 minute and add to the *blanquette* 5 minutes before taking out of the oven. Just before serving, take out the *bouquet garni* and add the cream mixed with the egg yolks, stirring briefly with a wooden spoon. Serve in a deep dish. Boiled rice or boiled potatoes go well with it, as a side dish.

Bouquet garni: Tied together—1 branch of celery, 1 bay leaf, a pinch of thyme leaves, 1 leek, some parsley branches. *Serves 6.*

GOURMET ROOM

Pheasant en Casserole, Vallée d'Auge

    1 PHEASANT
      SLICED SALT PORK
      BUTTER
    4 CUPS DICED APPLES
    2 TABLESPOONS CALVADOS (APPLEJACK)
    2 CUPS SOUR CREAM
      SALT AND PEPPER

Wrap the pheasant in salt pork and tie securely.

Brown pheasant in butter in deep casserole. Cover and let simmer over low heat until tender.

Add apples, Calvados, cream and cook over slow heat until ready to serve.

AMBASSADOR INN

Boneless Breast of Chicken

Debone chicken breast and flatten to a cutlet. Dip in flour then in eggs, and bread with white cubed bread.

Sauté in butter to a golden brown. Then cook in the oven at 300 degrees. Cooking time 15 minutes. Serve with green noodles and red currant jelly.

THE PATIO

Breast of Capon on Ham with Truffle Sauce

Dip breast of capon in seasoned flour and sauté in equal amounts of oil and butter until golden brown.

Cream Sauce with Truffles:

Sauté truffles gently for 2 or 3 minutes in butter, add a bit of brandy, combine equal parts of cream and béchamel sauce. Mix in the truffles and add a lump of butter.

Place a slice of cooked thin ham on a plate and top with the breast of capon. Cover the breast with the truffle sauce. (Can be served under glass.)

COPAIN

Sweetbreads à la Mode de Copain

Select a fine pair of sweetbreads and poach for 45 minutes with a little vinegar added. Clean well.

Prepare a Supreme sauce (any self-respecting cookbook will tell you how to make it), to which add some cooked sliced mushrooms and a little sherry. Let sweetbreads warm in sauce. Serve on a bed of lightly cooked leaf spinach.

BEAU SÉJOUR

Guinea Hen with Brandy Sauce

Put a pinch each of salt, pepper and leaf thyme inside an oven-ready guinea hen, baste it with butter and corn oil, place it on its back in a shallow roasting pan and roast at 350-375 degrees. After 10 minutes the hen should be basted and turned on its side, and 10 minutes later likewise on the other side. After 30 minutes it should be golden brown. Transfer it to a French oval cocotte with a tight-fitting cover. At this time add a lump of butter and a half cup of consommé or wine. Return to the oven with a reduced temperature of 300 degrees.

The sauce is made in the roasting pan, first removing all the cooking oils. Into the pan put a cup of consommé, a chicken-bouillon cube, a lump of butter, a pinch of thyme, a clove of garlic, 1 tablespoon of currant jelly and a tablespoon of sour or sweet cream. Blend and bring to a boil. To thicken the sauce, dissolve a tablespoon of cornstarch in a half a cup of water, and add to the sauce a little at a time, stirring all the while. When it reaches the desired thickness, strain over the guinea hen, add an ounce of brandy, and serve.

Desserts

BLUE SPRUCE INN

Bavarian Cream with Rum

½ PINT OF MILK

4 EGG YOLKS

4 OUNCES SUGAR

8 TEASPOONS GELATIN

1 QUART HEAVY CREAM

2 OUNCES JAMAICA RUM

Dissolve the gelatin in half a cup of water. Scald milk, yolks and sugar. Remove from fire, add the gelatin and strain. Put in cool place and just before it starts to set add the cream, whipped stiff, and the rum. Fill into pudding cups and place in refrigerator to set. To serve, remove from molds into individual dishes with an extra dash or two of rum.

JOHN BARTRAM HOTEL

Pêche Macéré au Cognac

PEACHES (IN SEASON PREFERRED) FRESH ORANGES WITH SKIN
PLAIN SYRUP CINNAMON STICKS
HONEY FRENCH ICE CREAM
2 QUARTS WATER COGNAC
CLOVES

Take 2 quarts water and boil with peaches, honey, cloves, fresh oranges (with skin), cinnamon sticks, for 10 minutes. Remove peaches and allow to cool. When cool, remove the peach skins, split peach and remove the stones.

Place large scoop of ice cream in terrapin plate. Place peaches in chafing dish in front of guests, add cognac for flaming. Cover peaches and French ice cream with sauce.

LOCKE-OBER

Cherries Jubilee

14 BLACK BING CHERRIES—CANNED
2 OUNCES OF CHERRY JUICE
2 TEASPOONS SUGAR
¾ OUNCE KIRSCHWASSER
¾ OUNCE BRANDY, IMPORTED
1 LARGE SCOOP VANILLA ICE CREAM

Place cherries, cherry juice and sugar in chafing dish and bring to a slow boil. Cook slowly until liquid is reduced by one half. Add Kirschwasser and brandy. Place ice cream in deep serving dish, ignite cherry mixture with a match and spoon it over ice cream. *One portion.*

STOCK YARD INN

Strawberries Romanoff

1 PINT FRESH STRAWBERRIES	1½ CUPS SOUR CREAM
3 OUNCES BRANDY	1 QUART ICE CREAM

Cut berries and mix in cream. Add brandy and blend in ice cream just before serving.

CHASEN'S

Coupe Alexander

1 scoop of vanilla ice cream.
Cover with fresh toasted coconut. Sprinkle lightly with imported Anisette.

COVENTRY FORGE INN

Wine Jelly

Dissolve 4 tablespoons plain gelatin in ½ cup cold water. Add to this 1½ cups boiling water and a generous cup sugar. Allow to cool. Then add 3½ cups orange juice (fresh or made from 1 can frozen juice), ½ cup lemon juice, 1 cup tawny port and 1 cup Madeira. Tint delicately with red coloring. Pour in molds and chill. Serve with *Crème Chantilly*.

GALATOIRE'S

Princess Cup

One large spoonful of fruit cocktail in an old fashioned glass; one large scoop of vanilla ice cream placed over the fruit cocktail; crown ice cream with a cherry and pour over one ounce of orange Cointreau liqueur or any other sweet liqueur if the above is unavailable.

LE CAFÉ CHAMBORD

Soufflé Rothschild

4 EGGS
½ CUP SUGAR
1½ CUPS MILK
2 TABLESPOONS FLOUR
3 OUNCES SWEET BUTTER
1 TEASPOON VANILLA
2 OUNCES COINTREAU
1 TABLESPOON MIXED DRIED FRUITS

Place sugar and milk in copper casserole, bring to boil, lower flame and allow to simmer for a few minutes.

In separate pan melt half of the original 3 ounces of butter, mix with the flour, forming a paste. Fold into sugar and milk mixture and place in casserole.

Allow to cook for 2 minutes. Remove from heat and add 4 egg yolks, the remainder of the butter together with the vanilla, Cointreau and fruit.

Beat egg whites until stiff. Fold into the casserole with a wooden spoon.

Grease Pyrex baking dish with butter thoroughly. Place mixture in baking dish and place in oven 320 degrees Fahrenheit for 20 minutes.

STONEHENGE

Rice Pudding, Candied Fruits

Wash and blanch ½ pound white rice. Cook in oven for 40 minutes having added 1 quart of milk and ½ vanilla stick. Withdraw vanilla stick, add 3 ounces of sugar, 2 ounces butter and pinch of salt. Mix thoroughly 6 egg yolks and 1 whole egg with 6 ounces of diced candied fruit, such as pears, pineapple, cherry, etc., and stir into this 3 well-beaten whites of egg. Butter and sugar deep pan or bowl 4/5ths full. Place in saucepan half filled with water. Place over flame until brought to a boil, then move to slow oven for 50 minutes. Remove from oven, let stand for 5 minutes, unmold and cover with a simple cream vanilla sauce.

PARK SCHENLEY

Pear Mimi

Mix in double boiler (not aluminum) the yolks of 3 eggs, 3 table-spoons of granulated sugar and 3 ounces of sherry wine. Whip until fluffy (firm) over a slow fire. Put into a glass container to cool. Serve as a sauce over 4 halves of ice cold Bartlett pears. *Serves* 4.

THE PUMP ROOM

Ice Cream Gertrude Lawrence

½ ORANGE PEEL
2 OUNCES JAMAICA RUM
2 OUNCES CHOCOLATE SAUCE
VANILLA ICE CREAM (SIZE OF PORTION AS DESIRED)

Grate ½ orange peel into a chafing dish. Add two ounces of Jamaica rum and flame.

While rum is flaming, add two ounces of chocolate sauce and pour over vanilla ice cream. *One serving.*

THE WARWICK

Strawberry Charlotte

I PINT RIPE STRAWBERRIES   I OUNCE GELATIN
8 OUNCES SUGAR   I PINT HEAVY CREAM (WHIPPED)

Soak gelatin in a little cold water, press berries through a sieve and mix with sugar. Beat cream. Dissolve gelatin on fire and add to it the crushed strawberries. Stir this mixture on ice until it begins to set and mix lightly with whipped cream.

Fill oiled molds and set on ice until firm. Turn from molds and serve decorated with whipped cream, ladyfingers and whole berries.

GOURMET ROOM

Soufflé au Chocolat

Blend together 3 tablespoons melted butter and 3 tablespoons flour. Add 1 cup milk, a dash of salt, stir over medium heat until the sauce is thick and smooth.

Add 2 squares baking chocolate to the butter, flour, and milk mixture and stir until the chocolate is melted and the sauce thoroughly blended. Stir in 3 beaten yolks of eggs, 1 at a time, and cool the mixture. Fold in 4 stiffly beaten whites and turn the batter at once into a buttered baking dish. Bake in a moderately hot oven (375 degrees) for 30 minutes, or until the soufflé is well puffed and browned.

If the soufflé dish is put into a pan of hot water (not boiling) it will have no crust on bottom or sides. Soufflés in the French manner are moist and even slightly runny in the center; for a soufflé that is firm through, bake 10 to 15 minutes longer. Serve with Sauce Sabayon.

Sauce Sabayon:

Whip together 6 yolks and ⅔ cup sugar. Stir in 1 cup Marsala wine. Cook, stirring constantly, in the top of a double boiler, starting over cold water, until the water reaches the boiling point or until the mixture is thick and creamy. Add 1 tablespoon of liqueur. Serve hot.

PIGALL'S

Pêche Flambée "Holiday"

With a pinch of fresh butter warm up in a chafing dish 2 halves peeled fresh peaches. Add few pieces sliced orange peel, some sliced almonds, a tablespoon of orange juice, a tablespoon of sugar. Let the sugar melt and cook for about 2 to 3 minutes. Then add a little kirsch and Grand Marnier. Set it aflame.

Serve very quickly with vanilla ice cream; sprinkle with good cognac.

Serve with some petits fours and a glass of good sauterne or Barsac wine, well chilled.

It is a very simple dessert but with a very delicate flavor.

CHARLIE'S CAFÉ EXCEPTIONALE

Apple Pie

1 QUART PEELED AND SLICED APPLES
4 TEASPOONS FLOUR
⅛ TEASPOON CINNAMON
1 CUP SUGAR
1 TABLESPOON BUTTER
JUICE OF ½ LEMON
PASTRY FOR A TWO-CRUST PIE

Fill pastry-lined pie plate with prepared apples. Sift together dry ingredients and sprinkle over apples. Squeeze the juice of ½ lemon over the apples and then top with bits of butter. Wet edge of lower crust, put on top crust and seal edges with fork and trim.

Perforate top to allow steam to escape. Brush top crust with milk and a sprinkle of sugar. Bake at 375 degrees for approximately 1 hour. Serve with cheddar cheese, whipped cream, or ice cream.

ANTOINE'S

Omelette au Rhum

For each omelette, beat separately white and yolk of 1 egg. Blend. Add 1 teaspoon water, ½ teaspoon sugar, pinch of salt. Heat ¼ ounce butter in pan, pour in egg mixture. Cook over medium flame, stirring sides with fork and tilting pan. When omelette sets, fold quickly and remove to hot, heat-proof platter. Sprinkle with powdered sugar. Pour ⅓ cup heated Puerto Rican rum—any brand—around omelette and ignite. While flaming, spoon some up and pour over omelette. When flame flickers, put out. Serve immediately.

THE BLUE FOX

Bunet Piemontese

Stir 1 cup sugar in dry heavy skillet over low heat until it melts. Add ½ cup water and boil syrup until well blended, stirring constantly. Pour this caramel syrup into bombe mold and keep turning the mold until inside surface is completely coated. When coating is set, pour custard filling into the mold, and set mold in pan of hot water. Bake in 350 degree oven for approximately 50 minutes, or until silver knife inserted comes out clean. Cool and unmold on serving dish. Refrigerate and serve very cold.

Custard Filling

Beat together 3 eggs and 3 egg yolks. Add ½ cup sugar and blend well. Scald 1 quart milk with ¾ cup sweetened powdered chocolate. Remove from fire, and add gradually to egg mixture, blending well after each addition. Add ¼ cup Grand Marnier liqueur, ½ teaspoon grated lemon rind, and 10 crushed macaroons. Blend well and strain. Pour into coated mold.

LA CRÉMAILLÈRE À LA CAMPAGNE

Omelette Soufflé au Grand Marnier

6 EGGS, SEPARATE THE WHITE FROM THE YOLKS
½ POUND GRANULATED SUGAR
2 OUNCES GRAND MARNIER
   RIND OF A LEMON, FINELY GRATED
6 LADYFINGERS

Put the yolks and sugar into electric mixer, beat at medium speed until thickened. Beat the whites separately until solid. Mix with the yolks, add grated lemon rind, 1 teaspoon of the juice of a lemon. Add Grand Marnier. Put the ladyfingers on the bottom of an ovenware platter, placing egg mixture on top. Spray some XXXX sugar on top, put into a 500-degree oven for 10 minutes. *Serves 4*

AMBASSADOR INN

Lemon Chiffon Pie

1 CUP SUGAR	5 LARGE EGGS
2 LEMONS	1 TABLESPOONFUL GELATIN

Put ½ cup sugar in a double boiler, add 5 egg yolks. (Grate the lemons and put grated parts aside.) Add the juice of the 2 lemons to the eggs and sugar. Put on fire and stir until mixture is to custard consistency.

Remove from fire, add the lemon rind and the gelatin, which should be dissolved in ½ cup of warm water. Stir and let cool.

Beat egg whites, adding the other ½ cup of sugar slowly to egg whites while beating them. When they form peaks add custard. Pour into 9-inch shell. Let set. *Serves 8.*

[375]

BEAU SÉJOUR

Almond Rum Layer Cake

10 EGG YOLKS	1 PINCH SALT
10 EGG WHITES	½ TEASPOON VANILLA
1 CUP POWDERED BLANCHED ALMONDS	JUICE OF 1 LEMON
½ CUP FINELY CHOPPED CANDIED	1 OUNCE RUM
CITRON	2 CUPS ZWIEBACK CRUMBS
½ TEASPOON BAKING SODA	1½ PINTS HEAVY CREAM

Mix egg yolks and one cup sugar until creamy. Add almonds, citron, soda, salt, vanilla, lemon juice, rum and finally the zwieback.

In another bowl beat egg whites. When almost stiff add 1 cup sugar, beat until stiff.

Add the egg-white mixture to batter, fold in carefully. Don't overmix.

Bake in a buttered crumb-lined eleven-inch (spring form) cake pan for one hour at 300 degrees. When cool, cut across cake twice, making 3 layers. Moisten layers with rum. Spread with whipped cream.

THE PATIO

Apple Pie Genoa Style

Slice the apples, make a mix of 1 cup of sugar, ¼ cup cinnamon and ½ teaspoon allspice, 1 ounce Cointreau and 1 tablespoon flour. Place in tins lined with pastry dough, moisten edge and cover with pastry top. When finished brush with mixed powdered sugar and a dash of cinnamon.

COPAIN

Baked Stuffed Apple, Royale

Use large greening apples; core, boil well for 15 minutes. Remove flesh carefully and mix well with 1 tablespoon sugar, 1 teaspoon finely chopped walnuts and a liberal pinch of cinnamon.

Put back in shell. Lightly cover with sugar. Put under hot broiler 3 minutes, remove and cover with sauce made of apple juice, sugar, grenadine, and cornstarch. Put under broiler again briefly. Serve cold.

Index of Restaurants

A NOTE ON MANUFACTURE

THE TEXT OF THIS BOOK was set on the Linotype in *Granjon,* a type designed under the supervision of George W. Jones. The face is based on the beautiful roman types cut by Claude Garamond (1510-1561) and is the best reproduction of that French master's designs.

The type is named in compliment to Robert Granjon, who was also active in sixteenth-century France and is best remembered for his *"caractères de civilité."* Also known as *"lettres françaises,"* these calligraphic types were based on the mannered courtly hand of the period.

This book was composed, printed and bound by THE HADDON CRAFTSMEN, INC., Scranton, Pennsylvania. The paper was manufactured by S. D. WARREN COMPANY, Boston. Typography and binding design are by GUY FLEMING.